PRAISE FOR *UNDERSTA*
ATTACKER MI1

C000156796

"There is so much rich content in this excellent and important book by Sarah Armstrong-Smith – why cybercrime is booming, how it works, and why so many of the approaches we've taken, like blaming poor, befuddled users, haven't worked. Anyone wondering about how and why their business might be at risk of cyber attacks, and what they can do about it, would be well advised to dip into it!"
Ciaran Martin, Professor of Practice at University of Oxford and former CEO of the UK National Cyber Security Centre

"Sarah Armstrong-Smith masterfully bridges the gap between technology and psychology of the adversary, exposing the vulnerabilities and desires that fuel cyber attacks. *Understand the Cyber Attacker Mindset* is as a powerful call for empathy and understanding and essential for charting a safer course through the ever-evolving world of cybercrime."
Miguel A Clarke, Retired Supervisory Special Agent, FBI and Cybersecurity Evangelist for Armor Defense

"*Understand the Cyber Attacker Mindset* offers a thorough and contextual look at cybercrime, analysing the conditions that allow it to flourish. Sarah Armstrong-Smith's insights demonstrate the complexity of the cyber attacker mindset, which is essential to understand if we want to overcome the growing scourge of cyber attacks."
James Coker, Deputy editor, *Infosecurity Magazine*

"Sarah Armstrong-Smith is a first-rate guide to where cybercrime lurks and how you can protect yourself from such attacks. *Understand the Cyber Attacker Mindset* is a very timely, very useful guide to not just how people attack computers, but why they do it. Understanding their motivation is half the battle."
Nicholas Booth, Former technology editor and author of *The Thieves of Threadneedle Street*

"*Understand the Cyber Attacker Mindset* sets out the landscape of cyber-crime, how we got here and most importantly what the mindset of the attacker actually is. Sarah Armstrong-Smith is a seasoned luminary in the field of cybersecurity and her latest work is testament to her dedication to shedding light on the intricacies of the cyber threat. I can confidently recommend it as a must-read for those who seek to understand the evolving threat landscape and take proactive steps to secure their digital estate."
Lisa Forte, Partner, Red Goat Security

"*Understand the Cyber Attacker Mindset* is what we've been waiting for! It genuinely captures all relevant and important aspects of the cyber attacker mindset and provides unique insight. Sarah Armstrong-Smith's book is an important knowledge source. A must read!"
Ulf Larsson, Security CTO, SEB

"Cybercrime is often mistakenly perceived as a problem that is solely related to technology. However, it is fundamentally driven by human motivations such as the desire for financial or professional gain, nationalism, greed, notoriety, or revenge. Sarah Armstrong-Smith's *Understand the Cyber Attacker Mindset* shows defenders how they can develop effective strategies and methods to combat cybercrime."
Shawn Loveland, Chief Operating Officer, ReSecurity

"Through terrifying real-life examples and hands-on advice, Sarah Armstrong-Smith's *Understand the Cyber Attacker Mindset* offers a thorough and practical survey of the growing cyber threat facing today's organizations, and how they can tackle it from the frontline to the boardroom."
Geoff White, Investigative journalist and author of *The Lazarus Heist*

"*Understand the Cyber Attacker Mindset* is essential reading for all practi-tioners involved in tackling fraud and cybercrime, academics, and anyone with an interest in understanding the hidden world of these criminal activi-ties, the darker sides of human behaviour and how to guard against them."
Dr Elisabeth Carter, Criminologist and forensic linguist

"*Understand the Cyber Attacker Mindset* is the ideal guide to revealing how different threat actors really operate with insight from experts in the field.

Sarah Armstrong-Smith raises the standard in recognizing the all-important human side of security to help make organizations and their people more resilient."
Martin Hill, Award-winning cyber security journalist and editor

"*Understand the Cyber Attacker Mindset* is an interesting, accessible read focussing on the human aspects of cybersecurity. The discussions concerning the motivations of digital criminals are illustrated with some great up-to-date case studies. There are some great suggestions for dealing with all of the issues considered."
Dr Paul Stephens, Director of Academic Studies in Law, Policing and Social Sciences and Principal Lecturer in Cybercrime and Digital Policing at Canterbury Christ Church University

"Sarah Armstrong-Smith expertly takes the reader through a comprehensive, but clear, journey leaving them with a path for creating security strategies that integrate both technology and people. Whether you have a technical, business, or human-centric background, *Understand the Cyber Attacker Mindset* demonstrates how to create a holistic security strategy."
Sarah Janes, Owner and CEO, Layer 8 Ltd

"The premise of *Understand the Cyber Attacker Mindset*, that the focus of cyber security strategy should be on humans and not just machines, is something that should resonate with any reader with an interest in cyber security. As a seasoned intelligence and cyber security practitioner I have learned a lot from reading this work, and I would suggest that others can do too."
Stuart Wiggins, Counter Adversary Practice Lead - Central and Northern Europe, CrowdStrike

"This is an absolute must read for anyone wanting a solid history of cybercrime and cyber security. *Understand the Cyber Attacker Mindset* brilliantly frames the key events in recent years that have helped shape the attacker mindset."
Phil Cracknell FCIIS, FBCS, CISSP, CISO - Defence Sector

Understand the Cyber Attacker Mindset

Build a strategic security programme to counteract threats

Sarah Armstrong-Smith

I hope you enjoy my book!

Best wishes

Sarah

KoganPage

First published in Great Britain and the United States in 2024 by Kogan Page Limited

2nd Floor, 45 Gee Street	8 W 38th Street, Suite 902	4737/23 Ansari Road
London	New York, NY 10018	Daryaganj
EC1V 3RS	USA	New Delhi 110002
United Kingdom		India

www.koganpage.com

Kogan Page books are printed on paper from sustainable forests.

ISBNs

Hardback	978 1 3986 1430 7
Paperback	978 1 3986 1428 4
Ebook	978 1 3986 1429 1

British Library Cataloguing-in-Publication Data

A CIP record for this book is available from the British Library.

Library of Congress Control Number

2023057366

Typeset by Integra Software Services, Pondicherry
Print production managed by Jellyfish
Printed and bound by CPI Group (UK) Ltd, Croydon CR0 4YY

To my partner David, for his love, understanding and support in working one too many weekends to research and author this book, and for always being my rock when I need it the most.

CONTENTS

PART ONE
Understanding types of attack, how they operate and why they are successful

LIST OF FIGURES AND TABLES

ABOUT THE AUTHOR

I have had a long and impactful career in business continuity, disaster recovery, cybersecurity and crisis management, which enables me to operate holistically to understand the threat landscape and how this can be proactively enabled to deliver effective resilience.

I have been recognized as one of the most influential leaders in cybersecurity and UK tech and have over 25 years' experience delivering and advising executives on large-scale business and ICT continuity, cybersecurity, data protection and resilience programmes.

I currently operate as the Chief Security Advisor in Microsoft, and act as an executive sponsor to strategic and major customers across Europe. Prior to joining Microsoft, I worked for several large institutions, including Thames Water, AXA, EY, Fujitsu and the London Stock Exchange Group. I have been on the front line of many major incidents including IT failures, data breaches and corporate fraud.

I am a trained PR spokesperson and international keynote speaker and talk passionately about the *human aspects* of cybersecurity and building trust and transparency through effective crisis management.

What motivated me to write this book?

Many books focus on the technical aspects of cybersecurity, such as how to deploy different tools, technologies and software to counteract cyber threats. While these have their place, it is also important to understand the will and motivation of attackers, and how they manipulate people to perform nefarious actions.

As technology evolves to automatically detect and block anomalies in the network, attackers are looking for workarounds and increasingly reverting to social engineering techniques, without the need for additional tools and software. Attackers prey on people's vulnerabilities, as well as utilizing current affairs and topical news stories to make their ruse more relevant, such as Covid-19 and the Russian invasion of Ukraine, to stir up deep emotions and propaganda. This is supported by an underground criminal network of syndicates and access brokers that have lowered the barriers to entry for would-be attackers by selling subscriptions and exploit kits on dark-web markets. Their ability to coordinate and collaborate across jurisdictions is at a scale that most government agencies can only dream about.

This book delves into the psychological and societal factors that drive individuals to engage in cybercrime, by examining the various types of attacker, and exploring their motivations, including financial gain, revenge and the desire for power and control.

Through interviews with academics, researchers and law enforcement personnel, and by profiling notable groups, this book provides a comprehensive look at the inner workings of the criminal mind in the digital age and provides a set of strategies that organizations can deploy to counteract it.

By understanding the mindset of attackers, and how they utilize such techniques, organizations will be able to develop *people-orientated* strategies that anticipate and fight against such attacks. The strategies consider how to avert some of the initial tactics used by attackers, through the power of education and by building a more cyber-aware and resilient culture. This includes tactics on training people to identify and resist manipulation, even when in the midst of a large-scale attack.

The human factors of cybersecurity have never been more critical.

FOREWORD

When we examine the balance of power in the fight against cybercrime, two recent dates represent significant changes and shifts in the balance of power: December 2019 and 24 February, 2022. The first stands for the start of the Covid pandemic, which sent every country in the world into an unprecedented state of lockdown. The second was the day on which we saw Russian military vehicles cross the border into Ukraine. Let's look at each in turn.

The Covid pandemic disrupted almost every business on the planet. Overnight, society had to change how it operated, and that included the ways in which we worked. A sudden shift to cloud-based working, previously regarded as impossible, now became essential. One of the many unwelcome consequences of the pandemic was that attacks increased in frequency and severity.

Attackers thrive on exploiting times of fear and uncertainty. Covid created the perfect storm of exploitable potential, more doors to open, more online activity to intercept and interfere with, and high levels of confusion and panic in the population to take advantage of. Attacks on hospitals and vaccine-producers were rife. The world has now settled into its new rhythm, but cyber attacks continue to increase at an uncomfortable rate. Chapter 4 of *Understand the Cyber Attacker Mindset* looks at this in detail and examines the wealth of factors that generated an ideal breeding ground for cybercrime.

The second date of significance was Russia's invasion of Ukraine. The developments observed were not the ones we anticipated. Many academics had commented that cyber warfare would be the fifth dimension of warfare. That has proved not to be the case, not in a state context at least. What we did see was the mobilization of well-resourced and capable threat actors in the form of hacktivist groups on both sides of the conflict. As activists in an armed conflict, their motivations have focused on disruption and sowing fear in the population of the enemy combatants. Unlike the organized crime groups profiting from Covid, their interests are not financial, but patriotic. This makes them much more difficult to deal with, rendering negotiation harder. Chapter 10 discusses the impacts of these attacks on nation states and their citizens.

These two dates highlight the volatility of the cyber landscape and the importance of understanding mindset and motivation when it comes to forming a proactive cybersecurity strategy, be it at the level of an organization or on national or international levels.

The most problematic adversaries that businesses face in the cyber world are organized crime groups (OCGs). I worked in one of the UK police cybercrime units and recall in my first week being astonished to discover just how organized these groups actually are.

In considering cyber OCGs, we are talking about groups that function in a manner resembling any legitimate business. They have job roles within the group that mirror the corporate structures with which we are familiar; they have salaries and holiday pay and they face similar business challenges to us. Motivated largely if not exclusively by profit, they adapt and evolve to fit the market as does any organization. Chapter 5 looks in detail at this business model as well as the more troublesome 'cybercrime as a service' structure.

Let's take ransomware groups as an example of just how agile OCGs have to be. They have adapted their 'business' strategies to exert the greatest possible pressure on their victims to make them pay the ransom; this includes aggressive attack and extortion strategies followed by more cooperative and collaborative language when negotiating the ransom. This alteration in approach, as Chapter 8 examines in detail, is not by accident but a deliberate and strategic move.

In 2021, the US Congress released a memorandum examining three large ransomware attacks on US victims: CNA Financial Corporation, Colonial Pipeline and JBS Foods ('Supplemental memo on committee's investigation into ransomware', 16 November). This followed the committee's investigation into the attacks and subsequent ransom payments by the three organizations. In all three cases, the attacks were not hugely sophisticated, the organizations all paid the ransom, they all managed to negotiate sizeable discounts on the ransom to be paid, and all obtained whatever had been promised to them by the attackers.

The communications between the attackers and the victims were examined, revealing a significant change in the attackers' direction so as to reframe the 'relationship' with the victims as being one of 'partnership'. In the case of *JBS Foods vs Revil*, for instance, they stated: 'we are in business not war' and offered the company additional benefits if they paid, such as a security report detailing how they were attacked. In the case of *Colonial*

Pipeline vs DarkSide, the attackers claimed they had 'helped more than one hundred companies'.

You may be asking yourself why they should move to portray themselves as friend rather than foe. This highlights the crucial need to fully understand the mindset and motivations behind the threat actors. Where OCGs are concerned, they need to apply the greatest possible effective pressure on their victims, they need to generate a high return on investment per attack and they need to paint themselves, bizarre as this may sound, as 'reliable' and likely to keep their word. This is not a technical skill; it is a business one.

A whole business model has grown up around organized cybercrime, from the ransomware groups to the 'as a service' crime groups to the money-laundering organizations operating in the cryptocurrency blockchain world. To fully understand the threat we are facing, you need to understand the interconnected 'businesses' operating in the digital underworld and their motivations and drivers. Chapter 9 looks at why law enforcement has struggled to keep pace with this business-minded criminal underworld and the challenges that need solving.

In contrast to these OCGs, we have hacktivist groups pursuing political goals and not necessarily motivated by money. These groups have caused a wealth of problems for organizations that work in, for or with causes to which they are opposed. Killnet and Anonymous Sudan are two of the most problematic for pro-Ukraine countries following the Russian invasion. Both are highly skilled, well-resourced and determined. Hacktivists, unlike OCGs, do not seek to apply pressure but to further a political goal. In the case of Killnet, this is for countries to cease funding and supplying Ukraine.

The way in which you build a security strategy depends on the threats you face. Cyber risk is volatile and not binary. The way you address risk, whether as an individual or as an organization, depends on the assets you hold, the profile you present, the exposure to risk and the appetite, or lack thereof, that you harbour for it. Looking into the threat actors that would be interested in attacking you or your organization requires you to understand their motives and mindsets, as well as their typical modus operandi and level of capability and resourcing.

One thing I have learnt in my career is never to underestimate what these attackers are capable of, or the moral boundaries they will be more than willing to cross. When examining the scope of this book, Sarah Armstrong-Smith has researched the human adversaries behind some of the most prolific threat actors. The candid interviews, from researchers, academics and those behind such attacks, really help to provide a rich insight on why some people are drawn into this life. What stands out is the sheer complexity of circumstances that has conspired to create a perfect storm for threat actors to thrive in. This includes the potential for high rewards, the low risk of arrest, reasonably low barriers to entry and a plethora of potential victims. In my experience, what is often not discussed in the cybersecurity profession is the real-world impact on victims.

This book requires us to consider not what the victim did wrong, but what the attacker did right, so that we may apply collective learning to counteract this capable and well-resourced adversary. That is what makes this book such an important read.

Lisa Forte,
Partner, Red Goat Cyber Security LLP

PREFACE

Understanding the cyber attacker mindset is crucial for organizations looking to defend against an array of cyber threats. Cyber attackers are not just malicious actors looking to cause harm or steal data; they are intelligent, motivated individuals who use a range of techniques and tactics to achieve their objectives. By understanding the motivations, methods and goals of cyber attackers, organizations can better prepare themselves to defend against cyber attacks.

The cyber attacker mindset is a complex one, and it can vary depending on the individual or group behind the attack. Some attackers are motivated by financial gain, seeking to steal data or extort money from their victims. Others may be driven by political or ideological goals, seeking to disrupt or undermine government or corporate entities, while some may be motivated by perceived wrath, seeking revenge against a particular individual or organization.

Regardless of their motivation, cyber attackers use a range of techniques to achieve their objectives. These include social engineering, phishing, impersonation, malware and other methods designed to exploit vulnerabilities in the target's systems or processes. Attackers may also use a combination of different techniques, working together in a coordinated effort to achieve their goals.

This book is important for the following reasons:

- It allows organizations to anticipate and prepare for a range of cyber attacks. By understanding the motivations and techniques of a range of attackers, organizations can take proactive steps to mitigate vulnerabilities and defend against threats.

- It enables the organization to build effective strategies in the event of an attack. Organizations must be able to respond quickly and effectively to mitigate damage and protect people and assets. This requires a deep understanding of attackers' will and motivations.

- By understanding the motivations and methods of attackers, organizations can develop more effective strategies for protecting their assets and mitigating risks. This includes implementing stronger security measures, understanding the evolving threat landscape and investing in employee education to ensure that all members of the organization are aware of potential threats and how to defend against them.

In summary, understanding the mindset of cyber attackers is critical for developing effective cybersecurity strategies and defending against cyber threats. By understanding the motivations and tactics of cyber attackers, organizations can identify potential threats and vulnerabilities, develop effective incident response plans and stay ahead of emerging threats.

This is not merely nice to have, but critical in the digital era.

ACKNOWLEDGEMENTS

I'm eternally grateful to each person that gave their time to be interviewed for this book, and who have given incredible insights into the attacker mindset to help understand what motivates people to do what they do, and how we can build stronger defences to counteract threats.

First, I wish to thank my dear friend **Lisa Forte**, Partner at Red Goat Cyber Security, for providing the foreword to this book. Lisa is no stranger to the cybersecurity industry, having previously worked in counterterrorism and the UK police. She now runs a successful business, training executives and running cyber crisis simulations to build their resilience to cyber attacks. She understands all too well the operational and reputational damage that can be caused by large-scale cyber attacks, and hence her insights are hugely valuable for setting the scene for this book.

This book would not have been possible without the candid interview from former criminal **Tony Sales**, once dubbed 'Britain's greatest fraudster' in the UK media, and founder of We Fight Fraud. In Chapter 2, Tony provides insights on his 'rags to riches' upbringing and what turned him into an expert manipulator and social engineer, which enabled him to perfect his cons. He describes the turning point during his life of crime, and why he has dedicated the last 10 years to educating businesses and fighting fraud.

Hacktivist **Lauri Love** reveals how untapped skills, and an exuberance for social justice, led him to join Anonymous. With the might of the US Justice Department bearing down, how does one man take up the fight to avoid extradition? Find out more in Chapter 6. Lauri now works as a security research and keynote speaker to reveal the inner workings of how he was able to utilize common vulnerabilities and exploits to gain access and deface government websites.

A big thank you to the security researchers and journalists, who delve deep into the underworld, to understand and reveal more about the attackers and their techniques:

- **Shawn Loveland,** Chief Operating Officer at Resecurity and former Microsoft dark web researcher, provides a fascinating insight into the criminal underworld and how attackers calculate a reliable return on investment by outsourcing and procuring services. When we can better understand the rationale and motivation behind the attacks, we might just have our biggest opportunity for disruption.

- **Microsoft** Digital Crimes Unit Lead Investigator **Peter Anaman** has dedicated over 20 years to the fight against cybercrime and dismantling criminal infrastructure. From the early days of software piracy to tracking some of the most prolific business email compromise and ransomware operators, Peter reveals the innovative and novel ways that Microsoft has used to disrupt attackers.

- **Geoff White**, investigative journalist and author of *The Lazarus Heist*, discusses how North Korea's 'cyber warriors' are some of the most talented and rewarded people within the regime, yet are merely 'state-backed slaves', who have little choice in what they are tasked to do. This requires us to re-evaluate our perception of certain attackers and their motivations.

Thank you to the academics who have dedicated their careers to understanding criminal behaviour, and who have published their research on how to avert the tactics and behaviour:

- **Dr Paul Stephens**, Director of Academic Studies in Law, Policing and Social Sciences, and Principal Lecturer in Cybercrime and Digital Policing at Canterbury Christ Church University, who researches the social issues and human factors of cybercrime. We discuss whether society itself has enabled cybercrime to proliferate in the way it has, and how culture plays such a pivotal role in what comes next.

- **Dr Elisabeth Carter**, Associate Professor of Criminology, and Forensic Linguist at **Kingston University**, London, whose research involves evaluating the language that romance fraudsters use to entice and hook their victims, which is at a level akin to domestic abuse. We discuss how to stop victim blaming and shaming and how a 'trauma-informed' approach might just be the key in how we speak with victims of cybercrime.

- **Sarah Morris**, Professor of Digital Forensics and Director of Enterprise for the School of Electronics and Computer Science at the University of Southampton, is engaged in complex police cases focused on digital forensics and evidence collation. In a twist of fate, we start with a tale of two halves, where two people with exceptional skills can make different life choices. We also discuss how having a deeper appreciation for how computers actually work can help to reveal the mistakes that attackers make when trying to cover their tracks.

- **James Sullivan,** Director of Cyber at the Royal United Services Institute, the UK's leading defence and security think tank, describes how psychological warfare has become a long-term objective for many nation-sponsored actors and is a pivotal part of their cyber influence operations. It requires us to think more holistically on the *who* and *why*.

Thank you to the members of law enforcement, intelligence agencies and military who work tirelessly across multiple jurisdictions to investigate, identify and apprehend some of the most prolific threat actors, including:

- **Milan Patel,** a former FBI cybercrime special agent and co-founder of the managed security provider Bluevoyant, describes the difficulties law enforcement has in compiling evidence and attributing incidents to a specific actor. We discuss a notable case and the steps taken by the FBI to dismantle and apprehend key members of Anonymous splinter group Lulz-Sec.

- **Andrew Gould,** Detective Chief Superintendent of the City of London Police, describes how, when faced with an array of criminal and terrorist threats, policing is stretched too thin, and prioritization needs to be levied at those committing the highest levels of harm. We discuss a new wave of cyber sanctions aimed at stopping those from profiteering from their crimes.

- **Wing Commander Paul Norry,** from the UK Ministry of Defence, Development, Concepts and Doctrine Centre, is researching the global strategic trends that will influence society over the next 30 years. We discuss the role of strategic culture and how it can influence how a nation perceives itself and may act in a given scenario. We examine how Russia's policy to remain a great power has influenced many of its decisions in its active targeting of Ukraine.

Finally, a big thank you to my friend **Nadja El Fertasi,** former stakeholder engagement executive with NATO Communications and Information Agency, and founder of Thrive with EQ, where she prioritizes building human resilience within the sphere of cybersecurity. We discuss her work with key decision-makers, such as ambassadors, military committees and private-sector entities, in making strategic decisions in times of crisis, and how she now trains executives in emotional resilience. We discuss board-level responses to cybersecurity and how executives can make strategic and rational decisions no matter what level of pressure they may be facing.

Understanding types of attack, how they operate and why they are successful

01

The evolution of cybercrime in the digital age

CHAPTER OBJECTIVES

The aim of this chapter is to highlight how changes in technology and social dynamics have contributed to the rise and proliferation of cybercrime.

The two key parts of interest in this chapter are *cyber* and *digital*, so we shall start with some definitions to help our understanding.

Information security has been around longer than cyber, and, as the name suggests, it is concerned with the protection and security of information and data. There are some trains of thought that see cybersecurity as a subset of information security, while others consider it a separate discipline. Some even suggest that cybersecurity doesn't exist as a concept and is merely security in its widest sense.

Cyber, for the purpose of this book, considers the level of connectivity required to link people, infrastructure and data together, and how the level of connectivity and collaboration has changed over time. *Digital* is about the use of electronic and computational power, driven by data insights and the extrapolation of the internet, as we shall explore.

It is this level of interconnectivity and accessibility of technology that brings the parallels of *cybersecurity* and *cybercrime* together; and the two really do go hand in hand.

Before we think about the types of cyber attack and why they work, let's first consider how technological advancements enabled cyber-related crime to boom and how attackers have evolved their tactics and techniques to take advantage of how we use technology.

A PC in every home

The first commercial mainframe was unveiled by IBM in 1964 and it revolutionized how organizations were able to consolidate disparate computer systems and applications into a single platform. IBM defined the mainframe, as 'a large computer, to which many more can be connected' (IBM, 2019). Getting access to a mainframe was normally through computer terminals connected throughout offices. People became accustomed to using networked computers to perform their work.

In 1971, Ray Tomlinson is credited with inventing what we now refer to as *email*. Initially an experiment to see whether two computers could exchange a message meant for a person, Tomlinson created the 'name@host' address format that has become ubiquitous today. I doubt even Tomlinson could predict that email would not only become the most popular method of communication but also one of the most popular methods of launching a cyber attack, as we discuss in Chapter 3.

The commercialization of computers into homes came in the 1970s with the advent of microprocessors that enabled stand-alone computers that could be operated by individuals. One of the first personal computers (PCs) was built by Apple, who we continue to associate with smart technologies today. IBM entered the PC market in the early 1980s and would become one of the most dominant manufacturers of PCs, initially using Microsoft's MS-DOS as its operating system (see Microsoft, 1981). It would be the vision of Microsoft founder, Bill Gates, that people would have 'a computer on every desk and in every home running Microsoft software' – a sign no doubt of what was to come (Microsoft, 2008).

The user-friendly interfaces and operating systems continued, and Microsoft Windows launched in 1985. This has become one of the most dominant and widely used operating systems for many PC manufacturers. Microsoft Office was subsequently launched in 1989, which paved a new way for people to work and collaborate.

With the multitude of networked computers also came the need for computer-based security standards and controls, framed around the key pillars of confidentiality, integrity and availability. As computer systems and networks became more sophisticated, this opened many possibilities for people to work with technology, but also to bypass security.

The illegal copying, distribution and piracy of software was set to become a big problem for technology providers in the 1980s, as well as big business for those profiting from it. Copyright laws, trademarks and patents were amended to protect the intellectual property associated with computer programs, books, music and films. It is estimated that copyright infringements cost the IT industry billions in lost revenue each year, and that is just the tip of the iceberg when it comes to people continuing to profit from cyber-enabled fraud.

Microsoft began online enforcement in 2008 to protect from online piracy, spam, phishing and malware. It created the Digital Crimes Unit (DCU) to protect against the rapid growth of cybercrime. The DCU is an international, cross-disciplinarian team of technical, legal and business experts who investigate online criminal networks, and file criminal referrals and civil actions, with the core mission of deterring and disrupting cybercrime. Initially set up to deal with the rapid increase in counterfeit Windows licences, it has expanded to disrupt attackers by dismantling the technical infrastructure used to target victims.

DCU Lead Investigator Peter Anaman has been with the team since it was founded and provided me with a fascinating insight into the world of cybercrime, how it developed and the novel techniques used to disrupt attackers. Examples include:

- In 2000, the team managed an Internet Enforcement programme to send takedown notices to online auction sites to remove Windows 2000 that was being offered for mail order.

- In 2004, the team brought a civil action under the CAN-SPAM Act (Controlling the Assault of Non-Solicited Pornography and Marketing). In the US, spam that contains sexual content viewable in the email preview violates the 'brown paper wrapper' provision. This requires the label 'sexually explicit' in both the subject line and the initially viewable area of the email to protect consumers from offensive and harmful material. Collectively, defendants in these cases allegedly sent hundreds of thousands of email messages to internet users, without appropriate labels and controls (Microsoft, 2004).

- In 2006, the team sent a criminal referral to Bulgarian law enforcement that led to the arrest of an international phishing operation. The group crafted emails to make them appear as if they were sent by Microsoft News (MSN) customer service representatives and created dozens of fake web pages that mimicked the design, logo and trademark of official MSN pages. The emails invited the target to update personal data such as credit card details and personal identification and verification numbers. That information was used to make purchases and receive money transfers, defrauding US, German and UK credit card holders of more than $50,000 (Kornblum and Evers, 2006).

We'll touch on more stories from the Microsoft DCU throughout the book. But first, let's explore how the internet took the world by storm, and enabled crime to proliferate to new levels.

Dawn of the World Wide Web

The *internet* was formed from a combination of researchers, engineers and scientists throughout the 1960s and 1970s, as scientists experimented with machine-to-machine communications and methods of data transfer. The World Wide Web, as we know it, came about after Sir Tim Berners-Lee in 1989 created an application to run on the internet that enabled people to access websites.

Despite the Web not becoming mainstream until the 1990s, cyber attacks were being experienced on the internet from malicious programs and software, which we commonly refer to as *malware*.

These can be *worms* – a stand-alone piece of malware capable of self-replicating to other connected machines, often utilizing a known vulnerability in the software program that an attacker has learnt to exploit.

Another form of malware is a *virus*, which inserts code into a legitimate program and relies on the system resources to copy and spread. The virus can often be dormant until it is activated by a human inadvertently opening an infected file, for example, that releases the program or 'payload' onto the machine.

A *trojan*, in comparison, is designed to mimic the legitimate software but does not replicate like a worm or virus. Once a person has 'executed' the trojan software, it sits on the machine and is used to copy and steal data, or credentials, and can also be used as a back door for attackers to launch other malware into the environment. The trojan is so named after the Trojan horse in Greek mythology. The tale is that Greek warriors were able to enter the fortified city of Troy by hiding inside a large wooden horse they had built. The Greeks tricked the Trojans into believing the horse was a gift, and it was taken inside the city walls, whereby the soldiers then seized control of the city from within. The 'trojan', in the context of security, is therefore known for its subversion and masquerade tactics.

The first example of a worm is believed to be the Morris worm – named after its creator Robert Morris – released in 1988 (FBI, 2023a). Morris initially created the worm to make the point to his peers that one machine could be utilized to infect another. Within 24 hours of the worm's release, it had infected over 6,000 Unix machines – which were principally used for hosting web servers – rendering them useless until they could be manually reprogrammed to remove the worm. As the internet was not in wide use at this time, it mainly impacted research facilities, universities and military installations across the US. Despite the Computer Fraud and Abuse Act of 1986, Morris was spared jail, instead receiving a fine and 400 hours' community service.

The incident highlighted how easy it might be for a stand-alone and malicious program to cause downtime to many institutions simultaneously. It served as a wake-up call to the perils associated with the internet. As a result, developers of hardware and software began to create programs to detect malicious programs – the forerunners to anti-malware software. Meanwhile, it also spurred on a generation of attackers, keen to understand how they could exploit malicious programs to cause mayhem to untold institutions.

The first commercial anti-malware products were made available in the late 1980s by Avast and McAfee. Anti-malware solutions evolved not only to detect malware but as mechanisms to remove malicious programs from the machines.

One of the fastest-spreading viruses came in the form of the Melissa virus in 1999 (FBI, 2023b), created by David Lee Smith and named after a stripper he met in Florida. People were enticed by the assumption that they could access and download free adult content by giving away free passwords to fee-paying sites. Once the person took the bait, a document was opened in Microsoft Word that unleashed the virus onto their computers by using a macro to hijack the Microsoft Outlook email system, which in turn sent messages to the first 50 people in the mailing list. It was designed like an automated chain letter, further enticing people to open more virus-laden documents with the promise of explicit materials. Email servers at more than 300 organizations and government agencies worldwide became overloaded, and some had to be shut down entirely, disrupting over a million email accounts. The clean-up and repair was estimated at over $80 million. The virus was not intended to steal information, but is an example of how attackers can use a virus to cause untold downtime. For his part in the crime, Smith was sentenced to 20 months in a federal prison.

Again, the Melissa virus was to serve as a wake-up call on how quickly a virus can disseminate and impact multiple systems. For law enforcement agencies, it emphasized the need to ramp up cybersecurity investigative capabilities. It also highlighted how people can be manipulated to 'click and open' documents and links with the promise of getting something in return. The evolving tactics used to induce people to perform specific actions are an area that we shall explore further in Chapter 3, and throughout the book.

During the 1990s, cybercrime was principally concentrated on gaining access to networks and data, potentially for the kudos factor by lone attackers looking to make a name for themselves. It is maybe where we draw the inference of the lone, shadowy figure sat behind a PC wearing a hoody that the media have latched on to and made mainstream, and which has become synonymous with the public's perception of cybercrime. This was perhaps first widely demonstrated in the 1995 film *Hackers* starring Angelina Jolie and Jonny Lee Miller as college kids looking to wreak havoc and revenge against the US government. The film became a cult classic, not just in terms of the 'hacker manifesto' that it portrays but how it could be said to glamorize the activists and anarchists rallying together for what they perceive as a greater good. The film's hacker manifesto states, 'This is our world now... the world of the electron and the switch... We exist without skin colour, without nationality, without religious bias... and you call us criminals... Yes, I am a criminal. My crime is that of curiosity.' The latter sentence seems to act as a beckoning cry to many teenagers to be curious, to experiment and to join the cybercrime revolution. We will explore the trials and tribulations of a former Anonymous activist in Chapter 6.

The dot.com bubble becomes lucrative

While many cyber attackers were causing untold financial damage because of their ability to shut down or deface websites and networks, there wasn't much financial gain for the attackers themselves. What changed was the need to monetize and reward their efforts. After all, simply hacking a few government websites and institutions to cause downtime won't pay the bills. They needed more motivation.

The link between cybercrime and fraud took off in earnest with e-commerce in the mid-1990s. No longer were websites just static sites providing information; people were buying goods and services online. It paved the way for many organizations to enter new markets and ship their products to different countries, and that required the ability for individuals to transact using credit cards. The 'buy now, pay later' model boomed, and investors were keen to take advantage of the excitement that was brewing around e-commerce, as retailers took to offering more services online. Amazon and eBay were both founded in 1995 and remain two of the largest online retailers today.

Meanwhile, not only did we see the rise of credit card fraud and identity theft, but the ease of downloading applications and services from the internet introduced a raft of banking trojans. As the name suggests, the trojan is designed to sit on someone's home PC to steal banking credentials and other forms of personal data. Consumers wanted to be assured of safer ways to pay and transfer money, and hence PayPal was launched in 1999 to act as an interface between the retailer and consumer.

In 2006 ZBot, or Zues-botnet, became one of the most prolific banking trojans. The malware was designed not just to steal bank accounts and other financial information, but to monitor the individual's web-browsing habits. This information was either used directly by the attacker or sold to other attackers through dark-web markets. What set Zbot apart was that, once the machine had become infected, it enabled it to be recruited to a botnet.

WHAT IS A BOTNET?

A botnet is a group of internet-connected devices that can be controlled by a 'command and control' server to perform various attacks such as denial-of-access, stealing data and other tasks determined by the attacker. These bots can transcend multiple different organizations, since they are connected via the internet, as opposed to the organization's own network. Botnets are often referred to as 'zombie armies' and have been used to perform Distributed-Denial-of-Service (DDOS) attacks: a command can be released to thousands of machines simultaneously requesting that they attempt to access a single resource on the victim's network, seeking to overwhelm it and cause it to fail. Because the botnet sits on multiple legitimate machines, it is hard to decipher real transactions from fake ones. Not only can attackers hijack and command machines, but they can do this at scale.

In 2011, the Zbot source code was leaked on a file-sharing site, and was capitalized upon by many attackers, who created customized variants of the underpinning malicious code that was amended to avoid detection, or perform other tasks. Its success, like many trojans, was its ability to operate in stealth mode, which made it a firm favourite with many attackers.

In fact, most strains of malware that we see today are variants of other malware families that preceded them, with tweaks designed to take advantage of gaps in known software vulnerabilities, to bypass anti-malware and other detections, or to perform specific tasks identified by groups of attackers. Those tasks are dependent on the overall objective of the attacker. So, the important thing to remember is that, as software develops, so does malware.

Rise of social media

Many of the websites developed in the 1990s also enabled people to communicate on websites through bulletin boards, which ultimately led to websites and applications designed solely for the purpose of communication and collaboration.

Friends Reunited is perhaps one of the earliest social sites. Launched in July 2000 in the UK by a husband and wife, it was designed to connect lost friends and family members (Hendelmann, 2023). It enabled people to set up personal profiles and include information such as schools, universities, workplaces, sports clubs, armed forces, that other people could search for and connect to. What made this platform interesting was that the company was forced to temporarily suspend the message board in November 2001 after students posted defamatory comments about their previous teachers. This was perhaps a sign of things to come, of how social media has enabled people to post misleading and inaccurate information for fun, revenge or other nefarious purposes.

In quick succession, some of the largest social media platforms in the world were launched (Anyaegbunam, 2023), between them amassing billions of active users (Figure 1.1).

The biggest appeal for the most part, is that these platforms are free for individual users. The platforms generate revenue by charging membership fees for specific content, charging organizations that have a presence on the platform, and through tailored advertising, enabled as a result of mass profiling on and off the platforms. The levels of profiling and advertising revenues are made possible by the sharing and oversharing of personal data performed by the individuals themselves.

FIGURE 1.1 Timeline of social media launches

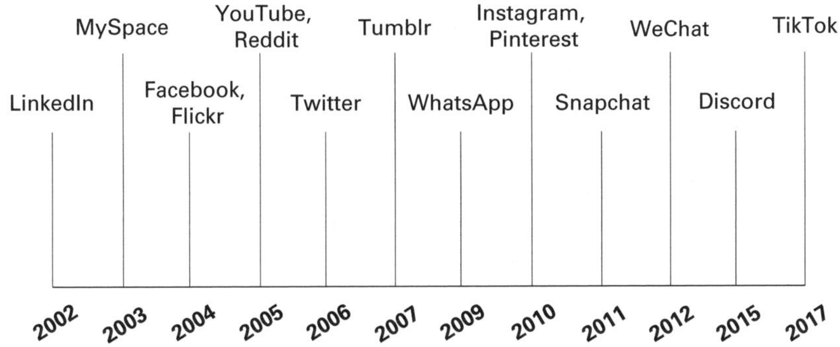

Not only has social media become big business for multiple organizations trying to reach specific demographics of the population, it has become an attacker's paradise, as they too use the platforms for collating information to enable them to target their victims through mass manipulation.

Regulators have tried to hold social media providers to account for abusing and violating data protection laws and ensuring they have appropriate security and privacy controls. Overall, however, this appears to have had little effect on the willingness and desire of individuals to continue to use these platforms, despite countless data breaches and regulatory fines.

One of the most infamous examples of mass manipulation through social media is attributed to the Cambridge Analytica scandal. First uncovered in 2018, the scandal highlighted how Cambridge Analytica, a UK political data analytics firm, had harvested personal data on Facebook relating to over 50 million people since 2015 (Weiss, 2018). A personality quiz called 'This is your political life' collated information entered through the quiz, as well as data from the connected profiles of the user's friends. This in turn was used to create algorithms designed to exploit and sway the political beliefs and opinions of millions of voters.

The scandal would open a Pandora's box on the scale of profiling and information that could be bought and sold on individuals. In 2019, the US Federal Trade Commission (FTC) slapped Facebook with a record fine of $5 billion and imposed restrictions on the company for deceiving users regarding their ability to control their privacy (FTC, 2019). The FTC alleged that Facebook failed to take appropriate action to deal with applications that it knew were violating its platform policies. We shall take a further look at how people can be psychologically manipulated to perform specific actions in Chapter 2.

Separate from the Cambridge Analytica scandal, the 2016 US presidential election was hit with further controversy as the Russian government was implicated in interference in the Hilary Clinton campaign. Thousands of private emails were published by WikiLeaks with the alleged aim of boosting Donald Trump's campaign and creating political disarray between US electorates. We shall circle back round to this in Chapter 10, where we explore Russia's strategic culture, and the role of nation-sponsored actors.

The ability to obtain information from multiple sources was taking off in a big way as even more services and data became digitally connected.

The internet of everything

The increased boom created by internet and social media platforms meant that many organizations were looking to curtail the rising costs associated with data storage and network bandwidth. The overheads to build and maintain on-premises data centres were high, and so the advent of cloud computing was a welcome relief for many.

The first hyper-scale public cloud offering was launched by Amazon in 2006 as Amazon Web Services (AWS). It was designed through its own necessity and the success of the retail arm of the business. It was taking too long to develop and build services because of the lead times in purchasing hardware and storage and designing the services to run on top. With multiple projects on the go at any one time, Amazon needed to build a common infrastructure that would allow multiple teams to collaborate. Not only did this revolutionize how Amazon managed its technology programs, but the company realized that this could also be commercialized. Hence the 'infrastructure as a service' (IaaS) model took off in a big way, as many organizations wanted cost-effective and scalable solutions.

By 2008, Google had launched its own cloud platform, the Google App Engine, which enabled developers to build and run applications on its infrastructure. Google continued to develop more cloud-enabled services and was formally adopted as Google Cloud Platform (GCP) in 2013. In 2008, Microsoft announced it would enter the cloud market, and hence Windows Azure was launched in 2010, renamed as Microsoft Azure in 2014. Although Alibaba Cloud was established in China in 2009, it was principally for local markets. In 2014, Alibaba became the first Chinese company to provide cloud services overseas, although it principally dominates the Asia-Pacific markets.

By the beginning of 2023, the most dominant cloud platforms by market share were Amazon (AWS), Microsoft (Azure), Google (GCP) and Alibaba Cloud, closely followed by Oracle and IBM (Kyndryl) (Zhang, 2023). Many smaller cloud service providers are growing to cater for market demands.

Simply put, the hyper-scale of the cloud has enabled multiple 'things' to be connected to the internet. This has become known as the Internet of Things, or IoT. In 2015, Cisco took this one step further by coining the phrase the 'internet of everything'. This is an apt term to describe how billions of devices are connected to the internet, enabling people to consume a huge array of online services, as smart technologies become embedded in multiple households and organizations. It is estimated that, by 2025, over half of the world's data will be stored in public clouds or on social media platforms. This equates to 100 zettabytes of data (1 zettabyte is 1 billion terabytes) (Morgan, 2020).

No longer is cybersecurity thought about as principally a technology issue, as it impacts everything that is connected to the internet, including the industrial systems that control the critical infrastructure that underpins the very fabric of society. The lines between the physical and digital spheres are becoming blurred. This hyper-scale of interconnected things has caused two realities:

- From the attacker's perspective, the attack surface is growing exponentially as new applications, devices and resources come online, every minute of every day. Each of these provides a potential new target, especially given the propensity for misconfiguration and vulnerabilities that can be exploited.

- From the defender's perspective, this level of connectivity has provided a hyper-scale level of visibility and threat intelligence. Each 'thing' is generating huge volumes of data and, when utilized in conjunction with vast levels of computational power, can provide deep insights on patterns of attacker behaviour and how their tactics and techniques are evolving.

Not only are deep levels of threat intelligence held by private organizations and government agencies, but the accessibility of available information held in public records, on social media, websites, online forums and in publications has created a wave of 'open-source intelligence' (OSINT). The process itself refers to the ability to collect, analyse and use information that has been legally and ethically accessed for research purposes. OSINT plays a significant role in how national security, law enforcement and cybersecurity providers obtain and use intelligence for legitimate purposes to provide evidence of wrongdoing by groups of attackers. This requires the ability to analyse and make sense of an array of disparate data sets. So how exactly do you make sense of so much data?

AI and automation

We often think of the advent of artificial intelligence (AI) as a relatively new phenomenon, but the idea was first considered in the 1950s, as scientists and researchers began to theorize whether it would be possible to one day have a computer that was as intelligent as a human. Although there was much excitement about the possibilities, there were not enough resources, computational power or know-how to make this a reality.

As the level of processing power and experimentation improved, so did the ability to create machine learning (ML) algorithms capable of processing large data sets. Cloud storage was a turning point in providing the level of computational power and data volumes that may be required to perform deep-learning capability and reasoning to complex problems. It was just a matter of time for the world to catch up with itself, as big tech, as well as research facilities, started to invest large sums of money in speech, language and image recognition and neural networks that are core to how a machine might make sense of a human's environment.

Generative AI, as an example, can create text, images and other media in response to written prompts and doesn't require specific coding. As the levels of computation and data sets grew, so did the quality of the output. When OpenAI released its generative pre-trained transformed platform GPT-3 in November 2022 it overtook TikTok as the most downloaded application in history, amassing 100 million subscribers in just two months (Hu, 2023). It is not surprising, therefore, that one of the largest supercomputers is hosted on Microsoft Azure and runs OpenAI's GPT platform. What made GPT-3 a game changer is that it was trained on 45 terabytes of open-source data held on the internet, utilizing ingested content from books, academic papers and the entirety of Wikipedia. GPT was about to enter its biggest testing phase in which anyone could pose questions to it. When OpenAI released GPT-4 in March 2023, it took this to the next level with a second wave of creativity and advanced reasoning capabilities that enabled the system to generate more sophisticated language models and outputs (OpenAI, 2023).

Critics of generative AI argue that such technologies can be used for nefarious purposes, including finding ways to bypass systems, creating malicious code that could be injected into software programs, and envisaging more elaborate ways to manipulate people. It could be counterargued, however, that such information is already available on the internet. The difference perhaps is that AI can generate in seconds. Another example is the use of 'deep fakes' to create images or voice skins of real people in unreal situations, which can be used to spread disinformation.

By September 2023, work had already begun on GPT-5, which may deliver the next phase of 'artificial general intelligence'. This refers to AI's ability to comprehend and learn any task or idea that humans can, and in an almost indistinguishable way (Blale, 2023). Many questions are being raised on the ethical dilemmas of using AI, and whether we have a good comprehension of the risks.

To some extent, it is irrelevant whether the source of a cyber attack is from a human or a machine because it is, ultimately, generated to fulfil the objective of a human adversary. In much the same way as attackers have created malware or scripting to make different phases of their assault more efficient and cost-effective, to utilize such technology for nefarious purposes still requires financial outlay and resources, as well as a deep understanding of the technology itself. The issue from a cybersecurity perspective is twofold: understanding the AI models themselves and how the algorithms can be manipulated, with misinformation and false data, to alter the outcome.

Such advances in technology and research become high-value targets for espionage, due to the competitive edge it can provide organizations, as well as nations. The trade in information has become akin to the 'new oil' in its diversity, richness and potential and the insights that it can generate.

Conclusion

In this chapter, we have looked at how cybercrime has evolved in line with technology, and how widely it has scaled. What we can say for sure is that the proliferation of technology shows no sign of slowing down, and attackers will continue to find ways to use it for nefarious purposes. It is the reason this book is centred on counteracting the human adversary, as opposed to specific technologies.

The ability to take advantage of new and emerging technologies, and how they could be utilized, is discussed in the next chapters. When we have a deeper understanding of the *why*, the *how* also starts to make a lot more sense.

References

Anyaegbunam, D (2023) 'The top 20+ social media platforms for 2023', Mirasee, mirasee.com/blog/social-media-platforms-2 (archived at https://perma.cc/U85A-4V5K)

Blale, A (2023) 'GPT-5 could soon change the world in one incredible way', Digital Trends, 28 March, digitaltrends.com/computing/gpt-5-artificial-general-intelligence (archived at https://perma.cc/L27K-5MNC)

FBI (2023a) 'Morris worm', History: Famous Cases & Criminals, fbi.gov/history/famous-cases/morris-worm (archived at https://perma.cc/S6HN-7BC7)

FBI (2023b) 'Melissa virus', History: Famous Cases & Criminals, fbi.gov/history/famous-cases/melissa-virus (archived at https://perma.cc/57LP-4GQ6)

FTC (2019) 'FTC imposes $5 billion penalty and sweeping new privacy restrictions on Facebook', press release, 24 May, ftc.gov/news-events/news/press-releases/2019/07/ftc-imposes-5-billion-penalty-sweeping-new-privacy-restrictions-facebook (archived at https://perma.cc/4H25-SDCM)

Hendelmann, V (2023) 'What happed to Friends Reunited? Here's why the UK-based social network failed', Productmint, productmint.com/what-happened-to-friends-reunited (archived at https://perma.cc/L7SD-47TW)

Hu, K (2023) 'ChatGPT sets records for fast-growing user base', Reuters, 2 February, reuters.com/technology/chatgpt-sets-record-fastest-growing-user-base-analyst-note-2023-02-01 (archived at https://perma.cc/5ABY-TWVV)

IBM (2019) 'A brief history of the mainframe', IBM Community, 23 December, community.ibm.com/community/user/ibmz-and-linuxone/blogs/destination-z1/2019/12/23/a-brief-history-of-the-mainframe-world (archived at https://perma.cc/P9AD-EU8N)

Kornblum, A and Evers, J (2006) 'Microsoft helps net Bulgarian phishers', CNET, 23 January, cnet.com/news/privacy/microsoft-helps-net-bulgarian-phishers (archived at https://perma.cc/8ZXB-LHNU)

Microsoft (1981) 'Timeline', microsoft.com/en-gb/about/timeline (archived at https://perma.cc/D6EF-2RFZ)

Microsoft (2004) 'Microsoft sues spammers who violate CAN-SPAM "Brown Paper Wrapper" rule', 2 December, news.microsoft.com/2004/12/02/microsoft-sues-spammers-who-violate-can-spam-brown-paper-wrapper-rule (archived at https://perma.cc/B6CU-QM9C)

Microsoft (2008) 'Iconic Albuquerque photo re-created', news.microsoft.com/2008/06/25/iconic-albuquerque-photo-re-created (archived at https://perma.cc/563G-5PKA)

Morgan, S (2020) 'The world will store 200 zettabytes of data by 2025', Cybercrime Magazine, 8 June, cybersecurityventures.com/the-world-will-store-200-zettabytes-of-data-by-2025 (archived at https://perma.cc/PB7K-8CU9)

OpenAI (2023) 'GPT-4 is OpenAI's most advanced system, producing safer and more useful responses', openai.com/product/gpt-4 (archived at https://perma.cc/5TUD-ZTH2)

Weiss, B (2018) 'Trump-linked firm Cambridge Analytica collected personal information from 50 million Facebook users without permission', Business Insider, 17 March, businessinsider.com/cambridge-analytica-trump-firm-facebook-data-50-million-users-2018-3?r=US&IR=T (archived at https://perma.cc/4MHG-HWSQ)

Zhang, M (2023) 'Top 10 cloud service providers globally in 2023', Dgtl Infra, 1 January, dgtlinfra.com/top-10-cloud-service-providers-2022 (archived at https://perma.cc/EZ8S-JQHF)

02

Understanding the will and motivation of attackers

CHAPTER OBJECTIVES

In this chapter, we shall explore the humans behind the attacks, and what motivates them to do what they do.

The single biggest question we can ask when it comes to understanding the evolving tactics and techniques of cyber attackers is to ask *why*. Contrary to widespread belief, not all attackers are motivated by financial gain. Often, it is driven by opportunity and to prove a point, and it quickly escalates, whether intentional or not.

Before we get into the types of attack and why they work, we need to consider the will and motivation behind different individuals and groups. When we understand the who, the what and the why, as well as the methods and outcomes of attacks, they start to make more sense. When we understand the will of the attackers, we can start to consider how to counteract them.

Understanding the social sciences

This is an area where scholars, academics and researchers tend to thrive. At a high level, it involves the principle of examining human behaviour in the context of an individual's social environment, standing and culture. Simply examining human behaviour by itself is not enough; we also need to understand the circumstances of the individual that drove them to exhibit the behaviour in the way they did.

Social sciences can include aspects of sociology, psychology, anthropology and economics. The *International Journal of Cybersecurity Intelligence and Cybercrime* highlights that research into the field of *cyber-criminology* needs to be considered from two perspectives: general crime-related theories around society, self-control, lifestyle and delinquency; and computer science, technical knowledge and capability. The two must come together to be most effective, especially when considering the tactics and techniques deployed (Wu et al, 2023).

Much academic research tends to be very compartmentalized in that it either consists of analysing the social aspects or cybersecurity aspects, but rarely both together. Hence, more emphasis on cybercriminality is required. Criminologists and computer scientists need to build collaborative relationships. Otherwise, cybercrime and cybersecurity research will continue to exist in silos, thus missing the wider opportunity to integrate key insights and lessons learnt from major cyber events. This is why I wrote this book: to try to bring some of these thoughts and perspectives together.

Arguably, it requires someone who has worked in cybersecurity, and can join some of the disparate areas together, to widen the conversation and to address the challenges that many organizations and individuals are facing. Many cyber attacks are indiscriminate and often with no regard for the impact on the end consumer who may be most affected by such crimes.

The art of social engineering

Social engineering, by contrast to the wider discipline of social science, is the ability to manipulate a person's or group's behaviour at scale in order to produce a desired outcome or action. Depending on the degree of manipulation, this can also lead to a level of coercion and control over the intended targets. It is most intricately linked to the field of psychology.

The term *sociale ingeniurs* was first coined by Dutch industrialist JC Van Marken in 1894 (CompTIA, 2023) from studying employers that needed specialists who understood human challenges, as well as technical specialists to manage non-human challenges. It was perhaps simplistic in its early principles, but perspectives and studies on social engineering have continued to evolve, to gain a deeper understanding of human behaviour.

For social engineering to be most successful, it requires a body of knowledge about the culture and social dynamics of the person or company to be engineered, as well as an appreciation of the tools and techniques that will work in each situation. This requires a degree of reconnaissance and information gathering on the subject(s), before attempting to manipulate the social dynamics of the situation.

Cybercrime

Cybercrime is largely considered a reflection or redirection of crime from a physical space to a virtual space, given that most crimes committed in person can be translated to those online, and whether this is a *cyber-enabled* or a *cyber-dependent* crime. The UK Crown Prosecution Service (CPS) offers useful guidance and examples to describe the difference, from a criminal and law enforcement perspective (CPS, 2019). Other countries may have variations of these.

WHAT IS CYBER-ENABLED CRIME?

This generally refers to crimes that can be delivered in cyberspace. The CPS describes them as 'traditional crimes which can be increased in scale or reach by the use of computers, computer networks or other forms of ICT, such as cyber-enabled fraud and data theft'.

WHAT IS CYBER-DEPENDENT CRIME?

This generally refers to crimes that need to be delivered in cyberspace. The CPS describes these as 'crimes that can be committed only through the use of ICT devices, where the devices are both the tool for committing the crime, and the target of the crime'. These fall broadly into two areas:

- illicit intrusions into computer networks, for the purposes of stealing, damaging, distorting or destroying data
- disruption or downgrading of computer functionality and network space, such as malware and DDOS attacks.

The level of criminality and the intended outcomes generally do not change, even if the attacker changes their modus operandi. It is an important consideration in relation to discussions in the previous chapter where we explored how cybercrime has evolved as technology has evolved, and how organizations as well as individuals have adapted to new ways of working and collaborating.

This is a position echoed by Tony Sales, once dubbed 'Britain's greatest fraudster' by the British media, as we shall discover...

The fraudster's mindset

I became intrigued by Tony Sales after reading several media articles about his life as a fraudster, and there were two particular things that caught my attention:

- First, Sales' opinion that 'there are no new frauds' – everything that we see today has been tried before.

- Second, how Sales changed his ways by effectively 'growing up and wanting a positive role model for his children', something that he never had, and which he claims had a profound impact on *why* he inadvertently chose a life of crime from an early age.

I was delighted when Sales agreed to talk candidly with me about his background. So, let me introduce you to Tony Sales – what started him on his journey, how he became a self-declared 'social engineering expert' and why he now educates people and organizations on fraud prevention.

Escalating to a life of crime

The biggest impact on Sales' childhood was not having a father figure. His biological father left when he was just a baby, and he recalls it being an extremely difficult childhood. He did not have anyone in particular to tell him right from wrong, did not have anyone to look up to, and no one did the typical 'Dad' things that you might expect.

Tony learnt from an early age how to socially manipulate his environment and family. He emphasized the need to try to outsmart those around you when you are on your own and can only rely on yourself. He found that his peer group and friends were in comparable situations, with one or more absent parents, and all having difficult experiences, so they sought kinship in each other. No matter who you are and where you have come from, there is still an innate need for the feeling of social belonging. We are, after all, social beings that need a sense of community.

You might learn that you need money to buy things you want, but your family does not have money, and so you need to make it. You take the legal route first, like washing cars or working in a shop, and then realize it is not enough…

In Sales' opinion, if you come from a working-class background, no one expects you to amount to anything. You will probably enter a service industry, and it is almost impossible to pull yourself out of that situation alone, without monetary support and guidance. Many people in that situation accept that this is their position in life. But what if you want more? You have no prospects, no qualifications, so what do you do?

Sales learnt that petty theft was not the answer, having been caught stealing items from a shop at a young age. He decided that he needed his independence, to be able to do what he wanted and buy the things that others had, but without having to ask for it. He also identified that he did not want to be stuck in this life, in this environment, and that to get out was going to require fundamental change.

Sales explained that, ultimately, what drives someone, drives them all the way through life. This is embedded, in terms of what gives you motivation, and, when you realize you are good at something, you want more, you want the kudos, in the same way that someone does in a legitimate job. You get a taste for money and the finer things, and you do not want to lose it or go back; so you establish what you are good at, and you build on that drive and skill.

There is also an assumption that you will not get caught, so you are willing to take more risk each time. By taking more risks, however, and going for higher targets, you are more likely to be noticed – and caught.

Learning how to engineer an outcome

Sales believes that his aptitude and skill for social engineering was a result of being highly observant – watching people, taking in information and learning their mannerisms.

What he observed is that each of us has a pattern of what we do and how we do it. You follow your own routine and way of doing things to the point where it becomes subconscious because you fall into a natural rhythm that is normal for you.

Sales identified that being quick witted and calm is important when dealing with people. The need to be able to quickly answer a question came from being stopped by the police and being asked what he was up to. If you hesitate or say the wrong thing, you know you are going to be in trouble, so Sales learnt how to answer the questions in ways that would mean the least amount of trouble. So, he learnt to tell people what they wanted to hear. After a while, it became second nature for Sales to be able to think on his feet and anticipate answers to key questions before they were even asked.

Sales' theory is that 'it takes one to know one' to spot how a fraudster or attacker might operate: you need to have walked in their shoes to consider how they think and how they use 'workarounds' to establish a relationship with an individual or organization. In his own words, '*I just don't care as a criminal. I will do what I need to do.*'

Sales explained that traditional security testing does not work because you need to know what you are really facing. He believes that there is a difference between an actual criminal and someone who is trying to be one. There is an extra level of deviance that security testers may not consider, or they may have a moral compass, which differs from a criminal.

Understanding motivations

Tony Sales highlights that, with a criminal mindset, learning how to manipulate situations is easy to do, and he can almost predict what the next move or outcome will be based on how he has engineered the situation. In some ways, we all can do this, since we may have a gut feeling or intuition for how we react in different scenarios, but what Sales describes is the ability to hone this innate skill.

Sales identified two fundamental traits that we, as humans, are driven by. The first is *fear* and the second is *love*. Whether you are frozen in fear or blinded by love, these fundamental emotions make people think irrationally and do things that may not make sense because of clouded or misplaced judgement.

I asked Sales to explain a comment he made to the media, that 'there are no new frauds'. He described that, from his perspective, it is such an easy thing to do. He needs to find a way to achieve his objectives, and that is just the way it is. He may adopt a slightly different ruse, dependent on the person or situation but, by and large, it has all been done before.

Sales stated that criminals are unrestricted in how a crime is committed. Sometimes, it is opportunistic by firstly obtaining information and then deciding what to do with it; other times, it can be a need to find and extract specific information, to aid a specific objective. There are many ways to do this, based on who you are, what you know and how much time and effort is needed to build a level of trust with someone.

Sales argues that everyone has interacted with the criminal underworld at some point in their life – perhaps experimenting with drugs at college, or buying recreational drugs or fake designer products. It is not just those from poorer socio-economic backgrounds that are susceptible, but the affluent too. When thinking about people at university in particular, they may become doctors, lawyers and politicians, and may have skeletons in the cupboard that they do not want exposed.

Such fear of being exposed, whether through embarrassment or loss of social standing, makes some people prone to extortion. Sales highlights that, with the sheer volume of information and pictures being shared on social media, there is always going to be something out there that you would prefer to stay hidden. Someone else just needs to be determined enough to find out what and why. This principle can also be replicated with an organization.

Learning about a target

As Tony Sales highlights, people are creatures of habit. Especially those, perhaps, that work in a traditional 9 to 5, Monday to Friday routine in an office environment. What Sales identified is that people start to let their guard down by Thursday, as they are looking forward to the weekend, and they may go for a few drinks on a Friday at an establishment close to the office. And they talk – about a lot of things that are going on, about projects, about other people at work, about their boss. It is not malicious, it is just office chat, but it is ripe with information. You are not going to stop people talking in their perceived safe social groups, and you can tap into it. As Sales points out, 'as a criminal, I don't care who you are, or where you are – it's all fair game'.

This is why traditional security vulnerability and penetration testing just does not work in Sales' opinion. Management will not allow testers to have casual conversations with employees in case it violates their privacy, but this potentially misses all the normal social interactions that people have inside and outside work, and how easy it can be to extract information from people with extremely limited effort, especially when their guard is down.

This is a crucial point, which we will circle back to in Chapter 12, that serves as a wake-up call for organizations to really consider how they educate and train people, and whether it is having the desired outcome.

Evolving tactics and techniques

Tony Sales explains that, despite the lifestyle, and despite the tricks, trust is difficult to obtain. After all, you are a criminal, and are prone to looking out for yourself and your needs. This is why most things are operated on a need-to-know basis. The less you know about the specifics of an operation you are involved in, the less danger you are in if you are caught; and you have little chance of trying to take over the operation.

Sales explained that most frauds he committed were by him and his childhood best friend. Only Sales and this person knew everything. Other people were employed only to perform specific tasks, and no one else knew the details of the end-to-end plan. At the height of his fraudulent activity, Sales' crew were moving plasma TV screens or Rolex watches to order. Marks and buyers were lined up in advance, and goods and money were moved quickly, paying each person for their part as they went. For Sales in particular, this was never about physically stealing the goods, but playing the system to 'smash and grab' in a unique way.

Invariably, this meant having an insider who collected information on individuals with high credit ratings. This was then used to make fake IDs, and the team also learnt answers to security questions. The core principle was that people with impeccable records of credit would have few issues with getting loans, and this is what was relied on. The objective was to hit as many stores as possible in succession, to buy goods on credit, before anyone noticed.

Sales points out that, before digitalization and real-time cross-referencing of data sources and credit reference agencies, many processes were performed manually. For example, when creating fake IDs, the driving licence number was invented. But the process changed, which meant institutions could verify that level of identification at source. Simply having an ID was not enough; the data also had to match, which took more time and effort.

In addition, when financial institutions started to introduce security questions, if someone got it wrong in one store, they just went into the next one, where they would be asked the same question, and would eventually have the correct answer. At that time, banks or credit agencies were not recognizing quickly enough that someone had failed a security check, and they were not rotating questions, or asking for other information. There was no automatic lock on the accounts, so a thief could just try again until successful.

Moving fraud online

From Tony Sales' perspective, 'fraud is fraud', and it is just a case of 'horses for courses' in that you adapt to a new situation and what is going to work best in that environment. So, committing fraud online follows the same principle as committing fraud in person.

As Sales highlights, if the bank or organization has changed its processes, the criminal must adapt too if they are to continue to achieve the intended outcomes. It used to be that, to buy goods on credit, you had to go in store, fill out a form, maybe run a credit check, and it could be days or weeks before the paperwork was approved. Now it can all be done online, and financial institutions can give you an instant decision, as they cross-check and correlate information in real time. So, does that mean fraud is prevented? No – it just means that criminals must learn how to circumvent the process.

How fraud differs in person versus online

Tony Sales believes that you need more confidence to commit a fraud in person than online. You must be able to stand right in front of someone, behave normally and be convincing. That is not required online. You do, however, need to understand the fraud: what to do and how to do it. According to Sales, you just work it out, based on whether you need to take or receive money. Sales learnt the pitfalls and errors from earlier attempts and adjusted. He found that 'phone spoofing' provided an easy way to confirm and verify trust, by pretending to be the bank and contacting the person directly. Vulnerable people tend to give a lot of information away over the phone when they believe they are talking to someone in authority. This collated information can be shared online quickly and easily.

Fraudster versus cybercriminal

In Sales' opinion, a cybercriminal is of a different class compared with someone who commits fraud in person. He believes that cybercrime starts at a level above 'traditional' working-class crime, as young people in that environment tend not to have access to computers. Sales also believes, however, that, despite these different backgrounds, the majority of criminals are still financially motivated: to make more money and to do this for as long as possible without being caught. As Sales highlighted, when the two meet and learn to work in unison, it can lead to big trouble!

Sales sees the difference between committing a crime in person and online as volume and scale. Online, you do not have to be near the target, not even in the same country, and that offers a whole new realm of opportunities. There is less likelihood that you will be 'caught in the act', as you might be in person. We shall discuss some of the further challenges that law enforcement have with traditional lines of enquiry in Chapter 5.

As Sales argues, if you can make millions through cybercrime, you will push every button because: 'Why wouldn't you? What have you got to lose when the stakes are so high?' Ultimately, what is that person or group prepared to do to make it happen? They want fear and, often, they want everyone to be talking about them. Cybercriminals are tuned in to the frenzy that has erupted around the stigma of being a victim of an attack. They use this fear to their advantage, to try to back someone into a corner so they do not think rationally.

Disconnecting from the victim

Tony Sales highlighted that, for a large portion of the time, he did not consider the end victim, and there were no feelings of guilt or remorse, as there was a level of dissociation. He recalled a television interview in which he was asked a question on victimology and empathy. He explained that, when he was using someone else's identity and data, he didn't notice who they were or even what they looked like. For example, it might have been Sales' photograph or someone else's on a driving licence: it was just a fake name and ID to be used to commit a fraud. In Sales' mind, if he did think about it, he believed that, despite his fraud, the person would get their money back, and it would not cost them anything.

He identified that, when you truly understand the reality, identity theft is extremely intrusive. People often feel violated by the attack on their privacy in a worse way than if someone had broken into their home – as your identity is unique to you – and it may have taken a long time to build their reputation and social standing, to have such good credit history and credit ratings. To have this shattered can be traumatic, especially when considering how private some people are. Then there are the personal losses on top of that, and the stigma. In many instances, the victims do not get their money back. For Sales, finally speaking this aloud and connecting all the dots together was a first, and it forced him to acknowledge the true impact his life of crime had on his victims.

Sales stated that it can be hard for someone honest to comprehend the level of disconnection that fraudsters and other criminals may have, but it is something that people need to be aware of, and that the level of disconnection is even greater when operating online. We shall further explore the victim impact of cybercrime in Chapter 3.

The turning point

Tony Sales highlighted that, when you don't care, you don't fear consequences. Even prison was not a deterrent. Despite mixing with violent criminals and ex-cons, he just saw it as another social situation to understand and adjust to. He says that he could not help but see it as a game, a challenge, with a need to be resourceful to control the situation.

Later, he realized that, to make a change, you must ultimately break the cycle and the routine. That came as a result of having his own wife and children and needing to be the father that he never had, and the heart-breaking understanding that his child was crying because they did not want to see him in prison any more.

Changing mindsets

When Sales came out of prison, he vowed to make a complete change, and to work in fraud prevention. He found out, however, that it was easier said than done. Even ten years after founding his company We Fight Fraud, there is a stigma that 'once a criminal, always a criminal'. There is a level of atonement that people expect long after the crime has been committed and time has been served.

Sales thoroughly believes that 'education educates out crime', and that training people on social engineering and behaviour, how people can be manipulated and how to protect themselves, is so important. He suggests that there is no separation between your personal life, work life or online persona and your physical being. It is a single identity and attack vector. We shall revisit this in Part Three, where we delve deeper into the organizational strategies to counteract the criminal mindset and build resilience to attacks.

The seven sins of attackers

Now that we have had the opportunity to understand how a fraudster's mind may work, I want to delve further into the principles of human emotions, motivators and levels of morality, which can differ based on an individual's personal belief system, social dynamics and culture. To do this, I would like to have a conversation about cardinal sins and whether they are motivators for why people are drawn into committing specific types of crime, and how that becomes a way of life for so many.

The seven 'cardinal sins' were first referred to by the Roman Catholic church in the fourth century as a way of teaching morality and ethics and the consequences for our decisions and actions (Britannica, 2023b). The theology is that these cardinal sins can lead people to want to commit other sins and further immoral behaviour through further temptation.

When thinking about the list of sins in Table 2.1 and the explanations, consider how they might be applied and what resonates most when considering what may motivate an attacker. We can see how one might lead to another and how quickly things might escalate.

In addition, the theology posited that the seven 'cardinal sins' could be overcome by the seven 'heavenly virtues', which are almost the opposites. One might propose that, by enabling people to be more observant in each of the virtues, it would lead people less to temptation and desire to engage in such activity. Of course, there are many factors that influence a person's capacity for change, and, for some, there may be limited deterrents.

TABLE 2.1 The seven sins of cyber attackers

Sin	Explanations	Potential motivator for attackers
Pride	A feeling of pleasure related to self-worth and often derived from personal achievements or talents, desirable possessions, or membership in an ethnic, religious, gender, social, political or professional community or organization (Britannica, 2023a). Those that boast about their achievements or an aspect of themselves, such as their physical appearance, are said to have too much pride or vanity. Pride is closely related to conceit and makes people highly competitive. It can lead to destructive behaviour to strip others of their worth, to promote ourselves and to be pleased at others' misfortune. The opposite virtue is 'humility' and respecting the talents and abilities of others.	Could be expressed as wanting kudos, fame and notoriety in belonging to a specific group and taking responsibility for a specific action or outcome. Attackers may be spurred on by the level of competition between groups, upping the stakes on the resulting target or victim.

(continued)

TABLE 2.1 (Continued)

Sin	Explanations	Potential motivator for attackers
Greed	The insatiable desire to always want more. No matter what we have, we think that it is not enough, and want more still. It leads to a blindness when we can't tell the difference between our wants and needs and leads to excessive consumption, as we fulfil an endless battle to acquire and possess more (Pope, 2019). The 'daughters of greed' are considered to be: o fraud o lying (especially under oath) o dissatisfaction o violence o hardheartedness. Despite its false promises, more wealth does not bring peace, but more anxiety. The opposite virtue is 'charity' and being more liberal with giving money away.	Could be expressed as an attacker driven by monetary gain. Attackers may be spurred on by the amount of money that can be made by going after bigger targets, or a willingness to take bigger risks to achieve the intended outcomes.
Lust	An overwhelmingly intense desire for something or someone. Lust, as opposed to love, can be used to objectify and control a person. It leads to a level of selfishness, for having no regard for anyone beyond ourself and what we want (Jeske, 2014). We place our own desires above another person's livelihood and worth and can lose perspective on our integrity. The opposite virtue is 'chastity' and an abstinence from what you most desire.	Could be expressed as an attacker driven by sexual desire and gratification of the harm they cause. Attackers may be spurred on by their infatuation with a specific person, or outcome, by thinking of more elaborate ruses to target the same victim or group of victims.

(continued)

TABLE 2.1 (Continued)

Sin	Explanations	Potential motivator for attackers
Envy	The feeling of acute jealousy over the achievements of others, with a desire to achieve the same level of advantage, position, power or possessions. This can lead to a level of rivalry and may lead to destructive behaviour that causes issues with physical and emotional well-being (Warren, 2019). Linked to levels of unrest and rebellion. The opposite virtue is 'gratitude' and to practise giving without receiving.	Could be expressed as being driven by acute jealousy of a specific individual or organization. Attackers may be spurred on by the amount of damage or harm caused to the social standing of an individual or organization by destroying their reputation.
Gluttony	Associated with an unhealthy indulgence in wanting to consume material things. Historically this was linked to overeating and drinking to excess, as this is what people were able to consume most readily (Verrett, 2021). In modern times, this is linked to obsessive behaviour, to indulging to excess, often at the expense of others, and it becomes a main priority and focus; consuming more of what they don't need to the point of constant cycles of debt, for example, or gambling. The opposite virtue is 'temperance' and practising self-discipline.	Could be expressed as the need to acquire material possessions, and is closely linked to greed. Attackers may be spurred on by the perception of others in the level of wealth and possessions they have and the status this may afford them.
Wrath	The feeling of anger and wanting to hurt someone physically or emotionally, in response to a real or perceived injustice. The level of resentment and anger feels justified, and stirs up bursts of emotion even long after the initial event has subsided (Tamayo, 2014). The level of 'righteous' anger can be out of control, demonstrated through irrational behaviour and actions. The opposite virtue is 'patience' despite provocation.	Could be expressed as the need to cause harm, based on the social group or organization that the target belongs to. Attackers may be spurred on by the perception that increased anger and harm is justified, even over prolonged periods.

(continued)

TABLE 2.1 (Continued)

Sin	Explanations	Potential motivator for attackers
Sloth	A deep level of idleness and laziness, and lacking enthusiasm or energy. Considered to be a lack of self-worth, and to live without empathy for others, as they lack a sense of identity and purpose (Blevin, 2019). A tendency to want to walk away from the things and people that serve us well. Avoiding things that take dedication and effort, leading to a level of complacency, and indifference to others. Can spiral into bouts of depression and anxiety, in attempts to get back a sense of control and belonging. The opposite virtue is 'diligence' and being persistent in setting and achieving goals.	Could be expressed as an attacker who lacks any specific objective but can be swayed into joining a cause. Attackers may be spurred on by the need to be accepted into a group, irrespective of the motive or outcome of the attacks they participate in.

If we consider some of the explanations offered by Tony Sales, we can see that one of his main drivers was greed. As Sales freely admits, not only did he want money, but he had a taste for the finer things in life, often to the detriment of others with how he disassociated his actions from his victims.

It should be noted that the propensity for committing such 'sins' is not just a motivator for attackers but for victims too. For example, a person that is driven by greed might be more willing to sell their credentials for the right price, as opposed to an attacker having to steal them. We shall further consider the *powers of persuasion* in Chapter 3. But first, what makes cybercrime so attractive to attackers?

Why cybercrime?

As Tony Sales has noted, moving crime online provides a level of scale and anonymity that traditional crime may not offer. It is easier for attackers to dissociate from their victims and it enables them to take on an alternative persona, or alter ego. Not only are the rewards high, and deterrents low, cyber enables criminals to experiment and try different things, as we shall discuss in Chapter 5.

It may also explain why many cybercriminals start young, since, it can be argued, they are easily influenced and potentially lack self-control and self-awareness, but have a strong desire for social acceptance among their peers. According to the UK Ministry of Justice (2023), juveniles tend to have a higher reoffending rate for committing fraud (around 34 per cent) than many adults (around 20 per cent). It is perhaps hard to quantify against cyber-enabled fraud, given that many people and organizations do not report a cybercrime, and many perpetrators are not caught. In comparison, juveniles convicted of a sexual offence tend to have the lowest levels of recidivism.

The level of anonymity given online means that some young people illicit more aggressive behaviour through their social interactions, in the form of cyberbullying. They may also be more prone to engaging in or sharing hateful or harmful content if they are not made aware of or don't understand the consequences of their actions. The proliferation of and access to harmful content on social media can also sway young people into believing specific ideologies, which may make them susceptible to want to join, or be manipulated into joining, specific groups or behaving in certain ways.

Conclusion

In this chapter, we have explored some of the motivations behind cybercrime, and whether this is cyber-enabled or cyber-dependent. While monetary and material gain is a prime motivator for many, there are those driven by the kudos and pride that comes from bringing large 'faceless' corporations to their knees. Those driven by wrath or envy may feel that they must avenge a personal vendetta. Those driven by sloth may join in for the ride, just to be socially accepted.

While some people are drawn into crime through necessity, there are also fewer deterrents to committing crime online than there are in person. That is not to say that some criminals may not choose both, but technology has become a key component in how they research and target their victims.

We have examined how cyber enables crime at scale, and across borders, and how one thing may escalate to another when there are the means, motive and resources. Cyber provides a level of anonymity that enables perpetrators to disconnect themselves from their victims and the impact and devastation that they cause.

It may also explain how a cyber attacker develops from being an opportunist into being recruited into organized crime. Just like any role, a cybercriminal needs to develop a skill and aptitude and someone needs to see their value. This will be brought to life in Chapter 9, where we examine one of the most successful organized cybercrime gangs in history.

References

Blevin, K (2019) 'What is the sin of sloth, and why is it worse than laziness?', Crosswalk, 12 April, crosswalk.com/faith/spiritual-life/what-is-the-sin-of-sloth-and-why-is-it-worse-than-laziness.html (archived at https://perma.cc/T5MV-G4UK)

Britannica (2023a) 'Pride: human behaviour', Science & Tech, britannica.com/topic/pride-human-behaviour (archived at https://perma.cc/6XPZ-YH9R)

Britannica (2023b) 'Seven deadly sins: theology', History & Society, britannica.com/topic/seven-deadly-sins (archived at https://perma.cc/GHX3-KAS6)

CompTIA (2023) 'What is social engineering? The human element in the technology scam', comptia.org/content/articles/what-is-social-engineering (archived at https://perma.cc/MT8V-WDU6)

CPS (2019) 'Cybercrime – prosecution guidance', 26 September, cps.gov.uk/legal-guidance/cybercrime-prosecution-guidance (archived at https://perma.cc/ML7M-F99Q)

Jeske, A (2014) 'The seven deadly sins: lust', InterVarsity, 15 September, intervarsity.org/blog/seven-deadly-sins-lust (archived at https://perma.cc/96DA-MU4Y)

Ministry of Justice (2023) 'Proven reoffending statistics', National Statistics, 27 April, gov.uk/government/statistics/proven-reoffending-statistics-april-to-june-2021/proven-reoffending-statistics-april-to-june-2021 (archived at https://perma.cc/HNL8-WV86)

Pope, C (2019) 'The seven deadly sins: greed', *Catholic Standard*, 2 April, cathstan.org/posts/the-seven-deadly-sins-greed-2 (archived at https://perma.cc/3YXA-SELU)

Tamayo, S (2014) 'The seven deadly sins: wrath', InterVarsity, 6 October, https://intervarsity.org/blog/seven-deadly-sins-wrath (archived at https://perma.cc/CP9H-FATP)

Verrett, B (2021) 'What is gluttony, and is it a sin?', Bible Study Tools, 15 June, biblestudytools.com/bible-study/topical-studies/what-is-gluttony-and-is-it-a-sin.html (archived at https://perma.cc/78LB-DQBU)

Warren, R (2019) 'What is envy? The definitions and consequences of this deadly sin', Christianity.com, 22 March, christianity.com/wiki/sin/what-is-envy-the-definition-and-consequence-of-this-deadly-sin.html (archived at https://perma.cc/RP5Y-MEKY)

Wu, L, Peng, Q and Lemke, M (2023) 'Research trends in cybercrime and cybersecurity', *International Journal of Cybersecurity Intelligence and Cybercrime*, 6 (1), vc.bridgew.edu/cgi/viewcontent.cgi?article=1154&context=ijcic (archived at https://perma.cc/Q8EW-93ZZ)

03

Types of cyber attack and why they work

CHAPTER OBJECTIVES

In the previous chapter, we explored what motivates some attackers: why they do what they do. Simply being highly motivated is not enough, and hence a level of social engineering is required to drive a specific outcome, and at a scale that will warrant the level of investment and time needed to achieve that outcome.

The main objective of this chapter is to consider specific tactics that an attacker may use to entice an individual or organization to perform a specific action. For many, the type of attack, and often the technology deployed to support the task, is often just a means to an end and has been developed to bypass existing controls.

As we have seen, often, the thrill and fame that comes from a successful strike may be enough motivation for an attacker to try more elaborate ruses. For some, it becomes a game of cat and mouse, while for others it is a vocation.

The power of persuasion

In his book *Influence: The Psychology of Persuasion*, Robert Cialdini (2006) highlights several factors that can affect how and why people react to situations in the way they do. This is important when considering the art of social engineering and the ability to influence and engineer a specific outcome. These influencing factors can be summarized into six key areas, in Table 3.1.

TABLE 3.1 The six powers of persuasion

Influencing factor	Explanations	How it might be used by attackers
Reciprocation	<ul><li>The requirement to repay what another person has provided.</li><li>This can be the assumption that, by giving something, we will receive something in return, as a 'quid pro quo', meaning 'a favour for a favour'.</li><li>From a legal perspective, this may assume that goods or services have been traded for an item of similar value.</li></ul>	<ul><li>Attackers may persuade people to click links or provide information in exchange for a special offer or discount code.</li><li>The level of attacks increases during seasonal demands and holidays, such as Black Friday, when many retailers typically offer discounted products and services.</li></ul>
Consistency	<ul><li>Once we make a choice or take a stand, we are often steadfast in our commitment to justify our decisions.</li><li>Being consistent in the message and instruction by following up and reiterating the request can persuade people to believe it is genuine.</li></ul>	<ul><li>Attackers may send more than one message or use more than one channel.</li><li>Attackers may express a level of urgency in their message if pretending that they need to contact their victim.</li><li>Phone spoofing, for example, can fool people into thinking they have an urgent message from their bank or doctor.</li></ul>
Consensus	<ul><li>When we are unsure of a situation, we look to others to suggest the correct actions to take.</li><li>The more people that undertake the action, the more we might consider it to be correct.</li><li>This can include our innate inclination to trust and follow good causes, such as charitable people and endeavours.</li></ul>	<ul><li>Attackers may look to impersonate respected brands and institutions, where we are more likely to trust and believe what is said.</li><li>In times of crisis, fraudsters may spoof charities or funding pages to entice people to give money to what they believe is a good cause.</li></ul>

(continued)

TABLE 3.1 (Continued)

Influencing factor	Explanations	How it might be used by attackers
Liking	• The propensity to agree with people we like, such as friends and family, and, just as important, the propensity for others to agree if they like us. • This can include our willingness and desire to believe or follow social influencers or religious leaders.	• Attackers may look to impersonate friends and family by using contact details listed in social media accounts or directories. • People may be more prone to give information or click on a link if a message is from someone they have a trusting relationship with. • Some attackers have been known to impersonate a child in trouble to illicit a specific response from a parent or guardian.
Authority	• We are more likely to say yes to those in a position of authority, who may yield greater power and expertise. • This can lead to a fear of being reprimanded because of failing to obey an instruction or order.	• Attackers may impersonate people in authority in a work or similar environment. • Attackers may illicit specific demands, and instructions to subordinates, on the premise that they are more likely to react to someone in authority, especially if they are much higher up. • Some fraudsters have been known to impersonate government tax authorities, with threats of prosecution or fines.
Scarcity	• We may be more likely to act when we believe that time is of the essence, and there is limited time within which to act. • The scarcity of a resource or offer can influence someone to act, particularly if we feel that it may benefit us.	• Attackers may look to place time limits on their messages or offers. • Attackers may state that this is a one-time offer, or that if they don't respond within a given timeline, it may lead to subsequent action or penalties. • Some people may feel under increased pressure to respond quickly, which is another tactic that the attacker is reliant on.

Finding an influencing factor and scenario that works is not only dependent on the individual, but several factors at play at the time. The level of distraction and timing could affect how and when people react to a situation. For example, is it a busy or stressful time, are they overloaded, or are they not fully concentrating on the task at hand? This can explain why it can be hit and miss for those who are simply opportunists, rather than those that specifically target an individual or organization.

The level of manipulation can be so subtle so as not to be noticeable; may be done for a specific purpose, to establish persistence, or can be just a one-off. If you have burnt bridges, or gone too far, a door may be permanently closed, and so, sometimes, it pays to have an open door that you can return to. For more experienced attackers, they will learn what is required to elicit a specific response. This may involve learning more about the specific culture, understanding the key people and ingraining themselves into the situation.

Our desire to help, to be kind to strangers, and to rally round when things go wrong are key features that the attacker relies on. For example, if someone is kind or charitable to us, we are more likely to react favourably to that person or their actions. We may even let our guard down and welcome them in.

Think back to our discussion in the previous chapter about *sins and virtues* and how they could be used to turn someone on to, or off, a situation. When performed at a distance, it is harder to read visual cues and body language, such as someone smiling at you, so the online attacker arguably must work harder to win favour and trust; hence the level of time, persistence or patience they may need.

Victimology and impact

While researching for this book, I had the opportunity to speak to Dr Paul Stephens, Director of Academic Studies in Law, Policing and Social Sciences and Principal Lecturer in Cybercrime and Digital Policing at Canterbury Christ Church University. Dr Stephens researches the social issues and human factors of cybercrime. I wanted to explore the level of disassociation that exists between some attackers and the end victim, and how some people have almost convinced themselves that cybercrime is victimless. Given that attackers are driven to satisfy their particular objectives, it is important, when considering different types of attack and why they work, that we also consider the level of trust that has been destroyed as a result.

Dr Stephens argues that there are many people with the technical skills and aptitude to undertake cybercrime, but they don't, even though it is by far the easiest way for them to make money. Some of these people may be in low-paid jobs and have low prospects. So, do these people have other social circumstances and ties that reduce the temptation? We explore this question in Chapter 12, with a tale of two paths – how two people who received a similar education went in different directions.

The key question on Dr Stephens' mind is whether we have socially and culturally enabled cybercrimes like this to happen, as, from an attacker's perspective, why wouldn't you? If there is low deterrent and high reward, and low likelihood of being prosecuted, then for some it may feel like a natural thing to do. And it is arguably much easier to target a big, faceless institution, or ideology, than it is to go face to face with an individual.

In Dr Stephens' opinion, the reframing and disconnecting from the target organization is a way of attackers justifying to themselves what they are doing and why they are doing it. If they really understood the impact, would they still do it?

As we shall go on to highlight, romance scams and sextortion are different because the attacker has to get close to the victim, and be one on one with them, so, while they may disconnect some of their emotions, it is perhaps another level of cruelty to inflict harm on a specific individual, even if it is seen as a means to an end.

A report by His Majesty's Inspectorate of Constabulary (HMICFRS, 2018), *Real lives, real crimes*, looked at the impact that cybercrime has on the UK economy and the personal impact that digital crime has on victims. The report highlights that cybercrime is just as pernicious and disruptive as other crimes and merits an equal response from law enforcement.

In their interviews, victims were broadly unaware of the threat that cybercrime posed to them, and of the prevalence of such crimes. This uncertainty meant that they were unable to take steps to prevent the crime or its repetition, and many were unsure about what actions to take in response to what happened to them. This included whether they should contact the police, and whether what had happened to them amounted to a crime at all. In instances of fraud, people were more likely to tell their bank than the police. Some extracts from individual victim statements have been included in the following section to illustrate the emotional impact of such crimes.

Return on investment

There is a myriad of different attacks, ranging from high-commodity, low-yield attacks not strikes that are indiscriminate in nature, to those that are highly targeted.

For those potential victims who are a bit sceptical or less inclined to perform an action without clarity, additional work may be required by the attacker to build trust and rapport. This inevitably takes time and comes down to the will and motivation of the attacker, and the outcome required. For example, what do they need that person to do, and what information or sway does that person have over others? In some circumstances, an individual may be part of a wider strategy – the final target, the person they are trying to impersonate – or just a cog in a wheel, with only a small part to play in the overall objective.

Any attack requires a level of commitment and cost to the attacker, so, for an attack to be successful, it requires a return on investment. If the effort is more than the reward, then the issue is one of value. Much in the same way as legitimate enterprises, the question becomes one of *'Do I build, or buy?'* Is it more cost effective to outsource all or part of the attack to another party, or do I invest the time to build myself? In Chapter 5, we discuss the rise of 'cybercrime as a service' in overcoming this dilemma.

The use of malware (malicious software) or botnets (multiple machines infected with malicious software) as a means of aiding the attacker to perform their tasks can act as a 'force-multiplier' to speed up elements of the attack or to enable multiple simultaneous attacks. For example, such programs may use automated scripts, and the individual or organization may be unaware of its existence until such time as the attacker uses it to perform a specific element of the assault.

But first let's consider some key methods, why an attacker might use them and why they work in the context of a human-orientated attack. In Part Two we shall look at some real-life case studies on how different attackers targeted and manipulated their victims; and then the strategies to overcome them in Part Three.

Phishing

The principle of phishing is synonymous with fishing, and is the favourite and most common tool among cyber attackers of all kinds. Before we consider why it is so successful, and the methods that attackers might use to lure their target to perform a specific action, let's first understand some of the similarities and principles to fishing itself (Table 3.2).

TABLE 3.2 Similarities between fishing and phishing

Question	Key considerations	How this could be used by attackers
What type of fish are you trying to catch?	• For those starting out, it can be a thrill to catch anything, no matter how small. • The issue when trying to catch any fish that will bite is that you're not prepared. You're more than likely relying on luck, rather than skill. • It may be ok to experiment when you're a novice, to determine whether this is right for you, but it takes time and effort, and money for the right equipment, so it pays to research first, rather than just hope for the best. • To be most successful, it's a good idea to concentrate on a specific type of fish until you master your technique and try different things. • For some, the overarching objective might be big-game fishing. It can often be a case of 80% waiting around and 20% adrenaline rush when the big fish is finally hooked. • Keeping the fish interested may require a degree of teasing, to make the fish want to follow the lure. • The time, effort and resources to undertake big-game fishing may just be too far out of reach for some, and, though it may sound like fun, fishing for big game is only going to be feasible in certain waters and conditions.	• This will depend on whether they are opportunistic or highly focused on targeting a specific individual and what the outcome may be. • For some, it will be high volume, low yield by casting the net as far and wide as possible to see who bites and why. • There will be an element of trial and error. • While the overall objective may be to catch a high-value target, or big fish, it would be extremely rare to achieve this without experience.

(continued)

TABLE 3.2 (Continued)

Question	Key considerations	How this could be used by attackers
Why are you trying to catch this fish?	• Are you just starting out? • Is this a prize catch, and is there kudos attached to a specific fish? • What happens once you have caught it? • What is the ultimate objective?	• There may be a level of experimentation when attempting to phish for the first time – perhaps the thrill of the chase when they start to hone and perfect their techniques. • The key is whether this is just a means to an end or whether it was the intended outcome from the outset, for example collating as many credentials as possible, to be able to move up towards higher-value targets. • For some attackers, it is pot luck who they access and why, and they may need to keep moving laterally before they find something of value.
Where are you trying to fish?	• Are you even fishing in the right area? • There is a big difference between fishing in a pond and fishing in an ocean. This can feel overwhelming if you go from one to the other. • Have you done your research, learnt from others, joined the right discussion groups and forums to find out and learn about the right techniques and tools? • Do you trust the sources of information, and can you spot those that may be trying to lead you in the wrong direction, so they can have all the fish for themselves?	• For opportunists, there may be no specific objective on who or why. Arguably, when you cast the net wide, without a clear objective, it can waste a lot of time and resources. • Those that take the time to learn and refine their craft will get better results, but this can take time, effort and skill that some don't have. Either they need to accept that, or invest in new ways of operating, which means buying in or outsourcing elements of the attack.

(continued)

TABLE 3.2 (Continued)

Question	Key considerations	How this could be used by attackers
What method will you use to fish?	• It is not a case of one size fits all – there are different requirements for different types of fish. For example, are you fishing in a pond, river, lake or ocean? This will dictate how you gain access to the fish, and how far you might need to cast before you reach the intended target.	• Many attackers favour the tried and tested when it comes to what has been used before. • Most attacks will be delivered by email (phishing), text message (known as smishing) or phone and voice messages (vishing) – the most common forms of communication used by individuals and organizations. • The adage 'if it isn't broke, don't fix it' fits perfectly here in that, if a specific technique is proven to be successful, there is little motivation to change. • However, the more a specific tactic or lure is used, the more people will get wise to it and learn to counteract it. The attacker may not have an option but to refine their methods. • Some attackers have evolved to use every means of communication and access into the organization, which may include social media channels and customer feedback forms. • Establishing a level of entry and access is the core objective of many attackers, and phishing is a first-stage attack that enables this.

(continued)

TABLE 3.2 (Continued)

Question	Key considerations	How this could be used by attackers
When do you intend to fish?	• There are big differences in the time of day as to whether the fish is interested in the lure. If the weather is too hot or cold they may also be distracted, and not interested in biting.	• Attackers need to determine the general location and time zone of the individuals and organizations they are attempting to access. • Sending a phishing message during the middle of the night will not yield the same results as during the day when there are more people at work or online. • Understanding the hemisphere is important because some people's summer is others' winter, so the same lure will not have the same effect. • An appreciation for culture, and what is happening in the specific country or organization and why people act differently, is important to know.
What lure or bait will you use?	• The success of the bait comes down to how attractive the fish finds the lure and whether it stands out from other bait. • Just because fish are tempted by a certain thing, doesn't mean they want the same over and over, so it pays to mix things up to see what makes them bite on a specific day. • You can't assume that any bait will work on any fish – a good angler will know that different fish are attracted to different lures.	• A one-size-fits-all message that targets a large part of the population is unlikely to yield the same results as a carefully crafted message unique to the individual or organization. • Attempts to spoof a well-known brand or person can take time and effort. • People have been trained to look for poorly written messages, with bad grammar, spelling and language. This can happen when an attacker is a non-native speaker or may not appreciate the dialects or cultures of certain areas. • While some people will inevitably be caught off guard, attackers still need to consider the specific bait that is needed for a range of scenarios and situations.

(continued)

TABLE 3.2 (Continued)

Question	Key considerations	How this could be used by attackers
Do you intend to switch the lure, or stick with what you have?	• Are you prepared to try new tools and techniques, or are you sticking with tried-and-tested methods? • Once you have found something that really works, and the fish are biting, are you prepared to use that for as long as possible, before the fish get bored and you need to try a different approach?	• For some attackers, it may be a case of hitting at the opportune moment, and to go as hard and fast as possible before they are detected and the lure or method of attack no longer works. • For some opportunists, and for more established groups, an exploit or lure is so successful that others want to get in on the act and use the same method. • The potential issue is that, as the type and style of attack is used multiple times, it is only successful for a short time until individuals and organizations learn to counteract it. • This means that the lure or exploit becomes unusable or needs to go dormant for a while.
Do you intend to cast wide, or target a specific fish?	• Are you even fishing in the right place? There can be a tendency to want to throw out the bait to the first fish we see, but a good angler will take time to watch and learn the movements of the fish and the optimum places to fish from. • When you cast far and wide without a purpose or objective, it is a waste of bait and means you're probably less likely to catch, and so become frustrated.	• For many opportunists, or those wanting to test a specific element of their attack, it may be a good idea to cast far and wide to see how things land in different areas. • The issue is just how far the net can be cast and whether the approach is effective. • For those targeting a specific individual or organization, far and wide may not yield the required results unless ring-fenced to a specific area. • If transfixed on a specific target or outcome, more work is required to understand the conditions in order to lure in and hook the target.

(continued)

TABLE 3.2 (Continued)

Question	Key considerations	How this could be used by attackers
What hook will you use?	• Has the hook been sized to the fish? • Do you use the same hook over and over, or do you sharpen or replace it to make sure it's more likely to hook the fish first time, and correctly? • What happens if a hook suddenly breaks? Can you easily switch to another one? • A failure to properly look after equipment will make it less efficient and can be counterproductive as you may be less likely to hook or retain the fish. • Remember that bigger fish need a bigger hook, so consider your toolkit and whether you're fully prepared. • Make sure you're not being too aggressive, as you may be at risk of harming the fish.	• The attack is only successful if you have been able to hook and reel in the target. • The lure or bait is only one element – the attacker needs the individual or organization to take some affirmative action. Typically, this means opening an attachment (which may run a malicious program) or clicking a link to manually enter information into an online form or fake domain. • If this action is not performed, the attack is not successful.
How will you keep the fish hooked?	• Hooking and catching the fish is the final objective, as otherwise you are just wasting time on lures, bait and feeding the fish. • Once you've managed to hook the fish, what is the right level of tension to keep it on the hook for long enough to reel it in? Too little or too much could mean that you lose the fish completely or it becomes harder to reel in as it starts to fight against you.	• Many will bite, only a few will be hooked, and even fewer successfully reeled in. • Many people will ignore a phishing message, some will open and read it, some will take the bait and open the attachment or enter their information. • Some will need additional levels of persuasion, whether that is sending multiple messages or convincing them in other ways. • It requires a degree of tenacity. If you go too hard, it is more likely to raise suspicion and alarm.

(continued)

TABLE 3.2 (Continued)

Question	Key considerations	How this could be used by attackers
Will you catch and release, or tag the fish?	• Sometimes, the fish may hold so much significance, or is so rare, that researchers wish to study its movements and patterns. • For some, it may just be enough to collect data and obtain insights on what the fish does or how it does it, so that others may also learn from it. • They may wish to operate in a stealthy way, to be able to monitor the fish in its natural habitat without forcing it to change direction or behave out of character.	• The objective may be to collect as many credentials or to release as much malware into the environment as possible. There may be no further use for that individual or organization, so they either leave or provide a back door for other attackers, with different objectives (typically at a price). • If the individual or organization is the ultimate target, they will need to maintain a level of presence. This may be done in such a way as to go unnoticed, for example when the attacker is exfiltrating information or attempting to learn more about the target. • In some cases, the attacker may need the target to perform additional actions as part of subsequent stages of an attack.
How committed are you?	• Fishing requires a level of commitment and patience. • Sometimes no matter what you do and how hard you try, the fish won't bite that day, so how much persistence do you have? • Are you prepared to pack up and go home, knowing that you caught nothing, or will you keep going until you've exhausted everything at your disposal?	• For many attackers, there must be a return on investment, and they therefore need to decide on the level of resources, time and money they're prepared to commit. • Even if monetary gain is not the end game, there is still a cost – which means the attacker is being funded in other ways. • Arguably, organized crime and nation-sponsored actors have access to more resources, which enables them to be more committed. • Those who are driven by kudos will be determined to meet their objective in other ways. • A key factor is not just on the motivation, but who holds the skills.

(continued)

TABLE 3.2 (Continued)

Question	Key considerations	How this could be used by attackers
How much experience do you have?	• How many times have you fished before? • Are you a recreational angler, focused on catching bigger and bigger fish, or are you a professional angler focused on a specific fish? • The more experienced the angler, the higher rate of success. Even the best anglers know that it takes an incredible amount of time and effort to experiment and come up with something new, but the thrill can often be in finding a technique that has never been used before but has a very high success rate. • If you do find that new method, what then? Do you keep it to yourself or monetize it in some way? • When you think about the successes and the different fish that you may have reeled in, what happens if you need help? • How will you make sure that you don't lose the fish, or allow another predator, lurking in the background, to steal it from you?	• The more time and effort spent working in a particular area, the more experience is gained. • It is not an easy task to switch vocations and then become an expert in that field. • People will naturally excel in different areas and have specific skill sets and areas of interest that make them highly sought after. • While many attackers may be highly motivated, they may lack the skill and know-how to do all stages of the attack. For example, some attackers may be highly successful in writing code for malware, but have no skill to socially engineer someone to download it. • Attackers find that they are more successful in groups, or they need to procure 'packaged services' that enable them to fulfil different parts of their objective. • Attackers need to ensure they can trust those that they are working with, and can protect their intellectual property from being stolen. • In many ways, attackers must overcome the same supply chain issues as organizations if they are to be successful.

Now that we have established the key principles of phishing and how attackers might use it, let's consider it combined with social engineering to consider how phishing might be used in a second-stage attack. This means that the attacker now has access to the individual or organization, because of harvesting credentials or through the delivery of malware, but that is not enough to fulfil the final objective, whether that is politically, economically or socially motivated.

Impersonation

The art of impersonation is used as a method of pretending to be another person, to fulfil a specific action. This can include:

- **Identity impersonation,** to enable the creation of fake identities to obtain credit and loans. This may include *account takeovers* whereby the attacker has direct access to specific bank or credit accounts where they can elicit the transfer of money or procurement of goods.
- **Brand impersonation,** to fool someone into believing they are liaising with a bank or other trusted party to extract information from that individual or organization. We shall explore an example of how Microsoft's brand was used to fool people into providing permission to access their accounts in Chapter 4.
- **Organization impersonation,** to fool someone within the organization, or their supply chain, into believing they are a representative of that organization to extract information or money.

The principle of pretexting, from a social engineering perspective, includes the act of masquerading as a legitimate person or organization to create fake scenarios that aim to legitimize who they are to elicit the information they need. The objective is to do this in such a way that the target is unaware of the action.

Let's look at an example of organization impersonation, in the form of business email compromise (BEC). The FBI *Internet Crime Report 2022* (FBI, 2022) identified that BEC is one of the most financially impacting cybercrimes, with adjusted losses of $2.7 billion, an increase of over $500 million on the previous year.

Business email compromise

BEC is often referred to as a *second-stage attack*, whereby the attacker already has access to the organization and its business email. BEC stands out from other cybercrimes due to the emphasis on social engineering and the art of deception.

The objective of the attacker is to use powers of persuasion by impersonating someone in a position of authority, and to use that perceived authority to persuade someone within the organization, or who has a relationship with that organization, to take some kind of action. The principle is to target and manipulate the biggest fish in the organization, and from a phishing perspective, this is known as 'whaling' (you can ignore the fact that a whale is not a fish, but hopefully you get the point). This type of attack is often called 'CEO impersonation' because it often uses the most senior person in the organization. However, this is a misnomer, as it can make people believe that other senior people are not targets when they are.

The attacker has to spend time learning about the organization and the person or group they are trying to impersonate, including the relationships they have with other people within, and outside, their organization. As the attacker is in the target's business email account(s), this is usually full of information about who they communicate with, the content and context of those emails and whether they contain sensitive information about the organization. It is useful for attackers to know what the business-to-business (B2B) and business-to-consumer (B2C) relationships are, either to aid with this attack or to facilitate other subsequent attacks not strikes within the supply chain.

Part of the reconnaissance phase may include key-word searches or an auto-forwarding rule whereby the attacker can forward emails to their own nominated email account based on the content of the emails or the senders and receivers of the email. Key-word searches may include *invoice, acquisition, confidential* as examples, but can be specific projects or intellectual property.

In addition, for the attacker to impersonate their target, they need to understand their idiosyncrasies and the style and structure of their emails. For example, are they written in an authoritative manner, with specific commands and instructions for the recipient to follow, or are they more collaborative and conversational in asking for feedback and so on? The attacker is looking for an opportune moment to intercept a legitimate email message and conversation, and interject and replace it with a malicious one. To avoid arousing suspicion, it needs to be written in a style and format that the target would write and be given to a recipient who would normally receive such messages.

The objective might be to swap the bank account on a legitimate invoice, to request the procurement of goods, or to get the receiver to perform a specific action, such as the exfiltration of specific information.

The FBI highlighted how the scheme has evolved from simple spoofing of business and personal email accounts and a request to send wire payments to fraudulent bank accounts. Lately, fraudsters are more frequently utilizing custodial accounts held at financial institutions for cryptocurrency exchanges, or having victims send funds directly to cryptocurrency platforms where funds are quickly dispersed. There is also an increasingly used tactic to spoof legitimate business phone numbers to confirm fraudulent banking details with victims.

Between April 2022 and April 2023, Microsoft detected and investigated 35 million BEC attempts, with an average of 156,000 attempts daily. Tactics included contrived deadlines and urgency to spur recipients who may be distracted or already accustomed to such urgent requests. BEC operators have a quiet confidence, and spend time improving the scale and plausibility of malicious messages.

While the top targets are executives and senior leaders, BEC operators also target finance managers and human resources personnel who have access to social security numbers and other forms of personal data. New employees also make attractive targets as they are less familiar with business processes and less likely to challenge requests.

Unlocking why 'Nigerian prince' emails are so successful

I'm sure we have all received them at some point – the emails with outlandish claims about status, stolen millions, corrupt officials, wicked in-laws, near-death escapes and secret safety deposit boxes where the recipient of the emails are promised a share of millions for their help.

The concept is nothing new, and this form of social engineering can be traced back to the late 19th century and was often referred to as the 'Spanish prisoner' tactic – the fraudster tells the target victim that he is a wealthy person imprisoned in Spain under a false identity. The prisoner cannot reveal his identity without serious repercussions and is relying on a friend to raise money to secure his release. The fraudster offers to let the target put up some of the funds, with a promise of a greater monetary reward upon release from prison. The fraudster continues to press for more money until the victim is cleaned out or refuses to put up more funds.

Such fantastical stories of hidden riches and grandiose gestures have continued to evolve over the years, the most noteworthy of which tends to be the 'Nigerian prince'. These are so ridiculous, that people can't possibly fall for them, right? Wrong! In fact, such frauds have made an incredible amount of money, and have earned some attackers celebrity status, as we shall discuss in Chapter 9. But why are they so successful, and why don't the fraudsters just lie about their location, or come up with a better ruse?

Microsoft Research (Herley, 2016) highlights that assuming a level of stupidity on the attacker's part is not the answer. By contrast, the fraud requires skill in social engineering, and considerable inventiveness.

The fraud is entirely one of manipulation and is likely to work only on the most gullible. Since gullibility is unobservable, the best strategy is to get people to self-identify. Tales of fabulous amounts of money will strike all but the most gullible as bizarre. They will be recognized and ignored by anyone who has used the internet long enough, is savvy enough to use a search engine, has consulted family or friends or heeds the advice from banks.

Only when potential victims respond does the labour-intensive and costly effort of following up by email (and sometimes phone) begin. Of these, those who go the whole distance and eventually send money are 'true positives', while those who realize that it's fraud and back out are 'false positives'. Those who remain are the fraudster's ideal target. They represent a tiny subset of the overall population. The initial email is effectively the attacker's classifier: the goal is not to attract viable users, but to repel the non-viable ones. A less outlandish email would certainly gather more responses but yield lower profit.

As Peter Anaman, Microsoft Lead Investigator explains, so many people just want to be loved, they are inherently good people that want affection and trust people. They believe they are helping those in need, and that is what makes them vulnerable. We will circle back round to the work that Peter Anaman has done with Nigerian law enforcement in Chapter 9, but first, let's consider some of his comments further.

Honey trap

In Chapter 2, we explored how some attackers may be motivated by lust or a sexual desire, and how potential victims may be motivated by similar things. They are more likely to respond in a positive way if they find the person they think they are liaising with physically attractive.

Attackers might also use pride as a tactic to play to someone's ego. For example, giving high praise and admiration to a person who has high social standing or a position of power, such as a politician or company executive.

Catfishing

In a similar way to other types of phishing and impersonation, here the attacker will pretend to be someone else to elicit information from their target. The attacker will often set up a fake profile on social media or dating sites and use the photos, and possibly identity, of another person whose details they have stolen or whose pictures they have taken from other social media sites and platforms.

Often, catfishing includes a persona to go with the pictures, including a job, friends, hobbies. These may closely align to something that the attacker is already engaged in so they can talk convincingly about a specific subject, but they may embellish details to sound more exciting, or to fit in with images and videos they have stolen. It can often be difficult for attackers to keep up with the storytelling if there is not an element of truth to it, and they are more likely to slip up or be contradictory. It is likely that the attacker will have more than one persona and/or more than one target.

The objective of the catfish may simply be to gain trust and elicit personal information from the target that might be used for other attacks, or to convince the victim to send explicit images or engage in sexual activity. In some cases, the victim may feel that they are in a genuine relationship, which provides a level of reciprocity to the persuasion. Sexually explicit material may be just for the attacker's benefit, or sold on, or used as a method of coercion to get the victim to partake in additional activity. This would include extortion.

The victim is often unaware that they are being manipulated. For example, Microsoft (2023) identified how an Iranian state-sponsored group created fake social media profiles to target individuals on LinkedIn. Over a period of several months, the attackers attempted to establish romantic relationships using intelligence gathered from the targets' public profiles to build trust and rapport, before sending malicious BEC files disguised as videos or surveys. Because of the relationship that had developed, the target was more likely to trust the source and ignore the resulting security alerts.

Romance fraud

With some similarities to catfishing, romance fraud involves people being duped into sending money to attackers who go to great lengths to gain trust and convince them that they are in a genuine relationship (Action Fraud, 2023). They use language to manipulate, persuade and exploit the victim so that requests for money do not raise alarm bells. These requests might be highly emotive, such as attackers claiming they need money for emergency medical care or to pay for transport costs to visit the victim if they are overseas. The attackers will often build a relationship with their victims over time.

Attackers may prey on victims by joining a dating site and creating a fake profile to entice and lure their victims, as they will be aware that the target is looking for a relationship and know what sort of person they may be attracted to by some of the information they have freely given.

> 'As a result of my experience, I felt violated, both emotionally as well as financially. Had I been robbed/burgled, I would have been visited and questioned by someone. Because it was over the internet, with no hard evidence/fingerprints, etc, my complaint was as invisible as the person who had stolen from me – more so because the hard evidence I did have was of no interest to anyone.
>
> Ultimately, I have been left realizing that the emotional damage is as important, if not more so, than the financial. I lost some money, but, emotionally, the scars are a lot deeper.'
>
> Jane – victim of romance fraud

While researching for this book, I had the opportunity to speak with Dr Elisabeth Carter, Associate Professor of Criminology and Forensic Linguist at Kingston University, London. Dr Carter's research involves evaluating the language that fraudsters use to entice and hook their victims, using critical discourse analysis (Carter, 2023).

WHAT IS CRITICAL DISCOURSE ANALYSIS (CDA)?

CDA is a research method for studying the written or spoken language in a social context, including non-verbal aspects associated with tone and gestures. It is not just concerned with what you say, but how you say it. CDA is often applied in the fields of sociology, psychology, anthropology and cultural studies.

Dr Carter examines transcribed voice messages and reviews emails and social media messages between perpetrators and victims to look for commonalities. Dr Carter does not speak to the victims directly, as the written communication between the fraudster and the victim is effectively frozen in time, enabling her to see the 'crime scene' and how the fraud unravelled.

Part of the study of language includes genre-mapping by harnessing a communication style that provides contextual references to current affairs to make the misinformation seem more credible and which forms an emotional link to the victim by having a deep appreciation for local cultures. This acts as a way of establishing shared values and rapport.

Dr Carter identified that the tactics utilized are akin to the coercive control and grooming seen in victims of domestic abuse. One of the tactics includes moving the victim away from the platform that they originally started talking on, such as a dating site, so that they can engage in unmonitored conversations. This isolation then extends to additional sources of support, such as friends and families. The perpetrator will often accuse those in the support network of interference and this, rather than helping the situation, can force the victim further into the arms of the fraudster. The objective is to get the victim to comply with acts that culminate in their own exploitation, as if they are willing participants in what comes next.

The next tactic is to wear the victim down, often by sending multiple messages, day and night, while eating, working or sleeping. The objective is to dampen the rational decision-making in a way that comes with tiredness or stress.

To keep up the pretence, fraudsters will often work in teams, and across time zones, working from a playbook. This enables them to continue the bombardment of messages, as they work in shifts, handing over to the next member of the team. To them, it is a job and the chance of a pay day, but for the victim it is exhausting.

The trick to the scam, and what often trips up the victims is that the fraudster does not explicitly ask for money in the beginning. They may state that their phone is broken, or stolen, and wait for the victim to offer to pay, and it can build from there as the ruse gets more elaborate. From the victim's perspective, they may not realize it is fraud, as they willingly sent the money, but it is classified as 'misrepresentation' and is a form of advance-payment fraud.

The form of social engineering used in romance and investment scams is known as 'pig butchering' from the Chinese phrase *sha zhu pan* – to fatten a pig before slaughtering it – which was coined by Chinese fraudsters to describe their scam. The objective is to entice the victim before taking them for everything they've got. It shows the level of disdain that perpetrators have for their victims. The unfortunate reference to victims being 'fat pigs' also draws on the human emotions of greed, gluttony and lust used to lure victims and keep them hooked. Quite often, the victims are from affluent countries and thought to have 'more money than sense' and so deserve to be victims.

This often contributes to the shame that victims feel, and some may be hesitant to report the experience as a crime, which is what the perpetrator is hoping for. We will explore some ways to reduce victim shaming and blaming in Chapter 13.

The fraudsters themselves don't always get it right – they may pick up the script in the wrong place or forget who they are talking to. Sometimes they will send the same message again, word for word. Often this is just the wake-up call that the victim needed.

What is perhaps also surprising is that some of the attackers themselves may be victims. Some people in South East Asia, for example, are forced into modern-day slavery and forced to perform tasks by organized crime syndicates (Wong, 2022). People are lured in with the offer of a fake job. Their passports are taken from them, and they are forced to work in 'fraud factories'. As we discuss in the next chapter, many criminal enterprises learnt how to pivot their operations to working online during the Covid-19 pandemic, and adapted at scale.

Blackmail and extortion

Although such terms are used interchangeably, there is a difference between blackmail and extortion that is worth exploring for context. Different countries or jurisdictions may have different definitions.

WHAT IS BLACKMAIL?

Blackmail does not usually involve the attacker making threats of violence in order to coerce the victim to adhere to their unwarranted demands. The victim often consents to the surrender of money or property because of the perpetrator's other menaces.

WHAT IS EXTORTION?

Extortion involves the attacker making threats of physical harm or destruction of property in order to force their victim to adhere to their unwarranted demands. Extortion can be considered a form of robbery because the level of coercion is against their will.

Extortion is often used to hold part of an organization to ransom, for example, by threatening the release or destruction of data, or through the destruction or sabotage of infrastructure. There is often a debate around the moral, ethical and social dilemmas of paying such demands since this motivates the attackers further. The proceeds of such crimes can also be used to fund other illicit activity. This can include funding for drugs and weapons as well as human trafficking and child exploitation. As we explored previously, a cyber attack is often just a means to an end and is not the prime motivator. This is something that organizations must be cognisant of when formulating their strategy against extortion demands, as we shall discuss in Chapter 15.

Ransomware

Ransomware is another example of a second-stage attack whereby the attacker has already gained access to the organization, and the network, for them to perform reconnaissance, to determine the level of exploits that will be applicable. As highlighted earlier, a scattergun or one-size-fits-all approach may not yield the required results, so, depending on the stakes involved, the attacker may take their time.

As the name suggests, ransomware is a form of malware deployed on the organization's systems and networks that requires the payment of a ransom demand in exchange for the release of the hijacked systems or data. This may include a level of encryption or destructive and wiper elements to render all or parts of the infrastructure unusable.

Ransomware has been utilized as an attack vector for over 10 years. Many forms of ransomware started as commodity-based attacks that affected individuals in an indiscriminate way. The ransomware would encrypt a user's hard drive. Depending on the type of malware, the individual might be met with an affordable ransom demand, which they could pay by debit or credit card, with the promise of a decryption key. It would be hit-and-miss whether the attacker followed through with this decryption key or instructions on how to unlock the systems once a payment had been made. Again, individuals were also less likely to report such attacks to the police.

'I was completely overwhelmed, in total shock. I couldn't believe what was happening. I panicked and transferred the cash without thinking. I was embarrassed. It was so stupid. As soon as the police arrived, they said they had heard of similar cases, which made me feel that I'm not the only idiot.'

Daniel – victim of blackmail

Attackers realized they could obtain higher-value rewards, as well as notoriety, if they targeted organisations. Many organizations have higher levels of security and defences than individuals, which requires more work for attackers. Some opportunists may still favour small and medium enterprises, whereas other groups and organized crime may favour the larger enterprises, or 'big-game ransomware' as it is also known. Some relish the challenge and kudos that goes with obtaining such a trophy.

Most ransomware attackers opportunistically deploy ransomware to whatever network they get access to, and some even purchase access to networks from other cybercriminals, as we shall discuss in Chapter 5. Some attackers prioritize organizations that have higher revenues, while others prefer specific industries for the shock value or type of data they can exfiltrate.

Not only have attackers learnt to adjust their modus operandi, they have evolved their extortion models:

- **Traditional extortion model** – a single extortion demand to release a decryption key so that organizations may decrypt their network, systems and data.

- **Double extortion model** – as above, but attackers also exfiltrate data from the organization before encrypting the network and systems. A secondary ransom demand is placed to stop the release of data being published on the dark web or public forums. This usually comes with an expiration time, with some amounts of data being released to show that the attacker means business.

- **Triple extortion model** – as above, but attackers also go after the individuals whose data has been exfiltrated, to prevent the release of their data. Examples might include high-profile individuals who have had medical procedures such as plastic surgery.

Attackers use different elements of the infrastructure and data as the basis for the ransom demand. For example, they may have already established the level of sensitivity of the data and why organizations would pay for its return.

Attack patterns demonstrate that cybercriminals are acutely aware when there are change freezes, such as holidays, that will impact an organization's ability to make changes (such as patching) to harden their networks. They are hoping that organizations are more willing to pay a ransom than suffer downtime during key billing cycles in the health, finance and legal industries in particular.

Ultimately, the aim of the attacker is to apply significant pressure in relation to the level of threat and damage that may be incurred, to drive fear into organizations as a way of manipulating them further. Such tactics are part of the game plan, particularly if such attacks are played out in the public domain and media and a backlash follows for organizations not doing more to protect data. It is important for people to know how attackers use such threats and demands to force a reaction. Including an expiration time just applies more pressure, which is more likely to result in a rushed or irrational response.

The rise in destructive and wiper malware shows a willingness and desire to take this type of cybercrime to the next level, and is potentially being used as a 'parting gift' where other extortion demands have not worked, and as a warning to the next victim of what happens when someone doesn't pay. This is something that attackers are reliant upon, and which organizations need to be aware of, when training executives on how to deal with large-scale attacks and extortion demands. We shall discuss this further in Part Three, when we look at the type of strategy that organizations should implement to protect themselves from human adversaries.

Evolving extortion models

A change in tactics observed in some attacks shows that the perpetrators have honed the extortion model, by learning and observing human and organizational behaviour and reacting to it. This means that some attackers are forgoing deploying ransomware to encrypt or destruct networks and systems and are just concentrating on the exfiltration and ransoming of data instead. One dilemma for attackers is that, if you remove the operational impact of having systems down for prolonged periods, what prevents the organization simply saying no to the ransom demand?

Attackers need to spend more time on reconnaissance to learn the organization's business processes, the value of highly sensitive data, and how well organizations have prepared to prevent the release of data. Arguably, if the attacker doesn't have to invest time and effort getting malware into the environment, they have more time for research, irrespective of whether they do it themselves or through affiliates. In addition, for those attackers that are not motivated by monetary gain, there can be an increased incentive to use a similar technique to force policy changes, for example if a pharmaceutical company had not performed enough testing before the release of a new drug or had not published some of the known side-effects.

According to security research firm Redacted (2023), ransomware operator BianLian – a relatively new operator, first observed in 2021 – had already switched to a pure extortion model by tailoring their messages in such a way as to increase the pressure on the victim organization, even quoting specific legal and regulatory issues that the target may face, should such a breach be made public. These were relevant to the sector and jurisdiction in hand, highlighting that the message had been customized to fit the organization, rather than being generic. To apply additional pressure, BianLian also posted varying degrees of masked data onto a leak site, which included the victim's sector, geographical location and revenue. The time from initial compromise to leaking of masked data also sped up, ranging from 10 days to 48 hours. Removing the encryption phase meant that they could expedite the extortion demand.

As highlighted in Chapter 2, this is where social science plays a role in understanding social, political and economic conditions and the circumstances that may make the target more susceptible to attacks or demands. Having envy or wrath as motivators means that some attackers are more likely to go after specific target organizations, or release data, without a monetary extortion demand. Such attackers might demand instead a resignation or confession of wrongdoing from an executive or public official.

Unit 42 (2023) notes that attackers are evolving to use multiple extortion tactics to align with how organizations are evolving their defences. Harassment was a key factor in approximately 20 per cent of ransomware cases during 2022, compared with just 1 per cent the year before, often targeting specific individuals in the organization by making threatening communications and demands. This can make individuals feel more anxious if they are being specifically targeted, but also highlights how attackers have taken the time to determine the people in authority. Unit 42 predicts that extortion demands will become more politically motivated and be used as a distraction technique for other types of attacks.

Disinformation and propaganda

Lee and Choi (2018) in the *International Journal of Cybersecurity Intelligence & Cybercrime* highlight how the proliferation of hate speech and misinformation on social media has increased the volume of harmful interactions, in particular, the rise in illegal and harmful content relating to children, as well as racial or religious abuse.

The unwillingness and/or inability to effectively stem the flow of content only serves to exacerbate the problem. Even complaints raised against specific social media accounts and forums may only incur a ban on the content rather than the account. Attackers look to circumvent such actions by utilizing multiple accounts and handles or by burying further content in embedded links or private forums.

In addition, the deliberate targeting of subgroups of susceptible people can lead to radicalization, in which they start to support extreme ideologies and which can potentially draw them into acts of hate or terrorism. This is a form of psychological manipulation.

The rise and use of disinformation for the mass manipulation of people has been a growing trend. Unlike some cyber attacks on individuals or organizations, disinformation campaigns aim to target entire communities and even countries. The use of disinformation is often politically motivated, and, with widespread data sources and content, attackers utilize cyber influence operations that can cause large-scale social and economic unrest. This is a particular tactic that nation-sponsored actors have used to reignite severe right-wing or left-wing narratives. We shall discuss this further in Chapter 10.

While perhaps not as extreme, activists use disinformation to target subgroups of people to disrupt organizations through protest or sabotage. Organizations can find themselves targets through association due to the countries, companies or individuals they work or trade with.

An attempt to curtail freedom of speech can often have the opposite effect, where content is taken underground or the person is given a level of notoriety that inevitably means they attract more followers. Organizations need to be careful when banning content by way of 'access and deny' lists that they apply to certain websites or social forums.

Conclusion

In this chapter, we have delved further into the attack patterns and methods used to persuade and entice targets to act. We have explored the level of social engineering required to understand what will work under different situations, and why a one-size-fits-all approach may not achieve the required outcomes.

Rather than disconnect from the victims, we have given them a voice to express the devastating impact that cybercrime has; the invasion of privacy and the emotional turmoil they experience. Often, not only has their identity and/or money been stolen, but someone has entered their life with the sole intent of building and destroying trust, all to fulfil a selfish objective.

Organizations are not victimless, as they too must wrestle with the turmoil of being threatened with extortion and the release of sensitive data that may do more additional harm to people. While some attackers may see it as a game, a challenge, a means to an end – the level of disconnection means that inevitably some will take it too far and that we will continue to face incidents of increasing magnitude and devastation.

References

Action Fraud (2023) 'Romance fraud', actionfraud.police.uk/a-z-of-fraud/dating-fraud (archived at https://perma.cc/78DB-M8NC)

Carter, E (2023) 'Confirm not command: examining fraudsters' use of language to compel victim compliance in their own exploitation', *British Journal of Criminology*, 25 January, doi.org/10.1093/bjc/azac098 (archived at https://perma.cc/D3D3-2CGA)

Cialdini, R (2006) *Influence: The Psychology of Persuasion*, New York: Harper Business

FBI (2022) *Internet Crime Report 2022*, ic3.gov/Media/PDF/AnnualReport/2022_IC3Report.pdf (archived at https://perma.cc/AZ4K-XEF9)

Herley, C (2016) 'Why do Nigerian scammers say they are from Nigeria?', Microsoft Research, microsoft.com/en-us/research/wp-content/uploads/2016/02/WhyFromNigeria.pdf (archived at https://perma.cc/UQ7S-U3XB)

HMICFRS (2018) *Real lives, real crimes: A study of digital crime and policing*, justiceinspectorates.gov.uk/hmicfrs/our-work/article/digital-crime-and-policing/real-lives-real-crimes-study-digital (archived at https://perma.cc/7HBB-R8DX)

Lee, C and Choi, K (2018) 'The present and future of cybercrime, cyberterrorism and cybersecurity', *International Journal of Cybersecurity Intelligence & Cybercrime*, 1 (1), vc.bridgew.edu/cgi/viewcontent.cgi?article=1008&context=ijcic (archived at https://perma.cc/KN95-BA46)

Microsoft (2023) 'Cyber signals: shifting tactics fuel surge in business email compromise', 19 May, microsoft.com/en-us/security/blog/2023/05/19/cyber-signals-shifting-tactics-fuel-surge-in-business-email-compromise (archived at https://perma.cc/LK6Z-22LL)

Redacted (2023) 'BianLian ransomware gang continues to evolve', redacted.com/blog/bianlian-ransomware-gang-continues-to-evolve (archived at https://perma.cc/LC6C-RZ5F)

Unit 42 (2023) 'Ransomware and extortion report highlights: multi-extortion tactics continue to rise', 21 March, unit42.paloaltonetworks.com/multi-extortion-rise-ransomware-report (archived at https://perma.cc/7GRS-9ACZ)

Wong, T (2022) 'Cambodia scams: lured and trapped into slavery in Southeast Asia', BBC News, 21 September, bbc.co.uk/news/world-asia-62792875 (archived at https://perma.cc/56YK-SVQ9)

04

How Covid-19 created an epidemic of cybercrime

CHAPTER OBJECTIVES

In this chapter, we consider how seismic events have the power to shift the world in a different trajectory, for better or worse depending on your perspective.

We explore how world events and the news of the day enable attackers to prey on uncertainty and fear, and how they use this to manipulate people to act, often in irrational ways because of extreme stress or fatigue. That is what the attackers rely on.

One such event to take the world by storm was the COVID-19 global pandemic. This chapter takes a deep dive into how it fostered conditions that offered an ideal breeding ground for an epidemic of cybercrime.

A new pandemic is declared

When considering the profound impact that the pandemic had upon the world – and how it impacted cybercrime – it is useful to understand how it became one of the most significant events of the 21st century.

Once a global pandemic had been declared on 11 March 2020 by the World Health Organization (WHO), multiple countries started to take action to limit the spread of the virus by restricting international travel (WHO, 2020b). People started to be mandated to wear protective masks, and rules surrounding social distancing were enacted. Across many countries, police and law enforcement agencies were given additional powers to fine or imprison people who were found in violation of these strict rules.

The race started for government health agencies and pharmaceutical companies to create vaccines and to distribute these quickly. In December 2020, the UK became the first Western country to license a vaccine (from Pfizer/BioNTech), for those people most vulnerable from severe respiratory complications (UK Government, 2020). Critics as well as conspiracy theorists would later point to swathes of misinformation regarding the advocacy and effectiveness of the vaccines. The anti-vaxxer rhetoric was about to take off in earnest, which played right into the hands of those looking to capitalize on disinformation and cyber influence operations.

As the first lockdowns eased and countries took steps to start to reopen, Covid cases began to spike again, and so multiple cycles of full or partial lockdowns were instigated. The number of prolonged lockdowns began to take a heavy toll from a political, economic and social perspective as governments, organizations and the people most impacted were placed under extreme pressure.

How the pandemic impacted people's livelihoods

In October 2020, the WHO began to highlight the devastating impact that the pandemic was having on people. Not only did the pandemic cause a massive loss of life but it severely impacted people's physical, financial and psychological well-being (WHO, 2020a).

The WHO further laid bare the fragility and impact on the food system and the ripple effect that this caused to the global workforce. Border closures, trade restrictions and confinement measures prevented farmers from accessing key trade markets and selling their crops. This led to food shortages in many countries and agricultural industries were further hit by the lack of the itinerant and migrant workforce that tends to work in this sector. When experiencing income losses, farmers in some countries resorted to negative coping strategies, such as taking predatory loans or using child labour.

Fast forward to April 2023, and a study by the World Economic Forum noted how the pandemic had severely impacted people's perceptions of their general health and well-being over the three years since the pandemic had been declared. The study highlighted that, compared with how people were feeling prior to the pandemic, anxiety and depression had worsened, especially for those under 35 and women, whom they stated were over-represented in low-paid jobs and care roles (WEF, 2023).

Focusing the reporting primarily on Covid cases and deaths overlooked the burden of the pandemic and how differing levels of social isolation had affected the mental health and well-being of the global population. Countries that were able to offer greater financial support tended to fare slightly better overall, yet every person felt an impact.

Preying on the fear of the unknown

In many ways, the pandemic created a perfect storm for cyber attackers, not just in terms of the huge changes that were impacting people's livelihoods and general well-being, but organizations of all sizes had to adapt en masse, introducing an array of new processes and technologies at haste.

According to Microsoft (2020), the lives of up to 300 million information workers worldwide were upended, and many found themselves adjusting to remote working with limited resources and increased stress. For many organizations, security governance and controls started to slip, as many were left struggling with multiple rounds of missed critical patches and updates, which compounded the threat.

Attackers had to adjust their business model, as they too were feeling the strain. Organized crime groups were forced into moving large elements of their enterprises online as it was significantly harder to move and trade in illegal substances or goods because of border closures and limited transportation and logistics.

Fraudsters tend to favour tried-and-tested methods to maximize their return on investment, so the type of attacks didn't necessarily change but the tactics and lures did. Let's dive into some of these to find out how they evolved, particularly at the start of the pandemic, when the level of fear and uncertainty was as its highest and many organizations were in utter turmoil.

Phishing and impersonation

Attackers utilized a range of Covid-related lures principally through emails and text messages. They pretended to be legitimate organizations, such as government, health and public authorities, financial services and even charities. These were timed to follow the news of the day, depending on the type of messages being delivered by government and certain institutions, and the messages were altered to fall in line with these official communications.

In April 2020, Microsoft released a blog with several key observations (Lefferts, 2020):

- Covid-themed attacks were re-treads of existing attacks, slightly altered to tie in to the pandemic. This means a change in lure, as opposed to a surge in attacks.

- Every country in the world saw at least one Covid-themed attack, with China, USA and Russia hit the hardest.

- TrickBot and Emotet malware families were rebranded, with 76 recorded variants using Covid-themed lures.

- Of the millions of targeted emails each day, around 60,000 included Covid-related malicious attachments or malicious URLs.

- Attackers were impersonating established entities like WHO, the US Centers for Disease Control and Prevention and the UK Department of Health and Social Care to get into inboxes.

In June 2020, Microsoft Threat Intelligence issued a blog detailing how it had backtracked over the previous three months to see how attackers had evolved their tactics to follow the news of the day relating to Covid, at a global as well as national (US) level. This had started as early as 11 February 2020, when the WHO formally gave the coronavirus the name Covid-19. The following week saw Covid-themed cyber attacks increase 11-fold. While this accounted for less than 2 per cent of overall attacks, it was clear that cybercriminals wanted to exploit the situation.

This peaked in the first two weeks of March 2020, as many countries tried to curtail the virus with travel restrictions. Malware campaigns, attack infrastructure and phishing attacks all showed signs of opportunistic behaviour, categorized by the repurposing of attacks to include a Covid lure, as opposed to creating new ones. Attackers predominantly preyed on the fear and confusion of the situation and the need for a fast resolution. They did this by cycling through global and local news stories and adapting the same phishing email to be more relevant to different populations and what was going on at the time. This presented some early lessons:

- Cybercriminals adapt their tactics to take advantage of local events that are more likely to lure victims to their schemes. While the lure is quickly adapted, the underlying hook or method remains consistent.

- Security investments that raise the cost of attack or lower the likelihood of success are the optimal path forward, demonstrated by utilizing increased cyber awareness training, and monitoring for specific types of lure or attack.

- Focusing on the behaviours of attackers is more effective than just examining indicators of compromise.

Business email compromise

In July 2020, Microsoft Digital Crimes Unit (DCU) undertook its first legal action to disrupt a specific Covid-19 attack, which was attempting to defraud organizations across 62 countries. It resulted in a court order that enabled Microsoft to seize control of six key domains in the criminals' infrastructure (Burt infrastructure).

First observed in December 2019, the criminals had devised a sophisticated phishing campaign designed to compromise Microsoft customer accounts. The phishing emails looked like they originated from an employer or other trusted source and frequently targeted business leaders across a variety of industries, attempting to compromise accounts, steal information and redirect wire transfers. The emails contained references to Covid to exploit financial concerns and induce victims to click on malicious links, with terms such as 'Covid-19 Bonus'. When victims tried to open the file, they were redirected to the criminals' malicious web application that pretended to be Microsoft Office 365, where it asked the victim to unwittingly grant unwittingly:

- maintain access to data you have given it access to
- read your contacts
- sign in and read your profile
- read your mail
- read all Onebook notebooks you can access
- read and write to your mailbox settings
- have full access to all files you have access to.

This is 'consent phishing', in which attackers trick victims into granting malicious application access to sensitive data or other resources. Instead of trying to steal the user's password, an attacker is seeking permission for their application to access data. It is much more intrusive, as it enables the attacker to maintain access in the environment.

Since the attacker in this case was impersonating Microsoft, the DCU took a novel approach by seeking a court order to take control of the domain names that the cybercriminals used to launch their attacks. The US Federal Court granted the motion, and the malicious domains were turned over to Microsoft, preventing future attacks originating on the domains.

Online frauds

Linked to phishing as a method of delivery, the rate of online scams and fraudulent transactions increased during Covid, because of attackers pretending to offer access to services, such as the provision of PPE, testing kits and even vaccines.

Other scams included advance payment fees, where attackers pretended to be legitimate postal and courier services. They requested that the victim pay a nominal fee of £2 to £5 to release an item that was being held for them. Such online scams are deliberately low value – but high volume – as they are less likely to be reported to the banks or police. Based on the sheer volume of messages, it can be profitable for opportunists to perform such attacks with minimal outlay. As consumers from across the world adjusted their online behaviour and purchasing habits, criminals continued to capitalize on this method of attack.

Extortion and ransomware

Opportunists as well as organized crime groups took advantage of organizations that had to make changes quickly. New technology and processes, coupled with a lack of training and understanding, meant that there were more vulnerabilities to exploit and target because of the expanding attack surface.

It is estimated that over 1.6 billion children had their education disrupted because of school closures and staff absence. The pandemic exposed and deepened existing education inequalities that were never adequately addressed, impacting vulnerable and marginalized learners the hardest (UNESCO, 2021). The education sector became a key target because of attackers' ability to obtain access to large numbers of devices and data. In some cases, children's Covid test results and medical data were the subject of ransom. Education has continued to be the most targeted sector by attackers, at a rate 10 times higher than the retail and consumer goods sector (Microsoft, 2023).

Not only were people feeling the pressure at home and the impact on their livelihoods, but organizations offering critical provision, including healthcare and emergency services, were deemed easy targets, and one where providers may have been more susceptible and willing to pay ransom demands. In April 2020, Microsoft observed that a prolific ransomware criminal responsible for more than 100 major incidents suddenly switched to using the infamous trojan 'WannaCry' after attacking hospitals and healthcare organizations during the crisis.

Antivax campaigns seed disinformation

As well as attacks aimed at individuals and organizations, there was a significant rise in disinformation campaigns from activists, nation-sponsored actors, as well as prominent influencers and conspiracy theorists.

In the early days of the pandemic, there was much misinformation from an array of sources, which was amplified by social media. This provided a perfect opportunity for some groups to interject with deliberately false information, often targeted at specific subsets of the global population, in a bid to turn people on or off to a specific narrative, and for swathes of the population to then turn against their government or public health authority, inadvertently putting themselves and others at higher risk.

With more time on their hands, because of long and repeated cycles of lockdowns and social distancing, people were spending an exorbitant amount of time online, scrolling through different websites, social media sites and dedicated forums and reaffirming the rhetoric that was building. The more people like and search for specific content on social media, the more the algorithms work to provide similar content, which only perpetuates the conscious or unconscious bias that has built up; and when the whole world is dealing with a seismic event, it can feel like a merry-go-round, with no way off. And that is what cyber attackers and bad actors are reliant on – the seed of doubt has been sown, and they can sit back and watch the fallout from afar. We shall discuss further how nation-sponsored actors use cyber influence operations in Chapter 10.

A report published by Interpol in August 2020 highlighted the increasing amount of misinformation and fake news that was being consumed by the public. The level of unverified information, misunderstood threats and conspiracy theories not only increased levels of anxiety but helped to facilitate the rise in cyber attacks. One country reported 290 postings within a one-month period, with the majority containing concealed malware. There were also reports of misinformation being linked to the illegal trade of fraudulent medical and safety equipment.

In addition, a report issued by the Center for Countering Digital Hate (2021) highlighted how just 12 prominent anti-vaxxers were responsible for spreading two thirds of the disinformation relating to Covid vaccines, generating over 29 million impressions across social media platforms. The research shows that, while many people might share and spread content on social media, it is often generated by just a few limited sources intent on harm.

Conclusion

In this chapter, we have explored how global events can amplify the capacity, will and motivation of criminals. When emotions are running high and there is fear of the unknown and a dire need to obtain more information, it can create almost a frenzy for attackers. The attackers prey on people's fears, distractions or pain from the loss of loved ones and livelihoods, and they use it to their advantage. The impersonation of healthcare and charitable institutions to prey on the most vulnerable in society only shows the level of deprivation that some attackers will stoop to.

And while some may have a moral compass in times of crisis and forgo some of the typical types of attack we have come to expect, it is imperative for organizations to understand that no one is immune. Just like a virus, for attackers to thrive, they need to prey on the vulnerabilities of their hosts.

References

Burt, T (2020) 'Microsoft takes legal action against COVID-19 related cybercrime', Microsoft blog, 7 July, blogs.microsoft.com/on-the-issues/2020/07/07/digital-crimes-unit-covid-19-cybercrime (archived at https://perma.cc/W3GR-PS5M)

Center for Countering Digital Hate (2021) The Disinformation Dozen: Why platforms must act on twelve leading online anti-vaxxers, 24 March, counterhate.com/wp-content/uploads/2022/05/210324-The-Disinformation-Dozen.pdf (archived at https://perma.cc/KJG7-XWEG)

Interpol (2020) 'Report shows alarming rate of cyberattacks during COVID-19', 4 August, interpol.int/en/News-and-Events/News/2020/INTERPOL-report-shows-alarming-rate-of-cyberattacks-during-COVID-19 (archived at https://perma.cc/C3QK-6UZU)

Lefferts, R (2020) 'Microsoft shares new intelligence, security guidance during global crisis', 8 April, microsoft.com/en-us/security/blog/2020/04/08/microsoft-shares-new-threat-intelligence-security-guidance-during-global-crisis (archived at https://perma.cc/J328-GBHT)

Microsoft (2020) Microsoft Digital Defence Report 2020: Cyber threat sophistication on the rise, 29 September, microsoft.com/en-us/security/blog/2020/09/29/microsoft-digital-defense-report-2020-cyber-threat-sophistication-rise (archived at https://perma.cc/EY7Z-KBDD)

Microsoft (2023) 'Global threat activity', 30-day rolling graph, microsoft.com/en-us/wdsi/threats (archived at https://perma.cc/6D7F-K63R)

Microsoft Threat Intelligence (2020) 'Exploiting a crisis: how cybercriminals behaved during the outbreak', 16 June, microsoft.com/en-us/security/blog/2020/06/16/exploiting-a-crisis-how-cybercriminals-behaved-during-the-outbreak (archived at https://perma.cc/P2GH-QVVH)

UK Government (2020) 'UK medicines regulator gives approval for first UK COVID-19 vaccine', press release, 2 December, gov.uk/government/news/uk-medicines-regulator-gives-approval-for-first-uk-covid-19-vaccine (archived at https://perma.cc/6SQG-YHV8)

UNESCO (2021) 'One year into COVID-19 education disruption: where do we stand?', 19 March, unesco.org/en/articles/one-year-covid-19-education-disruption-where-do-we-stand (archived at https://perma.cc/X4AF-Q6RP)

WEF (2023) 'New research shows the significant health harms of the pandemic', 17 April, weforum.org/agenda/2023/04/why-focusing-on-covid-deaths-undercounts-the-health-harms-of-the-pandemic-new-research (archived at https://perma.cc/N3R3-WQEK)

WHO (2020a) 'Impact of COVID-19 on people's livelihoods, their health and our food systems', 13 October, who.int/news/item/13-10-2020-impact-of-covid-19-on-people%27s-livelihoods-their-health-and-our-food-systems (archived at https://perma.cc/3HWW-5TRU)

WHO (2020b) 'Listings of WHO's response to COVID-19', 29 June, who.int/news/item/29-06-2020-covidtimeline (archived at https://perma.cc/D6BJ-NEKG)

05

Cybercrime as a service – a booming enterprise

CHAPTER OBJECTIVES

In this chapter, we look at how the barriers to entry have diminished for nearly all attackers. Once the domain of highly skilled actors with deep technical skills, developers are now monetizing their skills by creating and selling exploits, kits and managed services on dark-web markets to a range of attackers.

With the maturity of the cybercrime ecosystem, offenders can utilize an array of services to easily perform, and adjust their attacks for nominal outlay, as 'cybercrime as a service' proliferates.

Establishing skill sets

Cyber-dependent crimes are committed for many different reasons by individuals, groups and nation-sponsored actors. Many cybercriminals have relatively low technical skills, but their attacks are increasingly enabled by a growing online marketplace that provides easy access to sophisticated and bespoke tools and expertise, allowing less skilled attackers to exploit a wide range of vulnerabilities. Highly skilled individuals or groups who can code and disseminate software to attack computer networks and systems are highly sought after and can command high fees as a result.

The cybercriminal network is a continuously evolving interconnected ecosystem of many players with different techniques, goals and skill sets. Attackers are learning that there is less work and less risk, as well as a higher return on investment (ROI), in hiring or selling their tools for a portion of the profits than performing the attack themselves. This industrialization of the cybercrime economy has made it easier for offenders to use ready-made tools to perform their attacks, with some even providing extra incentives such as profit share and managed-services schemes complete with help desks and human resources departments.

As Dr Paul Stephens highlighted in Chapter 3, given the right conditions, why wouldn't someone become an attacker? Perhaps a rhetorical question, but it seems the expected ROI outweighs the anticipated risk when it comes to the ability to gain access to new and evolving tools and techniques to help achieve the goals.

Before we explore the types of service and kit that are on offer, and how they might be utilized, let's first look at the criminal underworld where many of these services and transactions take place.

Navigating the criminal underworld

When conducting research for this book, I had the opportunity to speak with Shawn Loveland, former Microsoft threat researcher and now Chief Operating Officer of Resecurity, where he specializes in dark web intelligence. Loveland provided a fascinating insight into the criminal underworld and the array of services that can be bought and sold on the dark web and other forums, from a role that he has specialized in for over 10 years.

When Loveland first started researching the dark web and the roles of different actors, he assumed that the main factor that drives criminals was profit, but, after about a year, he identified that the most attractive driving factor was in fact a reliable ROI. How much effort, time and patience the attacker has depends on what they believe the ROI will be across different techniques and victims. Is the scheme tried and tested or new? The ROI can be money, kudos or the next promotion, especially if an attacker is looking to climb the ranks or join a specific group.

Many attackers will already be aware of what the different regulations and processes are with regard to attacking a US bank versus a German bank, or a citizen versus an organization; for example, how long it will take and whether they need to adapt and change tools to meet the needs of their campaign or monetization strategy. Part of the ROI is not to just consider who to target but the time, effort and cost involved in overcoming the associate complexities.

As an example, Loveland spoke about how many organizations have implemented multi-factor authentication (MFA) to counteract the use of credential theft, by requesting additional checks such as biometric authentication, one-time passcodes and so on. The counter-move for the attackers was to retool their process, even if it took several months, because, once they worked out how to bypass MFA, they could reuse that, sell the techniques to others or improve the kits and services they sell to others. For example, they may adjust the process to include more social engineering or adversary-in-the-middle attacks, which is where an attacker intercepts and reroutes a network communication between two parties.

As we discussed in Chapter 1, as technology evolves, so do the types of attack and the defence methodologies used against those attacks. So, while we can take steps to drive up the cost to the attacker, it does not mean that they just stop. As more of the exploits and workarounds become mainstream, that too drives up the level of security tools and processes required by organizations to counteract them.

Shawn Loveland gave the example of a botnet takedown. This can take months of research, and a huge amount of effort by law enforcement and other agencies to get a court order to seize the malicious infrastructure. For some criminals, they may take it as a vacation opportunity while they purchase and build more command-and-control servers, with 1 million botnet registrations. Loveland estimated that it might take the offender 6 to 18 hours to recoup the cost of downtime and infrastructure reinstallation and re-establish operations. The ability to scale is on the attackers' side, when considering how quickly they can move across jurisdictions to reset up infrastructure, compared with how much effort is required to dismantle it. The ROI for many attackers can be substantial, even with the downtime that may ensue. We will examine the challenges and opportunities faced by law enforcement in Chapter 8.

For many organizations, too much emphasis is placed on disrupting the *how* – the technology, infrastructure or exploits that attackers deploy – rather than *why* they are attacking.

The how is often a fixed transactional cost, perhaps calculated on a ratio of price per hit and determining whether it is more cost effective and efficient to use malware, a script or a human to do the work. The method is often a means to an end rather than the end objective itself. If you take one of those methods away, or block it, the attacker will just try another one, or tweak it to bypass the detections.

The why is perhaps the more interesting factor. When we consider the 'seven sins of attackers', there are only a finite number of 'whys', but there are countless 'hows'. The why suggests how much time, persistence and inclination an attacker has. Arguably, if you disrupt the rationale for the why, and curtail the motivation behind the attack, it will have a greater impact. Understandably, this requires a change of mindset in how cyber-crime is viewed, by all stakeholders, so that the deterrents, penalties and repercussions for attackers are much higher.

A look inside criminal networks

To understand the level of criminal networks, and how far they go, it is first necessary to understand the layers of the web and how they are accessed. Many people will be unaware of these different levels, or how to access them, so you need to be in the know, and that information is not available to just anyone. There is a vetted and trusted process that operates across different layers and domains, as one might expect since there is a need to hide illegal activity from law enforcement and intelligence agencies, as well as other competing groups. At a high level this can be described as in Table 5.1.

TABLE 5.1 Examining partitions of the web

Partition of the web	Explanation
Surface web	• This is the visible and searchable part of the web that can be accessed through standard search engines such as Google, Bing, Yahoo and so on. • It equates to around 4% of the web. The remainder is what lies beneath.
Dark web	• This is the invisible part of the web that most users don't know how to access. • It cannot be searched or crawled by traditional search engines and requires authorization and credentials to access. • It can include information that may be sensitive such as medical, financial, scientific and government records. • Much like how you would log in to your bank, or other accounts, you need to have an account, an identity and be authorized and authenticated to use it.

(continued)

TABLE 5.1 (Continued)

Partition of the web	Explanation
	• It can't be accessed by traditional search engines or crawlers. The purpose is to offer a level of anonymity and deep encryption, by using a special browser or software with decryption keys. This is often known as the TOR browser (the Onion Router) for its multiple layers that hide the user's IP address and location so that activity can't be tracked.
	• It is where individuals and groups engage in illicit activity by sharing information or engaging in the buying and selling of illegal goods and services.
	• It is the chosen platform for illegal trading of weapons, government or scientific secret information, malware, drugs, exotic animals, banned films/literature, fake documents, money-laundering and even human/animal organs.
Deep dark web	• This is a subset of the dark web.
	• It is where activity between professional cybercriminals is conducted and fresh content is shared, bartered, bought and sold.
	• There are believed to be multiple hidden layers that go even deeper with the trafficking of humans, child exploitation and even arranging to have people killed. Such forums and sites are difficult to find and access, and will be an invitation-only, tightly controlled network known only to a few hardened criminals.
	• It is sometimes referred to as the 'Mariana layer', named after the deepest undersea trench on the planet, some 10km beneath the surface and only hospitable to a few that dare to venture that deep.

Accessing the dark web

Shawn Loveland explained that Resecurity tracks tens of thousands of forums where cybercriminals and other threat actors conduct their business. There is a requirement within them to build trust, and it can take over 18 months before some attackers will gain access to some areas. They must be able to prove their worth, capability and credibility. They don't expect just to be let in or that others will readily talk to them, as, although there is a level of anonymity, people still need to know who they are dealing with, and there is still a paranoia about who else is watching.

The people communicating in such forums don't discuss things in the same way you would in person or other channels. They might use slang or code, so it is hard to decipher what they may be referring to. There are several vetted and paid forums, where the quality of what is provided goes up, but so does the effort to get in. In some ways, there are similarities between a drug cartel and a cybercriminal network, as someone might be challenged, for example to 'prove you're not a cop and go and do x'.

A newbie is more likely to get 'ripped off' or be sold inferior goods and services at above market prices because they don't know any better, much like someone who may be naïve in paying for overpriced items in an online marketplace. If someone tries this the other way around, they will probably be kicked out of such forums and groups and make a bad name for themselves. The sentiment that 'there is no honour among thieves' is not quite true here because many fraudsters and criminals rely on their reputation.

The vetted sites tend to be where the 'thought leaders' and strategists fraternize. These are the ones who had worked out the deep levels of exploits, but now, with added suspicions about who is who and who they are willing to do business with, the best intelligence and interaction is often taken offline and discussed in person.

Most of the criminals tend to be opportunistic, whereby, if they are trying to make money, they may not care where it comes from. As Loveland explained, it can cost as little as $1, with an average of $35, or much more to obtain someone's password and cookies. enabling them to log on through a user's PC. Some groups, however, may also place and advertise a bounty on a target organization, to steal specific data or research.

A successful cybercriminal – one that has credibility and is skilled at what they do, will not tend to provide or enact anything for less than $100,000 per transaction. Loveland is aware of one individual who breached 122 companies inside 45 days by honing a high-quality script. This person was averaging $250,000 per week through a cryptocurrency wallet.

Types of exploit

As we noted previously, the underpinning attack is often a means to an end, and the first stage is to gain access to the target's network. There are multiple ways to do this, but if it is collecting credentials to use for fraud, extortion, espionage or other nefarious purposes, attackers need an initial way into the environment to obtain this.

For some attackers, that means simply scanning the internet to establish what infrastructure is deployed, the operating system that may be running, and whether there are existing exploits or if new ones need to be created. So, let's consider some examples of these.

WHAT IS MEANT BY A ZERO-DAY?

The term '0-day', or 'zero-day', refers to the amount of time that a software developer must fix an issue. A vendor or developer has just learnt of a flaw and has 'zero days' to fix it before it can be exploited. There are a few terms that are commonly used alongside zero-day, but they mean different things on a cyber-attack timeline (Microsoft, 2022).

- **Zero-day *vulnerability*** is a flaw in software programming that has been discovered before a seller or programmer has been made aware of it. Because the programmers are unaware that this vulnerability exists, there are no patches or fixes, making an attack more likely to be successful. Software developers are constantly looking for vulnerabilities in code that they can fix with patches.
- **Zero-day *exploit*** is when an attacker takes advantage of the vulnerability, often by using malware that has been specially created.
- **Zero-day *attack*** happens when an attacker uses a zero-day exploit to attack or compromise an organization, often resulting in data loss and identity theft.

WHAT IS AN N-DAY?

In comparison to a 0-day that is unknown to a software developer, an N-day has been known for a specific number of days. In essence, there has been a delay of more than one day between the time of disclosure and the time of the attack. There is often a race against time for software developers to create and release a patch and for organizations to deploy the patch before attackers can exploit it. As a result, many entities have significant exposure to these types of exploit.

N-days tend to be a favoured area for attackers because much of the work to build an exploit has already been done. Once public disclosures have been performed by security researchers or software providers, it can indicate to attackers how they may use specific exploits to their advantage. Zero-days, in comparison, are time-consuming to create, take a great deal of skill and are expensive to obtain.

Often, it means scanning the internet for examples of specific networks or systems that may be running machines with the designated vulnerabilities and which have not yet applied the update and fix. Of course, many exploits will require that the attacker is already on the target network for it to be useable, which is why we see so many phishing and social engineering attacks – to trick the target into enabling the access.

As Shawn Loveland explains, there are several ecosystems for exploits:

- **Bug bounty researchers** – incentivized by the software developer or security researchers to identify and report vulnerabilities before they are identified by attackers. There is often a payment made to the researcher based on the severity of the vulnerability. Less reputable researchers may also be incentivized to play both sides by first reporting to the software vendor, then, while a patch is created, selling this information to attackers so they know what to exploit and when the door may be closed to them.

- **Zero-day attacks, sold on the dark web** – often labelled as a 0-day, and could be sold for $5,000 to $100,000. These are most likely not very useful, or they are in fact N-days where an available patch hasn't been deployed yet, and hence there can be a race against time to exploit it as quickly as possible.

- **Brokers, who broker 0-days from various sources, as commission** – often this is for specific software or operating systems such as Microsoft, Apple or Google. They take time and skill to build and create. There are some that may be built for or limited to the use of governments. They could be sold from $100,000 to over $10 million each.

Most zero-days are demand constrained, not supply constrained. Some may never be placed for sale. So as not to flood the market, brokers may also artificially increase the shelf life of a 0-day, by stating that they will report it to the researchers or software companies so that a patch is created. Not only does this push up the initial price but also ensures that new ones can come to the market. It becomes an issue of scale, not just in terms of who can afford to buy such an exploit, but in the ROI required by the attacker to justify when and how to deploy it for the most effect.

In April 2022, Mandiant reported that nation-sponsored espionage groups continue to be the primary actors exploiting 0-day vulnerabilities (Sadowski, 2022). It observed that, between 2012 and 2021, China exploited more 0-days than any other nation, although the proportion of financially motivated actors, such as ransomware operators, is increasing, as they can recruit or purchase the requisite skills to exploit 0-days. Shawn Loveland commented that, at one point, ransomware brokers were outbidding governments for access to 0-days because of the sheer volume of money they were making through cybercrime.

Exploit subscriptions

The most valuable O-day exploits are often those that are hard to fix, target commonly used software or hardware and involve a supplier that takes too long to resolve. For example, O-days on medical devices and industrial control systems may require hardware to be replaced before they can upgrade the software, so they can be exploited for longer.

For some attackers, commandeering a O-day is simply out of reach, so the lure of N-days is very attractive if utilized and operating efficiently to yield a ROI.

As Trend Micro reports (2021a and b), some cybercriminals offer exploit tools for a monthly fee, enabling attackers to launch their assaults relatively easily and with surprising regularity. These subscriptions are often reasonably priced, starting at $60. While relatively cheap for the attackers, such exploits can wreak havoc on organizations and be expensive to resolve.

The life of an exploit starts with its creation, either as an already working exploit or as a proof of concept that other developers could build upon. Once it can be weaponized, it is sold. Those sold on the dark web are often junk, while those sold in vetted forums tend to be better and sold at a higher price. After a patch for the affected vulnerability is released, the price inevitably drops for what is now an N-day exploit, which can be sold and bundled with other older exploits for years to come.

Shawn Loveland gave an example of how some exploits are designed with specific anti-malware products in mind. For example, if something had not been detected by one anti-malware product but had with another, the exploit developers could build a script or malware to run alongside that security product where it was less likely to be detected. So, the attacker can check what servers and operating system the target is hosting, as well as the security products installed, to see if an exploit is available to bypass them.

Subscription services are appealing for opportunists, as well as more advanced actors, as they drive efficiency and a higher ROI. These bundles of exploits often include automated scripts for deployment in phishing emails, to be launched into the environment by the users themselves. Some subscription services also promise subscribers periodic updates on their offerings.

As-a-service business models

Some groups have taken exploit subscriptions one step further by offering discrete packaged services for elements of the attack. For many attackers, the prospect of casting a wide net to see who bites is not a good use of time and resources, so outsourcing such services becomes an attractive proposition.

Just as cloud services and managed service providers offer 'on-demand' and 'pay-as-you-go' models to enable organizations to budget and plan their capital and operational costs, attackers are doing the same. These are often run as mini enterprises, with different people providing different aspects of the service, such as procurement and payroll. An interesting issue is that some salaried staff may not even know that they are working for a criminal organization, or at least the extent of the operations.

Initial access brokers

The most widely used and disruptive model to the exploitation market has been 'access as a service' where initial access brokers (IABs) provide access to the target organizations. Research conducted by Microsoft Threat Intelligence (2022) suggests that criminals are learning that there is less work and risk involved by renting or selling their tools rather than performing the attacks themselves. As in the industrial revolution described in Chapter 1, attackers are now industrializing their products. While some sellers rely on finding and capitalizing on working exploits, there are others who consider it a profession, offering a portfolio of services to loyal customers.

IABs principally focus on gaining privileged access to corporate networks, which they may auction off in dark web forums. Some IABs sell access for other purposes, such as ransomware. Such sellers may infect systems with malware or a botnet and then sell them as a 'load', which is designed to install other malware or back doors onto infected systems for other criminals to use. Other IABs scan the internet for vulnerable systems, such as exposed remote desktop protocol (RDP) systems with weak passwords or unpatched systems, and then compromise them to bank for later. Some advertisements even cite which systems are managed by an antivirus or endpoint detection and response (EDR) product, and how to bypass them, to command a higher price. Some IABs even call out where the target victim has a weak backup and recovery system (Flare, 2023).

The most-targeted countries are the United States, followed by Australia and the UK, indicating a strong bias towards English-speaking countries.

Phishing as a service

As we saw in Chapter 3, phishing (including email, text and phone messages) remains the most common form of attack, particularly for those cybercriminals looking to commoditize the ROI.

There was a time when attackers had to build their own phishing messages and brand-impersonating websites, requiring a level of skill to do so. Now, as for other types of attack, it has evolved its own service-based economy. From buying phishing kits to full end-to-end services, the barriers to entry for many attackers and opportunists are low. Basic levels of phishing require limited skill but there is often little money to be made. Attacks are evolving to include 'adversary in the middle', spear-phishing and consent-phishing.

WHAT IS A PHISHING KIT?

Pre-packaged phishing kits are sold on a one-time-use basis from sellers and resellers. They are ready-to-use templates designed to evade detection and are often accompanied by a portal from which to access them. The kit allows the buyer to set up websites and purchase domain names, and often provides a level of customization to suit.

In September 2021, Microsoft Threat Intelligence identified over 300,000 newly created and unique subdomains, which led them to unearth a large-scale *phishing-as-a-service* operation known as BulletProofLink that sells a range of phishing kits, hosting sites and automated services on a one-off or subscription-based model. The operators maintained multiple sites under the aliases BulletProftLink, BulletProofLink and Anthrax, including an online store, instructional videos and promotional materials for the 'dedicated spammer'.

This provided a fascinating insight into the type of services offered, including:

- a 10 per cent welcome discount on all new orders for subscribers to their newsletter

- a monthly service cost up to $800, or $50 for a one-time hosting link, mostly paid by Bitcoin

- customer support services for new and existing customers

- over 100 phishing templates that mimicked known brands and logos, with credential-capturing services, to be utilized for subsequent attacks.

The operators maximize monetization by ensuring that any stolen data, access and credentials are used in as many ways as possible. Victims' credentials are likely to end up in dark web forums, where they are bought and sold by other groups.

Ransomware as a service

Microsoft Threat Intelligence has noted a growing trend in human-operated ransomware. This term clarifies the difference between generic and automated commodity-style attacks, and those that are principally driven by humans who make decisions at every stage of the attack based on what they find in their target's network. Ransomware as a service (RaaS) is an arrangement between an operator (the seller) and an affiliate (the buyer).

WHAT IS A RANSOMWARE OPERATOR?

The ransomware operator develops and maintains tools to power the ransomware operation, including the builders that produce the ransomware payloads and payment portals for communicating with victims. This may include a leak site to share snippets of data that has allegedly been exfiltrated from the victim in order to entice a payment. Many RaaS offerings incorporate a suite of extortion support services, including leak site hosting and integration into ransom notes, as well as decryption negotiation and cryptocurrency transaction services. Some provide a dynamic pricing model, based on the geographical location of the victim, to establish what regulatory fines may be applicable for breached data, and whether to set the price higher or lower.

WHAT IS A RANSOMWARE AFFILIATE?

Affiliates are those that have bought a 'payload' from an IAB or have purchased the right to push the malware or ransomware to devices in selected demographics. The price can be as low as $25 per 1,000 PCs. They may not

---

know or care how the network was compromised, but will use it to perform other activities to understand the monetization potential. So, while some organizations may feel that they have been specifically targeted, the attacker may have just secured valid access to that network, with limited technical expertise.

Once on the target's network, the next stage is to perform reconnaissance to determine the next steps, based on knowledge of the target. Many of the initial access campaigns perform automated reconnaissance and exfiltration of information collected in the first few minutes of an attack, such as additional credentials because of laterally moving through the organization and elevating privilege. The attackers take note of security products in the environment and attempt to tamper with and disable these, using scripts or tools provided with the RaaS purchase or by using their own specific commands or techniques.

While some groups have access to large and highly resourced organizations, many prefer to attack small and medium enterprises (SMEs) for less overall ransom because they can execute the attack in a shorter timeframe. The ROI is often higher because the SME either can't respond or doesn't know how to respond effectively. The rising costs and pressures placed on SMEs make them more susceptible and vulnerable to the extortion demand and more willing to pay.

As ransomware deployment becomes more industrialized, it has become more difficult to link the tradecraft used in a specific attack to the ransomware payload developers. For example, identifying a ransomware attack by assigning it with the payload name gives the impression that a monolithic entity is behind all attacks using the same ransomware payload. However, the RaaS operator sells access to multiple affiliates, who, in turn, perform the network intrusion and deploy the payload. In some cases, the parties may agree to split the profit to make the services and offerings even more accessible.

Maintaining persistence

Once a target has been effectively compromised, the attacker will invariably want to maintain access, without the target knowing about it. This access can be utilized for their own purposes or sold to other attackers. The hand-offs and transitions between attackers mean that multiple attackers may retain persistence in a compromised environment, and so the cycle starts again, with access services and exploits offered to other attackers, with varying motivations and objectives. Unless attempts are made to evict the attackers once they have been detected, the organizations will continue to be seen as high-value targets.

Cyber weapons for hire

A worrying trend is that some exploits and zero-day attacks are not created just by cybercriminals, but by private-sector enterprises who build and sell offensive cyber-tools to an array of buyers. While they don't perform the actual attacks, they have the means, capability and resources to build dangerous tools. Such groups are often referred to as 'cyber mercenaries', effectively providing private offensive cyber weapons for hire. While such private sector actors may claim that they will not sell their services to certain governments and groups, it can be difficult to prove, as they are often incentivized to sell services to the highest bidder.

Offensive cyber-tools, often sold as O-days on legitimate infrastructure, can cause huge amounts of damage if they are misused or abused. Cyber-surveillance companies lower the barriers to entry by making spyware tools, for example, available to more countries. Even if the tools are sold to governments who use them for precisely targeted attacks, they can still fall into the wrong hands. In addition, private-sector actors are not subject to the same constraints as governments, since those governments with offensive capability are subject to diplomatic consequences, as we shall discuss further in Chapter 10.

One of the most widely known surveillance tools, Pegasus, was developed by the Israeli company NSO. In December 2020, Microsoft, along with Cisco, GitHub, Google, LinkedIn, VMWare and the Internet Association, filed an Amicus brief in a legal case brought by WhatsApp against the NSO Group (US Court of Appeal, 2020). According to WhatsApp, NSO enabled Pegasus to access more than 1,400 devices, including those belonging to journalists and human rights defenders (Burt, 2020).

Pegasus allowed the user to track someone's whereabouts, listen in on their conversations, read their texts and emails, look at their photographs, steal their contacts list, download their data, review their internet search history, and more. WhatsApp and Facebook (which handles cybersecurity for WhatsApp) eventually identified and closed the vulnerabilities NSO had used to install the spyware.

Concerned by the rising use of cyber-surveillance tools, in March 2023, the Biden administration gave an executive order to ban the use of commercial spyware that poses a risk to national security (The White House, 2023).

In April 2023, the *New York Times* highlighted how some countries continue to utilize and exploit such tools, and that Mexico was the biggest and most prolific user of Pegasus. The investigation showed how they wielded the surveillance tool against civilians who stood up to the state and defended human rights (Kitroeff and Bergman, 2023).

While Pegasus had been used for good, it had also created great harm. In helping to fight crime, it had broken up child-abuse rings and led to the arrest of drug lord El Chapo. But it had also been deployed to spy on human-rights defenders, democracy advocates, journalists and other citizens who challenged corruption and abuse.

As a result of Biden's executive order, members of the Cybersecurity Tech Accord (2023) agreed to a set of new principles to limit the harm caused by cyber mercenaries. The signatories committed to:

- take steps to counter cyber mercenaries' use of products and services to harm people
- identify ways to actively counter the cyber-mercenary market
- invest in cybersecurity awareness of customers, users and the public
- protect customers and users by maintaining the integrity and security of products and services
- develop processes for handling valid legal requests for information.

Conclusion

This chapter has explored different aspects of the cybercriminal underworld and how attackers are able to access the dark web to procure an array of exploits and services to aid their attack. It highlights that, for many, the target of the attack can be coincidental and just a means to an end, based on the procurement of access services, while, for others, they will be the intended target. Those with more resources and specialist requirements can deploy zero-day attacks for maximum ROI.

No longer just the domain of governments, organized crime gangs also have the capability to buy offensive cyber weapons from access brokers, who are not only being supplied by other criminal entities but with tools developed by private-sector actors, which have the potential to be released into the wild and cause great harm. In Chapter 10, we shall explore how a leaked cyber-tool went on to cause one of the most destructive cyber attacks in history, with NotPetya.

As we head towards Part Two, we take a deeper look at some of the different types of groups, the campaigns they have wielded, and what we can learn from this.

References

Burt, T (2020) 'Cyber mercenaries don't deserve immunity', Microsoft blog, 21 December, blogs.microsoft.com/on-the-issues/2020/12/21/cyber-immunity-nso (archived at https://perma.cc/3MMB-MHBB)

Cybersecurity Tech Accord (2023) 'New industry principles to curb cyber mercenaries', 27 March, cybertechaccord.org/new-industry-principles-to-curb-cyber-mercenaries (archived at https://perma.cc/9ME4-WNX8)

Flare (2023) 'The initial access broker economy: a deep dive into dark web hacking forums', Bleeping Computer, 7 September, bleepingcomputer.com/news/security/the-initial-access-broker-economy-a-deep-dive-into-dark-web-hacking-forums (archived at https://perma.cc/YH9F-VPB3)

Kitroeff, N and Bergman, R (2023) 'How Mexico became the biggest user of the world's most notorious spy tool', *New York Times*, 18 April, nytimes.com/2023/04/18/world/americas/pegasus-spyware-mexico.html (archived at https://perma.cc/TJ5F-QB4A)

Microsoft (2022) 'What is a zero-day vulnerability exploit?', 25 November, microsoft.com/en-us/microsoft-365-life-hacks/privacy-and-safety/zero-day-vulnerability-exploit (archived at https://perma.cc/U9RZ-4M66)

Microsoft Threat Intelligence (2021) 'Catching the big fish: analyzing a large-scale phishing-as-a-service operation', 21 September, microsoft.com/en-us/security/blog/2021/09/21/catching-the-big-fish-analyzing-a-large-scale-phishing-as-a-service-operation (archived at https://perma.cc/VD9U-B8NX)

Microsoft Threat Intelligence (2022) 'Ransomware as a service: understanding the cybercrime gig economy', 9 May, microsoft.com/en-us/security/blog/2022/05/09/ransomware-as-a-service-understanding-the-cybercrime-gig-economy-and-how-to-protect-yourself (archived at https://perma.cc/CBT3-FYWX)

Sadowski, J (2022) 'Zero tolerance: more zero-days exploited in 2021 than ever before', Mandiant, 21 April, mandiant.com/resources/blog/zero-days-exploited-2021 (archived at https://perma.cc/RG67-KKKV)

Trend Micro (2021a) 'N-Day exploit protection strategies', 19 November, trendmicro.com/en_us/ciso/21/k/n-day-exploit-protection-strategies.html (archived at https://perma.cc/2GU8-FPMS)

Trend Micro (2021b) 'Trends and shifts in the underground n-day exploit market', 13 July, trendmicro.com/vinfo/us/security/news/vulnerabilities-and-exploits/trends-and-shifts-in-the-underground-n-day-exploit-market (archived at https://perma.cc/9UCA-6FRB)

US Court of Appeal (2020) 'NSO Group Technologies Ltd et al v. WhatsApp Inc et al', 21 December, blogs.microsoft.com/wp-content/uploads/prod/sites/5/2020/12/NSO-v.-WhatsApp-Amicus-Brief-Microsoft-et-al.-as-filed.pdf (archived at https://perma.cc/U3FZ-SJ8U)

The White House (2023) 'Executive order on the prohibition on use by the United States Government of commercial spyware that poses risks to national security', 27 March, whitehouse.gov/briefing-room/presidenlunderworldtmodelstial-actions/2023/03/27/executive-order-on-prohibition-on-use-by-the-united-states-government-of-commercial-spyware-that-poses-risks-to-national-security (archived at https://perma.cc/YM8P-XCUJ)

PART TWO

Incidents, lessons learnt and the rise of the insider threat

06

Opportunists and activists – how anyone can become a cybercriminal

CHAPTER OBJECTIVES

As we head into Part Two, we take a closer look at the human adversaries and their motivations through various case studies.

In this chapter, we consider some of the opportunists and activists, how they went from teenagers with a deep curiosity for learning about computers into the early stages of experimentation through social interactions with peer groups.

We explore how different life experiences and ideologies can set people on different paths, and how their choices dictate what happens next.

At the end of Chapter 2, we started to look at why people commit cybercrime and why many attackers start young. Young people are often easily influenced and can sometimes have limited self-control and self-awareness. They also have a strong desire for social acceptance and a need to bond with peers.

The level of anonymity given online means that some young people display more aggressive behaviour through their social interactions, for example in the form of cyberbullying, and may be more prone to engaging or sharing in hateful or harmful content. They may not appreciate the gravity and consequences of their actions.

There are many tools and lots of information available online that enable people to learn and experiment: labs, guides and free tools that are easily discoverable (Robson, 2022). For some teenagers and young adults, learning digital skills and navigating the internet have become almost second nature. There is often a natural curiosity to join different chat forums and gaming platforms, where discussions can spin out into other, darker areas. Parents may not appreciate what their children are exposed to, or the type of discussions and activity they are engaged in, especially if they are being influenced by other group members.

Let us consider this further with some case studies, and examine why some people may not understand or even realize that what they are doing is unethical or illegal.

Establishing accountability for actions

While researching for this book, I took great interest in an article written by Stephanie Clifford in *The Economist* (2022) and specifically the subtitle: 'The criminal-justice system isn't ready for those wired to see the world differently'. Clifford provides a fascinating exposé into the case of two young adults, both of whom had been arrested for their crimes, and how the differences between the US and UK judicial systems would lead to very different outcomes.

CASE STUDY
The story of Brandon Fleury

Fleury had a tough childhood. At five years old, his mother died and his father became a full-time lone parent to him and his younger brother. After his mother's death, Brandon's father witnessed unusual elements of behaviour. Doctors diagnosed him with ADHD. When he was seven, they added OCD and Asperger's syndrome.

Fleury struggled with social interactions, often finding himself on the wrong side of bullies. They took his money and beat him up. As a result, he preferred to spend time at home, listening to music and surfing the internet.

When Fleury was 21, the FBI turned up at the family home to arrest him, having unearthed a series of disturbing social-media messages. He had created several Instagram accounts under different aliases. Most of these account names referred to Nikolas Cruz, a teenager who had killed 17 students and staff at a high school in Florida in early 2018. Fleury used these accounts to unleash a torrent of abuse at the friends and family of those murdered by Cruz. The messages included: 'I killed your loved ones haha.' 'Your grief is my joy.' 'I gave them no mercy.'

Fleury admitted to everything straight away, citing that he'd been inspired by an internet troll, 'Lynn Ann', who was obsessed with one of the Columbine High School shooters. Fleury told an FBI investigator that he had become interested in internet trolls because they were *popular*.

Prosecutors pointed out that Fleury's messages were crafted with specific information about the victims and made ongoing threats. He insisted that he didn't intend to hurt or scare people but to 'annoy' them and he didn't know that what he was doing was illegal.

Prosecutors painted Fleury as someone who might have gone on to commit mass murder himself if he hadn't been caught, though there was no evidence to suggest that. They went over his messages in detail to demonstrate the distress he had caused and did not accept that he was just a 'punk teenager' who may be trolling. The jury found Brandon Fleury guilty on three counts of 'cyberstalking' and one count of transmitting a 'kidnapping threat' (Padilla, 2022).

During the sentencing hearing, Fleury's father hired a new lawyer. They argued that Brandon was fundamentally a law-abiding person, pointing out that, when the court ordered him not to use social media as a condition of bail, he took it so seriously he wouldn't even touch a computer. The judge did not accept that Fleury 'didn't understand' the impact of his actions and sentenced him to five and a half years in prison, stating that he wanted to send a message to people who might do the same. The judge recommended that Fleury serve his time at a low-security prison, one of only two in the US with a skill-building programme offered to prisoners with different disabilities.

Stephanie Clifford's article also presented the plight of another man, Navinder Sarao, which was to have a drastically different outcome from Fleury's.

CASE STUDY
The story of Navinder Sarao

A few weeks before Brandon Fleury was sentenced, another federal case involving an autistic defendant was wrapping up.

This too had begun with a raid instigated by the FBI: agents were on the trail, they believed, of a criminal mastermind who was behind a huge financial market-manipulation scheme that briefly wiped $1 trillion off US stock markets in 2010. What they found in Hounslow in London was Navinder Sarao – a 'hoodie-wearing video-game addict who lived with his parents, had a bedroom full of stuffed animals and paid for his meals at McDonald's with coupons' (Clifford, 2022).

To Sarao's family, he was just a quirky, solitary maths whiz who had aced his degree, but his behaviour went beyond quirkiness. He was sensitive to light to the point that he hung blankets over his bedroom window, he still loved his stuffed-toy tiger, and he could be astonishingly blunt when speaking to people.

Sarao had an unusual eye for numbers and patterns. When he started the scheme that led to his arrest, he was working in one of London's trading arcades – a shared facility used by self-employed traders for a fee. Sarao was obsessed with the markets and became increasingly frustrated by high-speed algorithms and a dubious practice known as 'spoofing', which entails placing lots of orders to mimic a surge in buying or selling and then cancelling them at the last minute.

In 2009, Sarao began complaining about spoofing to officials at the Chicago Mercantile Exchange, on which he did most of his trades. Staff were not interested in his allegations of fraud, and eventually started to hang up on him. In response, Sarao commissioned someone to write a computer program that could beat the spoofing algorithms at their own game. It was a wild success: between 2009 and 2014 he made $70 million. Sarao was arrested in 2015 for his part in the 'flash crash'.

British media dubbed Sarao the 'Hound of Hounslow' as a quirky reference to the 'Wolf of Wallstreet' (Verity and Lawrie, 2020). Despite the nickname, his life could not have been more different from the character played by Leonardo DiCaprio in the 2013 film. Sarao made no ostentatious purchases and lost a great deal of money to fraudulent investors who took advantage of him.

Sarao initially spent four months in a UK prison before being extradited to the US. He also forfeited $7.6 million in illegal gains. Sarao was defended by some of the most sought-after lawyers in the business. One of whom was an expert in white-collar crime and was certain that, if prosecutors could get to know his client, they would see him as someone who was confused about rules and boundaries rather than a greedy fraudster. During his trial, Sarao was diagnosed with autism by Sir Simon Baron-Cohen, director of Cambridge University's Autism Research Centre and one of Britain's foremost psychologists, who also said this diagnosis was central to understanding Sarao's actions.

Sarao initially faced 22 charges with a maximum sentence of 380 years. However, his lawyer secured an agreement in which Sarao would help prosecutors with their inquiries in exchange for the possibility of a reduced sentence. Federal lawyers and agents came to spend a lot of time with Sarao, as he taught them how the markets worked and how to spot irregular trading patterns.

Sarao's defence team argued that he almost believed he was playing a highly sophisticated and complicated video game and, effectively, he had found the best 'cheat' to win the game. His motivation was never money, but the thrill of winning at his favourite game. Sarao's defence described him as a mathematical savant and 'singularly sunny, childlike, guileless, trusting person', who lived on benefit payouts and spent much of his time in his bedroom, surrounded by computer games and soft toys.

Sarao eventually pleaded guilty to one count of electronic fraud and one of spoofing – which is illegal in the US. By the time he was sentenced in 2020, he had met prosecutors ten times to explain spoofing, and served as a witness in another case. Prosecutors noticed Sarao's inability to maintain eye contact and his tendency to 'obsess' over certain details. In a highly unusual move, they requested that the judge give him no prison time, instead sentencing him to one year of home confinement. In their sentencing recommendation, prosecutors noted Sarao's medical diagnosis, his expressions of remorse and his assistance with other lawsuits. They said jail time would not serve as a deterrent, arguing that he had not been motivated by greed but by a desire to excel in an activity. The judge also considered his autism diagnosis, jail time already served, and that he had been helpful to the government for several years since his arrest.

Since his sentencing, Sarao has returned to a quiet life with his parents in Hounslow. Barred from trading, he spends much of his time gaming and playing with his nephews.

The impact of autism on some cybercriminals

There is no evidence of a 'criminal tendency' associated with the autism spectrum, and that is important to note – if anything, people with autism are often scrupulous about following rules. But a condition that makes it hard to read social cues puts people at risk of committing – or being accused of committing – certain crimes and makes it harder for them to navigate inter- actions with police and prosecutors when that happens. Some autism experts say they are seeing a growing number of people getting caught up in online crimes, both as victims and accused.

Stephanie Clifford notes that some people on the autistic spectrum lead fully independent, professional lives; while others may be non-verbal. She highlights that the diagnostic criteria are broad and vague, clustered around difficulties in social communication and interaction and repetitive behav- iours. Behind these generalities lies a range of complex symptoms that vary significantly from person to person.

THE RESEARCH OF SIR SIMON BARON-COHEN

Sir Simon Baron-Cohen has published multiple research articles on the theories of autism and how it can be diagnosed in children and adults. His prime focus has tended to be on highly functioning individuals who may sit on varying levels of the autistic spectrum.

Baron-Cohen (2008) suggests that the easiest way of seeing the distribution of autistic traits is using the 'autism spectrum quotient' (AQ). This is a questionnaire, either completed by a parent about their child or by self-report if the adult is high functioning. Such questionnaires can be subjective and interpreted differently by those completing and reviewing them, hence some critics think it broad and vague in its determination.

In addition to the AQ range, Baron-Cohen developed the mindfulness theory, in which he argues that some children on the autism spectrum are delayed in developing a theory of mind (ToM) – the ability to put oneself into someone else's shoes, to imagine their thoughts and feelings. Challengers to the theory highlight that the ability for some people to demonstrate empathy in social interactions is due to their social environment and learnt experiences, which Sir Simon has since acknowledged.

An additional theory of Baron-Cohen's is the 'empathizing-systemizing (E-S) theory'. This attempts to explain the social and communication difficulties in autism by reference to delays and deficits in empathy. The E-S theory proposes that people on the autism spectrum could potentially have lower tendencies to empathize but could have average or higher than average systemizing – which is the drive to analyse, govern or construct any kind of system and to predict how that system will behave. This may explain some of the narrow interests, repetitive behaviour and resistance to change that people with autism can demonstrate to varying degrees.

Insight into the mindset of an activist – Lauri Love

I first met Lauri Love in London, where we were speaking at the same conference organized by one of Microsoft's partners. He described his life as an activist, how it had started and how he had fought extradition to the United States.

I was intrigued by the fact that Love had only been diagnosed with autism during his extradition hearing. I was delighted when he agreed to be interviewed for this book and to share some of his background and experiences.

Navigating childhood

In a similar way to Tony Sales (Chapter 2), Love had navigated a difficult upbringing. But, unlike Sales, Love had a father figure in his life. He was raised by an authoritarian father who had strong views on values and morality, and some of that would be passed down to Lauri.

Love has a fondness for reading and loved science fiction. He was much happier reading books or playing on a computer than being around other children. His father was into computers too, and Love would often watch him changing disks, and hence he became interested in writing command lines. Love would also help his father to create church pamphlets on the computer, which he says was a window into a new world.

Diagnosis of autism

Although Love was not diagnosed with autism until his extradition hearing, he instinctively knew that he was different. As Love himself declared, he had an insatiable curiosity to see how things worked, and a need to challenge those who thought they already knew how things worked.

As Love described to me, there are different ways to be a human and each person has their strengths and weaknesses. Some people are very organized, and he is not. Love states that he is driven to think outside the box, and not make assumptions. When challenged by someone who states, 'This is the way it is,' his response is, 'No, that's the way you think it is, and I can think of many possible ways in which it isn't.' Love also shared that he suffers from extreme anxiety that can lead to depression in stressful situations. This manifested in a significant manner during his indictment.

Heading into a life of activism

Love stated that he fully comprehends and is cognisant of what he is doing and has a good sense of what is right and wrong, but his views about what he did may seem different from others.

Love explains that, when you go to university, you become more aware of things like politics; you start to question what is wrong with the world, you want to deliver change, and you end up meeting like-minded people.

You could think of it as an exuberance of youth, where you want to fight for people who are worse off than you and who might not have a voice.

But what if you find that people don't listen to you? When you are ignored, you find different ways to express yourself. You aspire to a world of power, where asking nicely no longer works, and where you decide that you must force a change. As Love states, when you have a certain personality disposition, you are not going to challenge and stand up to authority in traditional ways. You only find your boundaries when you keep pushing against them.

Love describes that he struggles with the balance between extreme arrogance and humility. While some people might take a stand by gluing themselves to monuments and shouting about things, this is not him. He likes to do things behind the scenes and for the most part have anonymity. People that take activism online are often known as 'hacktivists'.

Love states that the internet was his playground: 'When I see fences in the way, I step over them, and step back without damaging the garden. There was a sort of honour code – that if you don't delete or cause harm, it was kind of tolerated.' Things changed, however, when some attackers started to monetize the attacks this made it dangerous for everyone.

As Love explains, most attackers and their targets are opportunistic. There is a pyramid of scale, from the hobbyist through to organized crime and nation-sponsored actors, which determines the level of skill and determination. As we discussed in Chapter 3, it is often a case of casting the net far and wide to catch as many fish as possible, and putting back the ones you don't want or that are not interesting. It depends on what is presented, what software is used, what exploits are available and how many doors will open. When you have an agenda, or an operation, you will find a way in.

Joining Anonymous

Lauri Love's desire to change the world at university meant that he did not spend enough time on his studies or going to lectures, and, ultimately, was asked to leave. His was a noble aspiration, but, inevitably, he was not able to fulfil both ambitions. Love ended up moving back home with his parents, living on state benefits, and as a result he had a mental breakdown.

Being unemployed left Love disillusioned about what he wanted to do. He felt that he had so much frustrated potential, and the internet was at his disposal. When you have untapped skill, boredom and are at home, with no job, what do you do? As Love explains, 'you have the cards that you're dealt, and it is up to you how you play them'.

So, Love spent a lot of time hanging out as a newbie in chat rooms and internet relay chats, which were the predecessors to Slack and Discord. Ultimately, spend enough time online, and you come to know where interesting people hang out. One of those early groups was 4Chan, which Love describes as 'not a nice group', filled with racism, misogyny, antisemitism and other hateful things. Love didn't like it, or what it stood for. But, Anonymous fell out of it, as a splinter group focused on social justice.

WHO ARE ANONYMOUS?

The Anonymous group is a loosely affiliated international collective of hacktivists. The group is known for its digital activism, which often involves cyber attacks against governments, corporations and other organizations that it perceives as being corrupt or engaging in unethical behaviour.

An important aspect of Anonymous is its decentralized structure, which allows anyone to join or participate in its actions. This anonymity and lack of hierarchy make it difficult for authorities to track or arrest individual members.

Members of the group often use the Guy Fawkes mask as a symbol of their activism, which is a reference to the 2005 film *V for Vendetta*, in which the main character, who wears the mask, leads a revolution against the government.

While the group has faced criticism for its use of illegal hacking techniques, its activism has also sparked important debates about online privacy, government surveillance and the role of technology in shaping society.

As Love describes, Anonymous turned up with 'good branding' and he thought the group members were cool. Meanwhile, the media painted a picture of this sub-group of activists: there was a little bit of fear, they wanted to know more, they wanted to know what their agenda was. So, now, from Love's point of view, you have a platform, the media has given you a voice, you're getting noticed, and before you know it, you're back to wanting to change the world again.

There is a form of social and peer pressure because you still want to belong, you want to be part of the group, and sometimes it is hard to say no. There may even be a threat to 'dox' you (to identify or to publish private information about someone), but, mainly, you join in because you want to. Love stated that 'people play the internet like a video game, and it's hard to turn it off, and when you invest so much time and energy, you don't want to'. When you're operating as a group, you want to see the outcome.

It strikes me that this is very similar to how Navinder Sarao was portrayed and how prosecutors described what he was doing – as playing a favourite game, whether as a challenge or to prove a point, and that it is hard to turn away from, particularly when you have deep and untapped skills.

So, the people that Love worked with had named operations for each target. The one that he was allegedly accused of, and what he would ultimately be arrested for, was 'Operation Last Resort'.

WHAT WAS OPERATION LAST RESORT?

In January 2013, Anonymous commandeered several US websites, threatening to release sensitive government information unless there was legal reform (Blue, 2013).

In a massive show of force, the hacktivists wrestled with government operators to take control of USSC.gov – the United States Sentencing Commission – in which it placed links to encrypted files mirrored on multiple websites. Anonymous stated that the group had left a back door and made it editable, to encourage other attackers to attack the server. Anonymous changed the USSC website into a playable game of *Asteroids*. Shooting the website text caused the original image of the site to slowly shrink, revealing its iconic Guy Fawkes mask.

Anonymous claimed that the rationale for Operation Last Resort was in retaliation for the suicide of 26-year-old hacktivist Aaron Swartz, which many claimed was a result of the overzealous prosecution by the US Department of Justice, and the relentless and disproportionate persecution of hacktivists (Aarons ArkAngel, 2013; Naughton, 2015).

In September 2012, Swartz was charged with 13 counts of felony hacking, for allegedly trying to make Massachusetts Institute of Technology (MIT) academic journal articles public. The struggle to defend his name and pay mounting legal fees became too much for Swartz and he ended his life on 11 January 2013. His death acted as a rally call to many hacktivists, and he had almost become a martyr among his peers. Those people who believed in social justice and a desire for change became even more steadfast in their beliefs, and, rather than bringing an end to hacktivism, it only stoked the fires further. Anonymous stated that a line had been crossed, and hence the targeting of the USSC site was a symbolic action.

The indictment against Lauri Love

On 25 October 2013, Love was arrested at his home by the UK National Crimes Agency (NCA) under the Computer Misuse Act 1990, following an indictment issued by the US Federal Government. It was alleged that Love and co-conspirators had stolen military data and personal identifying information belonging to service personnel. The US government stressed that 'such conduct endangers the security of our country and is an affront to those who serve' (Halliday, 2013).

Love was charged with one count of hacking into a US department or agency computer and one count of conspiring to do the same. The US indictment described Love as a 'sophisticated and prolific computer hacker who *specialised* in gaining access to the computer networks of large organisations, including government agencies, collecting confidential data including personally identifiable information from within the compromised networks, and exfiltrating the data out of the compromised networks' (Halliday, 2013).

He was accused of targeting the computer networks of the US army, missile defence agency, environmental protection agency and NASA, with attacks between October 2012 and October 2013. He was subsequently released on bail, and never charged, despite the NCA seizing various equipment items, such as Love's computers, along with USB drives and old computing hardware, much of which belonged to his father (Parkin, 2017). This did not stop the US government from continuing to collect information, including chat logs, proxy servers, payment details and an IP address that led straight to Love's parent's home, and an extradition request.

In July 2015, Love was arrested again by the UK Metropolitan Police Extradition Unit on behalf of the US government. Love's US lawyer argued that 'the information he allegedly copied was never distributed anywhere, it was more a youthful prank. And the security exploit they allegedly used had been publicly disclosed months before and used by tens of thousands of people'. Love disputed the image the US Department of Justice painted of him: 'It has set this narrative that I'm some terrorist or some threat to the security of western civilization. I've held some radical political positions, but not bringing down the US government, because all hell would break loose' (McGoogan, 2016).

In addition, Love's US lawyer cited that if he were to face charges in the UK, the maximum sentence would be far less severe than in the US, and described the UK justice system as more civilized and humane. 'They don't generally destroy people's lives; the US system just crushes people'

(McGoogan, 2016). At the time, the longest sentence for a computer crime in the US was 20 years, whereas in the UK it was 2 years and 8 months.

In 2016, Love thwarted attempts by the NCA to force him to handover passwords and encryption keys to his devices. His lawyers challenged that such procedures would breach the Human Rights Act, including Love's right to 'respect for his private life and the right to the peaceful enjoyment of his possessions'. The judge presiding over the matter ruled in Love's favour, citing the NCA's failure to follow proper case management procedures to acquire and investigate the devices (City of Westminster Magistrates Court, 2016).

Fighting extradition

As the extradition hearing was not a criminal trial, Love was not required to respond to the specific allegations against him. However, as reported in *The Guardian* (Halliday, 2013), Love did not protest his innocence – he only pointed out that, without seeing the evidence, which the Department of Justice refused to reveal until he was on US soil, he could not say one way or the other, but he had the means, motive and opportunity to conduct the crimes of which he was accused.

Love spent four years fighting the NCA and the extradition request, which not only took a toll on his mental health but had a huge impact on his family, who spent a lot of time and money on helping his cause.

Love's case was crucial in establishing a precedent to prevent the US government from pursuing disproportionate and unjust claims against hacktivists and what have been described as 'unusually harsh punitive sanctions for computer crimes' (Parkin, 2017). In February 2018, the UK High Court of Justice approved a judgment that extradition to the United States 'would not be in the interests of justice' and that extradition would be 'oppressive by reason of his physical and mental condition'. The judgment included testimony from Sir Simon Baron-Cohen confirming that Love is high functioning and has the capacity to participate in a judgment approved by the court, but that Love's Asperger's syndrome is a 'very severe disability because it causes him to become so absorbed in his interests that he neglects important areas of his life, such as his studies, and even his health'.

As of December 2023, Love has not been prosecuted for his alleged role in 'Operation Last Resort', or for any other Anonymous operation.

Evaluating the case

When asked to reflect on the US assertions that Love had allegedly breached and exposed sensitive information, including social security numbers and other details relating to serving personnel, Lauri Love insists his intent was never to do harm. The prospect of going to prison preyed on his mental health, but concern for his family was of deep concern, as they had to raise money for his bail and other legal and medical costs. He explains that his brain compartmentalized things, but that would manifest itself as stress and anxiety, and he would scratch at his eczema, which led to painful sores.

He believes that he was right to fight the NCA, as well as his extradition. The need to fight and have a voice has not left him, and he feels compelled to take a stand when it comes to enabling privacy, using encryption.

As Love reflects, you can be moralistic about things, or you can be pragmatic. Love agrees that understanding the motivation behind a cyber attack is important. In his view, much of what he did was practical jokes in the form of satire, in ways that enabled a form of power. Yes, it came with high stakes, but the intent was never to monetize or exploit the cause. Some members may have discussed making money, but, ultimately, that was not what the group stood for.

When I asked Love whether he thinks the end justifies the means, he replied, 'I can't objectively answer yes, as what I think is different to what the companies think. They may see themselves as victims, but to me the victim is someone else.' He argues that you need people who are not afraid to call things out, who will highlight and expose wrongdoing.

When looking at the differences between activists and hacktivists and how they are treated by law enforcement and the media, Love argues: 'What is the difference between blockading a street and bringing London to a standstill, versus blockading a website or several of them? Both can cause nuisance and damage.' He understands, however, that there are no victimless crimes, as, otherwise, why the uproar?

Turning things around

Lauri Love highlights that society has given him the opportunity to reapply his skills in a different way, by working for security companies and speaking at events to share his experience and highlight how organizations should protect themselves. His case has opened as well as closed doors.

The stigma around his case wanes as time passes, and he believes that people can turn things around if given a chance, with many fellow Anonymous members now being security researchers. He appreciates that, for some employers, this may seem a high risk. Furthermore, he understands that some people will reoffend because it is the only life they know, and they don't have the same support structures around them. Love reflects on the fact that, if he had come from a place where crime was normalized, then things may have been different, since no one is a villain in their own story, and someone can always justify to themselves what they do and why.

Love believes that people can change. He highlights that his father still works as a chaplain in the UK prison system, and that he often brings perpetrators and victims of crime together to hear their different perspectives. Love thinks this is an important part of rehabilitation, to overcome some of the disconnection and barriers that attackers may have against their victims.

Finally, I asked Love about his thoughts on the 'seven sins of attackers' (discussed in Chapter 2). He admitted that he was perplexed, given his religious upbringing and how he sees the world, but suggested that *pride* was ultimately what led him into a life of hacktivism. The arrogance over his skill set, the overwhelming desire to think he could enable change, and the need for acceptance among his peers are what drew him in. Love was at pains to state, however, that people are not inherently bad – but they may make bad decisions – so the virtues should stand as an important counterbalance to help people understand their choices and how they can do less harm.

Conclusion

In this chapter, we have explored how some teenagers and young adults progress into cybercrime often by joining online forums and chat sites. This can lead them to be drawn into specific ideologies because of wanting to be socially accepted by their peers as they learn to experiment with their individuality and what they stand for.

We have further explored how some people demonstrate obsessive behaviour and systemizing that may compel them to perform delinquent or criminal activity, whether they intended to or not. Furthermore, some people with autism, for example, struggle with interpreting emotions and demonstrating empathy for others, which may help to explain why they feel a detachment from their victims – with some people perhaps not even comprehending that they are victims.

We shall reflect further on the power of education and support mechanisms that can enable people with high degrees of skills, and motivation, to seek alternative paths in Chapter 12. How we think about cybercrime and cybersecurity plays a large role in how we build such strategies.

References

Aarons ArkAngel (2013) 'Anonymous Operation Last Resort manifesto', youtube. com/watch?v=WaPni5O2YyI (archived at https://perma.cc/FZ26-VLW2)

Baron-Cohen, S (2008) 'Theories of the autistic mind', British Psychological Society, 15 February, www.bps.org.uk/psychologist/theories-autistic-mind (archived at https://perma.cc/KTQ5-9Y93)

Blue, V (2013) 'Feds stumbled after Anonymous launches "Operation Last Resort"', ZD Net, 30 January, zdnet.com/article/feds-stumbling-after-anonymous-launches-operation-last-resort (archived at https://perma.cc/W5FC-9BL3)

City of Westminster Magistrates Court (2016) 'Lauri Love and National Crime Agency', 10 May, documentcloud.org/documents/2828389-Lauri-Love-RIPA-10-May-2016.html (archived at https://perma.cc/3DHU-X4FN)

Clifford, S (2022) 'An autistic man was surfing the internet on his dad's sofa. Then the FBI turned up', *The Economist*, 21 November, economist.com/1843/2022/11/21/an-autistic-man-was-surfing-the-internet-on-his-dads-sofa-then-the-fbi-turned-up (archived at https://perma.cc/YC97-RWXY)

Halliday, J (2013) 'Briton Lauri Love faces hacking charges in the US', *The Guardian*, 29 October, theguardian.com/world/2013/oct/28/us-briton-hacking-charges-nasa-lauri-love (archived at https://perma.cc/RP4K-LZL7)

McCoogan, C (2016) 'The full story of Lauri Love's fight against extradition', *The Telegraph*, 27 June, s.telegraph.co.uk/graphics/projects/hacker-lauri-love-extradition/ (archived at https://perma.cc/V9F3-G68X)

Naughton, J (2015) 'Aaron Swartz stood up for freedom and fairness – and was hounded to death', *The Guardian*, 7 February, the guardian.com/commentisfree/2015/feb/07/aaron-swartz-suicide-internets-own-boy (archived at https://perma.cc/X6CT-Y3W5)

Padilla, M (2022) 'Man gets over 5 years in prison for stalking families of Parkland victims', *New York Times*, 2 March, nytimes.com/2020/03/02/us/parkland-shooting-brandon-fleury.html (archived at https://perma.cc/A35Z-R4EC)

Parkin, S (2017) 'Keyboard warrior: the British hacker fighting for his life', *The Guardian*, 8 September, theguardian.com/news/2017/sep/08/lauri-love-british-hacker-anonymous-extradition-us (archived at https://perma.cc/8DFB-5Q3E)

Robson, K (2022) 'Many of today's hackers are teenagers and access mass resources online are helping to train them', Verdict, 28 September, verdict.co.uk/most-of-todays-hackers-are-teenagers (archived at https://perma.cc/U3TE-H9L7)

UK High Court of Justice (2018) *Lauri Love and The Government of the United States of America and Liberty*, 5 February, judiciary.uk/wp-content/uploads/2018/02/lauri-love-v-usa.pdf (archived at https://perma.cc/QH23-NXGX)

Verity, A and Lawrie, E (2020) 'Hound of Hounslow: Who is Navinder Sarao, the "flash crash trader"?', BBC Business, bbc.co.uk/news/explainers-51265169 (archived at https://perma.cc/MNX2-R9TB)

07

New kids on the block – new groups making names for themselves

CHAPTER OBJECTIVES

In this chapter, we move beyond the opportunists and activists and look at how quickly new actors are appearing and striving to make a name for themselves, perhaps driven by a desire to be taken seriously and a level of notoriety that makes them stand out from the crowd.

This requires a new set of tactics and techniques that is guaranteed to get them noticed, and demonstrates a continuous evolution of cybercrime groups and how they are reacting to the world around them.

Naming and attribution of groups

Before we go any further, let's take a minute to discuss why cybercrime groups have different names and how they are tracked. Threat intelligence and law enforcement agencies use various techniques to locate and track specific groups and individuals across jurisdictions. As discussed in Chapter 5, different cybercrime groups can use the same exploit or ransomware payload, and linking to the ransomware name gives the impression that the group is much bigger and dominant than it in fact is. The reality is that attackers may use a variety of exploits and payloads to suit their objective.

To enable prosecutions, legal authorities need to track the individuals and link their activities to the crimes of specific groups. Some may even be moonlighting for others, or leave and join different groups at different stages. Some groups may be so large that people may not even know they are part of a wider group or be party to the wider strategy of that group, and so proving intent is also difficult.

Microsoft threat actor taxonomy

To help put this into perspective, let me explain how Microsoft tracks and names different groups of threat actors, and how these are arranged.

Microsoft Threat Intelligence has spent over a decade discovering, identifying and tracking targeted activity. Researchers actively track more than 300 unique threat actors, including 160 state-sponsored actors, 50 ransomware groups and hundreds of others. Microsoft categorizes these actors into five key groups (Lambert, 2023):

- **Nation-sponsored actors.** These are operators acting on behalf of or directed by a state-aligned programme, irrespective of whether this is for espionage, financial gain or retribution. Many nation-sponsored actors focus cyber operations on government agencies, intergovernmental organizations, non-governmental organizations and think tanks for traditional espionage or surveillance objectives. The big four nation-sponsored actors are grouped as:

  o Russia – 'Blizzard'

  o North Korea – 'Sleet'

  o Iran – 'Sandstorm'

  o China – 'Typhoon'.

- **Financially motivated actors – 'Tempest'.** These are cyber campaigns/ groups directed by a criminal organization or person with motivations for financial gain. This category includes ransomware operators, business email compromise, phishing.

- **Private sector offensive actors – 'Tsunami'.** This is cyber activity led by legitimate commercial entities that create and sell cyberweapons to customers. These tools threaten many global human rights efforts as they have been observed targeting and performing surveillance on dissidents, human rights defenders, journalists, civil society advocates and other private citizens.

- **Influence operations – 'Flood'.** These are information campaigns communicated online or offline in a manipulative manner, with the objective to shift perceptions, behaviours or decisions by target audiences to further a group or nation's interests and objectives.

- **Groups in development – 'Storm'.** This is a temporary designation given to an unknown, emerging or developing threat activity that Microsoft can track until there is high confidence about the origin or identity of the actor behind the operation. To meet the requirements of a fully named actor, Microsoft needs to obtain knowledge of the actor's infrastructure, tooling, victimology and motivation, based on telemetry data and industry reporting.

From disruption to destruction – Lapsus$

So, let's start with a group that has made a name for itself in a very short space of time, and which is financially motivated – a group known as Lapsus$ (which Microsoft tracks as 'Strawberry Tempest'). First appearing in 2021, the group quickly gained a reputation for being 'one of the most notorious cybercrime groups' (Jam Cyber, 2022). One security researcher even went as far as naming them 'Rookie of the Year' (Shriebman, 2022)

As reported by Microsoft Threat Intelligence (2022), unlike some attackers that wish to have a level of anonymity and stay under the radar, this actor does not seem to care, going as far as announcing its attacks on social media, and the organizations it wants to target. The tactics and objectives indicate that the attacks are motivated by theft and destruction, possibly to provide kudos.

What sets Lapsus$ apart from other attackers is the focus on large-scale social engineering and extortion operations, where it learns about the organization and the individuals that work there, to use this to its advantage.

Notable targets

As Microsoft highlights, Lapsus$ initially started out by targeting telecommunication, higher education and government organizations in South America. This expanded globally to cover a variety of sectors. Based on observed activity, this group understands the interconnected nature of the supply chain and trusted relationships, and pivoted into targeting technology, IT services and support companies – to leverage access from one organization to another.

The security research firm Flashpoint (2023) provides a timeline of some notable organizations that were targeted from December 2021 to March

2022, which highlights the pace with which they were able to identify and attack organizations across multiple countries (Table 7.1).

The attack on the Brazilian Ministry of Health is largely regarded as the first most prominent victim, which got law enforcement's attention. Some security researchers suggest that attacks may have started as far back as June 2021 because of similar social media usernames identified across other forums.

TABLE 7.1 Notable Lapsus$ attacks, December 21 to March 22

Date	Organization	Details of attack
		2021
10 December	Ministry of Health, Brazil	• The group deleted 50Tb of data, including millions of Covid-19 records, leaving the ministry unable to issue vaccination certificates as well as other services (Reuters, 2021). • The Brazilian police subsequently launched an investigation after it was identified that multiple government entities had been targeted.
12 December	Federal Police, Brazil	• The group offered to pay Federal Police insiders $15,000 for internal access to the police network, via the attackers' Telegram site.
		2022
3 January	Impresa, Portugal	• The websites of one of Portugal's biggest newspapers and broadcasters were taken down by a cyber attack (Reuters, 2022). • The attack also included a phishing email to subscribers and tweets from the newspaper's verified Twitter account. • The attacker published a message on the websites saying internal data would be leaked if the organization failed to pay a ransom.
11 January	Localisa, South and Central America	• The vehicle rental company confirmed that websites had been compromised. • Unlike previous attacks, no customer or sensitive information was stolen, and no ransom demands were made. Instead, consumers were redirected from the official website to a pornography site.

(continued)

TABLE 7.1 (Continued)

Date	Organization	Details of attack
8 February	Vodafone, Portugal	• The attack impacted its 4G and 5G services, causing nationwide service failures, including SMS messages and television services.
		• On 24 February, Lapsus$ admitted responsibility for the attack on its Telegram channel.
23 February	Nvidia, USA	• Lapsus$ successfully exfiltrated 1Tb of data from the company's networks, including proprietary information related to Nvidia's new graphics processing units, which was set to be publicly launched later that month.
		• In addition, Nvidia confirmed that the attacker stole credentials relating to 71,000 employees (Hope, 2022).
4 March	Samsung, South Korea	• Lapsus$ posted a message on Telegram informing subscribers that it had conducted an attack on Samsung.
		• Samsung revealed that it had suffered a data breach in which almost 200Gb of source code for Samsung Galaxy devices had been stolen. However, no personal customer or employee information was compromised (Savov and Kim, 2022).
20 March	Microsoft, USA	• Lapsus$ claimed to have breached one of Microsoft's Azure DevOps accounts and stolen partial source code for Bing, Bing Maps and Cortana.
		• Microsoft released a blog stating that the investigation had found a single account had been compromised, granting limited access.
		• Microsoft confirmed that it does not rely on the secrecy of code as a security measure and viewing source code does not lead to elevation of risk.
22 March	Okta, USA	• In a screenshot posted to the group's Telegram page, Lapsus$ claimed to have remote access and superuser and admin privileges on multiple Okta systems.
		• Okta released a statement revealing that, in late January 2022, it had detected an attempt to compromise an account belonging to a third-party customer support engineer.
		• Okta stated that the attacker's claims appeared to be related to the January compromise, and it had not identified other malicious activity.

Learning about its targets

Lapsus$ used extensive social engineering efforts to gather knowledge about its targets' business operations. This included intimate knowledge about employees, team structures, help desks, crisis response workflows and supply-chain relationships.

In some cases, the group first aimed at and compromised an individual's personal or private accounts to look for additional credentials that could be used to gain access to corporate systems.

Taking advantage of the insider threat

Microsoft found instances where the group successfully gained access to organizations through recruited employees (or employees of suppliers or business partners). In order to entice employees or contractors to take part in its operation, Lapsus$ advertised that it wanted to buy credentials for its targets. For a fee, the willing insider had to provide their credentials and approve the multi-factor authentication (MFA) prompt or install remote management software on a corporate workstation, allowing Lapsus$ to take control of an authenticated system.

Lapsus$ principally advertised on its social media site, Telegram, which has grown to have more than 45,000 subscribers (Krebs, 2022a). Adverts are typically posted in English and Portuguese.

WHAT WAS LAPSUS$ RECRUITING FOR?

The following examples are from an advert posted on Telegram on 10 March 2022.

- Any company providing telecommunications (Clara, Telefonica, ATT and similar others)
- Large software/gaming corporations (Microsoft, Apple, EA, IBM and similar others)
- Call centre / business process management (Atento, Teleperformance and similar others)
- Server Hosts (OVH, Locaweb and similar others).

  Note: we are not looking for data; we are looking for the employee to provide us with a VPN or Citrix to the network or some AnyDesk.

- If you are not sure if you are needed, DM and we will respond.
- If you are not an employee here, but have access such as VPN or VDI, we are still interested.

Additional adverts were posted on Reddit, offering employees at AT&T, T-Mobile and Verizon up to $20,000 a week to perform 'inside jobs'.

Lapsus$ ran two Telegram channels. The first was where only the group itself could post, and where it shared details about new breaches or links to released data. The second was a chat room where anyone could join and post messages. By doing so, Lapsus$ had an active and participative audience, as if its attacks were a game. The group chose three compromised victims and gave the followers the ability to choose which one to leak by running a poll (Cox, 2022).

Elevating and changing privileges

As well as using known tactics to move laterally and elevate privileges, the group were observed continuing the social engineering techniques once inside the organization. In some cases, the actor called the organization's help desk and attempted to convince the support personnel to reset a privileged account's credentials. The group used the previously gathered information and had a native-English-sounding caller speak with the help desk to enhance the social engineering lure. This included answering common security questions and account recovery prompts such as 'the first street you lived on' or 'your mother's maiden name' to convince the help desk of authenticity.

Data exfiltration and destruction

As Microsoft reported, the group appeared to be aware of detections such as impossible travel and thus picked VPN (virtual private network) egress points that were geographically similar to its targets. The group was observed downloading sensitive data from the target organization for future extortion or public release. In addition, it obtained access to cloud assets to create new virtual machines within the target's cloud environment, which it used to perform further attacks. This included setting a Microsoft Office 365 tenant level rule to send all mail in and out of the organization to the newly created account. It then removed all other global admin accounts, so only the actor had sole control of the cloud resources, effectively locking the organization out.

The exfiltration of data and deleting the target's systems and resources appeared to be a deliberate ploy to trigger the organization's incident and crisis response, so that Lapsus$ could observe what the organization did next. We shall discuss more on strategies to overcome attacker manipulation in Chapter 16, where we consider the board-level response.

Evolving extortion business models

The attacker took advantage of its newly gained privileges to monitor email, chats and communications to track incident-response efforts. This is used to gain insights into the victim's state of mind and their knowledge of the intrusion.

The attackers joined incident response calls, not just to observe the response, but unmuted themselves to demand a ransom while sharing their screens to show that they were deleting data and resources. In some cases, the group extorted victims to prevent the release of stolen data, and, in others, no extortion attempt was made – it moved straight to publicly leaking the data it had stolen.

Further research from NCC (2022) highlighted that, since not all victims or breaches appear to be announced via Telegram, nor are some victims approached with a ransom, it makes the attacks unpredictable.

The hunt for the attackers

UNITED STATES

- On 21 March 2022, the FBI issued an alert asking for public assistance involving the compromise of computer networks belonging to US-based technology companies: 'These unidentified individuals took credit for both the theft and dissemination of proprietary data that they claim to have illegally obtained.'

UNITED KINGDOM

- On 24 March 2022, the City of London Police stated that they had arrested seven teenagers in relation to the gang. One was 16 years old, and was reportedly one of the ring leaders, and had amassed a $14 million (£10.6 million) fortune.

- A report from the BBC claimed that the identification of the teenager was made as a result of being 'doxed' by rival attackers, revealing his real name, address and social media profile pictures. Security company Palo Alto also learnt of the teenager's identity through its own investigation, citing that the teenager had been instrumental in the most prominent attacks. A report from *Fortune* stated that 'the teen is so skilled at hacking – and so fast – that researchers initially thought the activity they were observing was automated' (Tidy, 2022).

- The boy's father told the BBC: 'I had never heard about any of this until recently. He's never talked about any hacking, but he is very good on computers and spends a lot of time on the computer. I always thought he was playing games. We're going to try to stop him from going on computers' (Tidy, 2022).

- On 1 April, the City of London Police confirmed that a 16-year-old and a 17-year-old had been charged with 'three counts of unauthorized access to a computer with intent to impair the reliability of data; one count of fraud by false representation and one count of unauthorized access to a computer with intent to hinder access to data. The 16-year-old has also been charged with one count of causing a computer to perform a function to secure unauthorized access to a program'. As they were both juveniles, the police prohibited the reporting of their identities. Prosecutors argued that the case should be sent to the Crown Court due to its complex nature and the sums allegedly involved (BBC News, 2022a).

- Having been previously released on bail, the younger teen was arrested again on 23 September, following an investigation by the NCA, in which he was accused of using his mobile phone to obtain information and codes from two companies in order to hold them to ransom. He was charged with breaching his bail conditions, and two charges relating to the misuse of a computer. He was remanded in youth detention (BBC News, 2022b).

BRAZIL

- On 16 August 2022, the Federal Police confirmed that they had triggered Operation Dark Cloud, with the objective to gather information related to cyber attacks against various federal organizations, including the Ministry of Health.

- A total of eight search and seizure warrants were served. The offences were: criminal organization; invasion of computer device; interruption or disturbance of telegraph, radiotelegraph or telephone service and preventing or hindering its restoration; in addition to the crime of corruption of minors and money laundering.

- On 20 October, the Federal Police confirmed that they had arrested a man suspected of being part of the 'transnational criminal organization'. Police believed the person to be the 'main Brazilian suspect' relating to Operation Dark Cloud.

Continuation of attacks

Despite several prominent arrests in the UK and Brazil, attacks continued to happen, suggesting that the group was much bigger than first anticipated and continued to wreak havoc (Table 7.2; Roth, 2022).

TABLE 7.2 Continued Lapsus$ attacks in 2022

Date	Organization	Details of attack
March	T-Mobile, USA	• As reported by Krebs on Security (2022b), copies of leaked chats show that Lapsus$ were discussing attacking T-Mobile right up to the arrests of the teenagers in the UK. • The attack breached T-Mobile multiple times in March, stealing 30Gb of source code. T-Mobile said no customer or government information was stolen in the intrusion.
15 September	Uber, USA	• The attack forced the company to take several of its internal systems offline, including Slack, Amazon and Google cloud platforms. • In a statement issued by Uber (2022), it revealed that an external contractor's account had been compromised. It is likely that the attacker purchased the contractor's corporate password on the dark web after the contractor's personal device had been infected with malware, exposing those credentials.

(continued)

TABLE 7.2 (Continued)

Date	Organization	Details of attack
		• The attacker repeatedly tried to log in to the contractor's Uber account. Each time, the contractor received a two-factor login approval request, which initially blocked access. Eventually, however, the contractor accepted one, and the attacker successfully logged in.
		• The attacker accessed several other employee accounts, which ultimately gave the attacker elevated permissions to a few tools, including G Suite and Slack.
18 September	Rockstar Games, USA	• In the early hours, the attacker posted about 90 videos, totalling 50 minutes of footage from *Grand Theft Auto* (GTA) (Macdonald et al, 2022).
		• Lapsus$ left a message on Telegram claiming it wanted to 'negotiate a deal' with Rockstar for the return of data – including source code for GTA5 and an in-development version of GTA6.
		• The attacker said the footage was obtained by breaking into Rockstar's Slack channel, and that videos were easily downloaded.
		• Rockstar confirmed: 'We recently suffered a network intrusion in which an unauthorized third party illegally accessed and downloaded confidential information from our systems, including early development footage for the next *Grand Theft Auto*.'
		• The parent company, Take-Two, issued takedown notices to social media channels and other websites posting the stolen footage.

On 2 December 2022, the US Department of Homeland Security (DHS) confirmed that its Cyber Review Board would investigate a series of high-profile breaches attributed to the Lapsus$ group, which it claimed was a 'prolific global data extortion gang run by teenagers'. The Homeland Security Secretary said during a press conference that the aim of the review board was to evaluate how the group had allegedly impacted some of the biggest companies in the world, 'in some cases with relatively unsophisticated techniques, and determine how we all can build resilience against

innovative social engineering tactics and address the role of international partnerships in combating criminal cyber actors'. He said that the ongoing Lapsus$ hacks 'represent just the type of activity that merits a fulsome review and can provide forward-looking recommendations to improve the nation's cybersecurity'.

In August 2023, the Cybersecurity and Infrastructure Security Agency (CISA) released a report in which it highlighted how Lapsus$ demonstrated an adeptness for identifying weak points in the system that allowed onward access to victims. The group also showed a special talent for social engineering and luring a target's employees to effectively open the gates to the corporate network. Most organizations were not prepared to prevent the attacks, but most rapidly changed their security programmes to account for vulnerabilities and make improvements to thwart future attacks. Those that had prepared for the possibility of these kinds of attacks, against their own infrastructure and that of their suppliers, proved most resilient.

The CISA report also identified that the young age of some of the actors limited law enforcement's role and would result in lighter penalties under the home countries' legal frameworks, which did little to deter them. This points to broader issues with systematic risk exposure that attackers can exploit.

As well as recommendations aimed at changing federal government and law enforcement, the report also made several recommendations for organizations, including:

- **Progress towards a passwordless society**: enabling secure identity and access management solutions by default and transitioning away from voice and SMS based two-step MFA.

- **Prioritize efforts to reduce the efficacy of social engineering**: implement more robust authentication capabilities by requiring phishing-resistant MFA for each sensitive system transaction and fostering a positive security culture that includes frequent education in a relatable and digestible manner on threat landscape trends, and how to prevent them.

- **Plan for disruptive cyber intrusions and invest in prevention, response and recovery capabilities**: create maps to rapidly adopt emerging modern architectures such as zero trust and strengthen authentication practices. Adopt best practices with an emphasis on identifying critical infrastructure, effective implementation of least privilege access, and monitoring capabilities to detect and respond to anomalies, to prevent future attacks.

We shall discuss the strategies to enable these recommendations in Part Three.

Bringing Lapsus$ to justice

On 23 August 2023, a UK court found two teenagers guilty of being part of the cybercrime gang after a seven-week trial. One was 18-year-old Arion Kurtaj. The other was not named, due to his age (17) (Tidy, 2023).

Jurors heard how Kurtaj and the other youth began their attacks in July 2021, having met online. The lead barrister highlighted how Kurtaj and his co-conspirators in the UK and Brazil showed a 'juvenile desire to stick two fingers up to those they are attacking' and referred to the gang as 'digital bandits'. The gang's actions were often erratic, swinging from notoriety, financial gain or amusement.

Kurtaj was found to be solely responsible for half the attacks, but was deemed unfit to stand trial by a judge, because of his complex autistic spectrum disorder. Kurtaj's doctor described him as a 'particularly impaired individual' who at best functions at a level of 1 per cent of his peers, adding that 'he doesn't want to be different, he wants to be like everyone else, wants to be seen as trendy and risky', and that the diagnosis didn't capture how vulnerable he is (Gemmel, 2023).

In a striking resemblance to the case of Navinder Sarao, Kurtaj's lawyer commented: 'There has to be a better system that enables the skills of such individuals to be utilised in a more positive way that protects corporations, acknowledges and supports the medical needs of vulnerable perpetrators and offers a more mutually beneficial outcome for all stakeholders in these situations.' We shall discuss the opportunities that may be available to help people find a different path in Chapter 12. Due to the complex needs and backgrounds of the defendants, the judge presiding over the case took 3 months to determine a suitable punishment.

In December 2023, the judge ordered that Arion Kurtaj should be detained for an indefinite time under the UK Mental Health Act, and can only be discharged from hospital if the justice secretary approves it. His co-conspirator was handed a youth rehabilitation order, including an 18-month supervision requirement, and a six-month prohibited activity requirement to stop him using a VPN. (Vaughan, 2023)

Analysing Lapsus$

Despite the arrests and convictions of Lapsus$ leaders in the UK in March 2022 and Brazil in August 2022, it was evident that attacks continued beyond these dates.

What we have seen here is just a snapshot of the organizations that were attacked and who made the headlines due to their size. It is evident from the money that was confiscated from the UK teenagers that the gang had a degree of success in its extortion demands, perhaps targeting much smaller organizations to refine the approach before hitting others. Despite apparently sitting on millions of dollars, it is unclear what the money had been spent on.

It is of interest that one of the charges made by the Brazilian Federal Police was in connection with 'corruption of minors'. It is not clear if this was in relation to the teenagers in the UK or if other minors were involved across Brazil and other countries. This may suggest that vulnerable, yet gifted, people might be manipulated into committing crimes.

The theft of data appears to be heavily focused on application source code or proprietary technical information. This contains commercially sensitive intellectual property, and in some cases, the attackers even suggested what changes the tech companies should make to their platforms if they wanted to avoid further data leakage.

The fact that Lapsus$ did not always follow through with ransom demands and did not always leak data is indicative that the attacks were not wholly financially motivated, often just wanting kudos for breaking into accounts and causing disruption to large companies. If we think back to the 'seven sins of attackers' that we explored in Chapter 2, there is evidence of pride and greed at play, and the temptation to try different things and wanting to be socially accepted.

From the leaked chats obtained by Krebs, there was evidence of infighting in the group as members refined their tactics and targets. Could that have just been illustrative of the age of some of the attackers, or was there a degree of coercion involved? There are certainly similarities with Lauri Love's experience in the previous chapter, with the reality of what happens when someone threatens to dox you and reveal your identity, which is what appears to have happened in the UK. It also suggests that rival gangs may be working against each other to unveil people's identities, perhaps because they want their own level of notoriety.

Conclusion

This chapter has explored how quickly new actors are appearing in cybercrime and striving to make a name for themselves, and how quickly they work to refine their approaches.

We have seen again that many attackers appear to be starting young, whether driven by a natural curiosity or because of generally spending more time online, making them tech savvy. Are we also perhaps seeing a level of grooming, whereby vulnerable young people are being manipulated into using their technical skills for illicit and fraudulent purposes?

Even if the teenagers are willing participants, and are completely cognisant of what they are doing, could it be that the rewards are so high and the deterrents so low that they just don't care about the consequences? Might it also be that they have an innate need to be socially accepted by their peers and will therefore take higher risks and temptations? Perhaps it is the start of a level of apathy that often leads people into further temptation, and, once they become embroiled in this life, it is hard to get out. What is clear is that society needs better mechanisms to identify and curtail such activity. Whether it is government, law enforcement, organizations or individuals, we require a different perspective and need to work collaboratively if we are going to be successful in thwarting such crimes.

The point is that we need to look at some of the attackers, what they do and how they do it *objectively*, as not everything is what it seems on the surface, and there can be wider issues at play. This links to the need to drive towards human-centric security, which we shall discuss further in Part Three.

References

BBC News (2022a) 'Lapsus$: Two UK teenagers charged with hacking crime', 1 April, bbc.co.uk/news/technology-60953527 (archived at https://perma.cc/F55L-WTZ5)

BBC News (2022b) 'Oxfordshire teen denies hacking companies for ransom', 27 September, bbc.com/news/uk-england-oxfordshire-63048518.amp (archived at https://perma.cc/G3MB-NLJQ)

CISA (2023) 'Review of the attacks associated with Lapsus$ and related threat groups report', 10 August, cisa.gov/resources-tools/resources/review-attacks-associated-lapsus-and-related-threat-groups-report (archived at https://perma.cc/A5AS-CDH7)

City of London Police, 'Two teenagers charged in connection with investigation into hacking group', press release, 1 April, cityoflondon.police.uk/news/city-of-london/news/2022/march/two-teenagers-charged-in-connection-with-investigation-into-hacking-group (archived at https://perma.cc/65DJ-GBJB)

Cox, J (2022) 'Lapsus$: how a sloppy extortion gang became one of the most prolific hacking groups', Vice, 24 March, vice.com/en/article/3abedn/who-is-lapsus-hacking-gang (archived at https://perma.cc/DT36-5BCZ)

DHS (2022) 'Cyber safety review board to conduct second review on Lapsus$', 2 December, dhs.gov/news/2022/12/02/cyber-safety-review-board-conduct-second-review-lapsus (archived at https://perma.cc/7XPM-PSYQ)

FBI Most Wanted (2022) 'Lapsus$: Cyber intrusions of United States-based technology companies', 21 March, fbi.gov/wanted/seeking-info/lapsus (archived at https://perma.cc/77RE-YB3K)

Flashpoint (2023) 'All about Lapsus$: what we know about the extortionist group', 23 March, flashpoint.io/blog/lapsus (archived at https://perma.cc/24T2-YMT3)

Gemmel, K (2023) 'How and why two British teenagers hacked several of the biggest tech companies in the world', *Time*, 25 August, time.com/6308370/british-teenagers-hack-tech-companies (archived at https://perma.cc/VC3P-P7H7)

Hope, A (2022) 'Nvidia data leak exposed proprietary information but wasn't a Russian ransomware attack, company says', CPO Magazine, 11 March, cpomagazine.com/cyber-security/nvidia-data-leak-exposed-proprietary-information-but-wasnt-a-russian-ransomware-attack-company-says (archived at https://perma.cc/Y76K-CQDJ)

Jam Cyber (2022) 'Notorious Cyber Crime Gangs', 11 August, jamcyber.com/blog/cyber-insights/cyber-crimes-gangs (archived at https://perma.cc/8D3G-6JL9)

Krebs, B (2022a) 'A closer look at the Lapsus$ data extortion group', Krebs on Security, 23 March, krebsonsecurity.com/2022/03/a-closer-look-at-the-lapsus-data-extortion-group (archived at https://perma.cc/XRW2-4ZKP)

Krebs, B (2022b) 'Leaked chats show Lapsus$ stole T-Mobile source code', Krebs on Security, 22 April, krebsonsecurity.com/2022/04/leaked-chats-show-lapsus-stole-t-mobile-source-code (archived at https://perma.cc/P8LA-RXK3)

Lambert, J (2023) 'Microsoft shifts to a new threat actor naming taxonomy', Microsoft Research, 18 April, microsoft.com/en-us/security/blog/2023/04/18/microsoft-shifts-to-a-new-threat-actor-naming-taxonomy (archived at https://perma.cc/EQ8L-QL6M)

MacDonald, K, Stuart, K and Hern, A (2022) 'Grand Theft Auto 6 leak: who hacked Rockstar and what was stolen?', *The Guardian*, 19 September, theguardian.com/games/2022/sep/19/grand-theft-auto-6-leak-who-hacked-rockstar-and-what-was-stolen (archived at https://perma.cc/7W79-QTZN)

Microsoft Threat Intelligence (2022) 'DEV-0537 criminal actor targeting organizations for data exfiltration and destruction', 22 March, microsoft.com/en-us/security/blog/2022/03/22/dev-0537-criminal-actor-targeting-organizations-for-data-exfiltration-and-destruction (archived at https://perma.cc/55VS-CTKD)

NCC (2022) 'Lapsus$: recent techniques, tactics and procedures', 28 April, research.nccgroup.com/2022/04/28/lapsus-recent-techniques-tactics-and-procedures (archived at https://perma.cc/VQ7Z-JUQM)

Okta (2022) 'Updated Okta statement on Lapsus$', 3 March, https://www.okta.com/blog/2022/03/updated-okta-statement-on-lapsus/#:~:text=The%20Okta%20service%20is%20fully,been%20viewed%20or%20acted%20upon. (archived at https://perma.cc/5723-TMSK)

Policia Federal Brazil (2022) 'PF conducts operation to investigate attacks on Federal Government sites', press release, 16 August, gov.br/pf/pt-br/assuntos/noticias/2022/08/pf-realiza-operacao-para-apurar-ataques-a-sites-do-governo-federal (archived at https://perma.cc/U2P3-SETU)

Reuters (2021) 'Brazil health ministry website hit by hackers, vaccination data targeted', 11 December, reuters.com/technology/brazils-health-ministry-website-hit-by-hacker-attack-systems-down-2021-12-10 (archived at https://perma.cc/9DEY-DTYF)

Reuters (2022) 'Portugal's Impresa media outlet hit by hackers', 3 January, reuters.com/business/media-telecom/portugals-impresa-media-outlets-hit-by-hackers-2022-01-03 (archived at https://perma.cc/DE43-M3XA)

Roth, E (2022) 'Lapsus$ cyberattacks: the latest news on the hacking group', The Verge, theverge.com/22998479/lapsus-hacking-group-cyberattacks-news-updates (archived at https://perma.cc/JA5K-WBJ6)

Savov, V and Kim, H (2022) 'Samsung says hackers breached company data, galaxy source code', 7 March, Bloomberg, bloomberg.com/news/articles/2022-03-07/samsung-says-hackers-breached-company-data-galaxy-source-code#xj4y7vzkg (archived at https://perma.cc/SNG9-YWPC)

Shriebman, Y (2022) 'Rookie of the year – Lapsus$ group', Cyberint, 23 March, cyberint.com/blog/uncategorized/lapsus-group (archived at https://perma.cc/CGP6-YGL9)

Tidy, J (2022) 'Lapsus$: 'Oxford teen accused of being multi-millionaire cybercriminal', BBC News, 24 March, bbc.co.uk/news/technology-60864283 (archived at https://perma.cc/G9UN-QEA6)

Tidy, J (2023) 'Lapsus$: court finds teenagers carried out hacking spree', BBC News, 23 August, bbc.co.uk/news/technology-66549159 (archived at https://perma.cc/L4MG-DUMW)

Uber (2022) 'Security update', 16 September, uber.com/newsroom/security-update (archived at https://perma.cc/4VLP-AAQU)

Vaughan, H (2023), 'Arion Kurtaj: Teenager sentenced over Grand Theft Auto VI hack', Sky News, 21 December 2023, https://news.sky.com/story/arion-kurtaj-teenager-sentenced-over-grand-theft-auto-vi-hack-13035718 (archived at https://perma.cc/AVU6-BGQF)

08

Syndicates – how groups work together to build services and avoid detection

CHAPTER OBJECTIVES

Once a threat actor has made a name for itself, how does it continue to remain relevant? Just like any enterprise, to stay relevant you need to adjust and adapt your business model to be successful, potentially opening new revenue streams and partnerships.

In this chapter, we explore not only how attackers exploit the niche they have found themselves in, but how they react to changing markets and conditions.

So, let's consider just that, with a study of how one organized crime group has remained active for over a decade by adjusting its business model and opening new revenue streams to make it one of the most successful and notorious cybercrime gangs in history.

Tracking the most successful cybercrime syndicate in history – FIN7

FIN7 (also referred to, or has strong ties with, Carbanak Group, Joker Stash, Navigator Group, Carbon Spider, Gold Niagara, ITG14, and Sangria Tempest, and possibly others) is an Eastern European group with links to Russia and Ukraine.

WHO IS FIN7?

FIN7 is one of the most sophisticated and aggressive cybercrime groups, consisting of dozens of attackers located over multiple countries. The group is known to use an array of constantly evolving tools and social engineering techniques, having reinvented itself multiple times over. During its tenure, the group has amassed billions of dollars.

The history of FIN7

In 2017, FIN7 was accused of being behind a cyber attack on corporations filed with the US Securities and Exchange Commission (SEC). This private data was exploited and utilized to extort a ransom, which was subsequently invested in the stock market.

As a result, the group profited handsomely from the trade of classified material. The cyber-enabled insider trading scam lasted for some time, so it is impossible to calculate the exact measure of financial damage. However, it is believed to be billions of dollars.

Unlocking a catalogue of attacks in the United States

On 1 August 2018, the US Justice Department announced the arrest of three Ukrainian nationals, who were accused of being leaders of FIN7. The conspirators were charged with 26 felony counts including 'conspiracy', 'wire fraud', 'computer hacking', 'access device fraud' and 'aggravated identity theft'.

From at least 2015, FIN7 members engaged in a highly sophisticated malware campaign targeting more than 100 US companies, predominantly in the restaurant, gaming and hospitality industries. As set out in the indictments, FIN7 hacked into thousands of computer systems and stole millions of customer credit and debit card numbers, which the group used itself or sold for profit.

In the United States alone, FIN7 stole more than 15 million customer credit card records from over 6,500 individual point-of-sale terminals, at more than 3,600 separate business locations, and then sold them on the dark web (Department of Justice, 2018a). The estimated impact was in the region of $3 billion.

We will have a deeper look at some of the individuals involved later in the chapter, but first we see how a supplemental document created by the FBI (2018) explains how the perpetrators were able to steal so much money.

The steps to success, and how FIN7 stole so much money

FIN7 used a false front company, Combi Security, purportedly headquartered in Russia and Israel, to provide a guise of legitimacy and to recruit hackers to join the criminal enterprise. Combi Security's website claimed that it provided several security services such as penetration testing. Ironically, the sham company's website listed many of its US victims among its purported clients.

UTILIZING SOPHISTICATED SOCIAL ENGINEERING TECHNIQUES

- Attacks were initiated by delivering a phishing email to an employee within the victim organization, with an attachment that included malware.

- The text of the email was written in such a way as to mimic a legitimate business-related message to get the recipient to open the attachment and unwittingly activate the malware that would infect the computer.

- Each email was bespoke to the sector that the organization was in. For example, when targeting a hotel chain, the sender might claim to be interested in making a reservation with details enclosed in the attachment. When targeting a restaurant, the email might refer to placing a large catering order or to complain about poor service or food quality, further described in an attachment.

- In many cases, the phishing emails were accompanied by a phone call to the company, which was intended to legitimize the email. The caller often directed the employee to the phishing email to entice them into opening the attachment and activating the malware.

- As Carr et al (2018) report, FIN7 had a particular prowess for social engineering, from leveraging web forms for initial contact to targeting and engaging directly with pre-determined store managers. As FIN7 matured so did the quality of their phishing lures and templates, which were most often sent from fake but well-disguised individuals, businesses and government entities, often taking the time to build highly customized graphics to mimic logos and typefaces.

NETWORK INTRUSION: CONTROL AND DATA EXFILTRATION

- Once malware had been released onto the machine, the compromised computer connected to one of FIN7's command-and-control servers located in various locations throughout the world.

- Through a control panel, FIN7 could download an array of additional malware to the computer, remotely send commands and move laterally through the company's network.

- Among other tools, FIN7 incorporated and adapted the notorious Carbanak malware, which allowed the attackers to conduct surveillance on company employees, including taking screenshots and video recordings, which enabled them to covertly steal credentials.

- FIN7 used this unauthorized access to locate and extract financial information and caches of customer payment card data. The objective was to focus on fast-food restaurants, hotels, casinos and businesses with a high frequency of point-of-sale transactions. FIN7 sought to steal credit, debit and gift card data used during legitimate customer purchases.

SELLING STOLEN CARDS

- Since 2015, FIN7 had successfully stolen data for more than 16 million payment cards, many of which have been offered for sale through underground online marketplaces. The purchasers could then use the stolen card numbers to make unauthorized charges on accounts belonging to the unsuspecting cardholders.

A look at some of the men behind the 2018 arrests

Let's look at two of the Ukrainian men arrested in conjunction with the crimes.

FEDIR HLADYR

- Hladyr allegedly served as FIN7's systems administrator. He maintained servers and communication channels used by the organization and held a managerial role by delegating tasks and providing instructions to other members.

- In September 2019, he pleaded guilty to conspiracy to commit wire fraud and conspiracy to commit computer hacking.

- Hladyr originally joined FIN7 via the front company Combi Security. He admitted in his plea agreement that he quickly realized that, far from being a legitimate company, Combi was part of a criminal enterprise. Hladyr played a central role in aggregating stolen payment card information, supervising FIN7's hackers and maintaining the elaborate network of servers that FIN7 used to attack and control victims' computers. He also controlled the organization's encrypted channels of communication.

- On 16 April 2021, Hladyr was sentenced to 10 years in prison, and ordered to pay $2.5 million in restitution.

ANDRII KOLPAKOV

- The US Department of Justice indictment (2018c) stated that, over a period of three years, Kolpakov, along with other co-conspirators, committed multiple instances of wire fraud, while he and Fedir Hladyr were directors of the company.

- On 1 June 2019, Kolpakov was extradited from Spain to the USA.

- In November 2020, Kolpakov pleaded guilty to conspiracy to commit wire and bank fraud and conspiracy to commit computer hacking (Stone, 2020).

- In June 2021, Kolpakov was sentenced to seven years in prison (Department of Justice, 2021). Court filings helped to explain why the group had been so successful:

  o By masquerading as Combi Security, FIN7 leaders organized their personnel into separate teams charged with developing malware, crafting phishing documents and collecting money from victims.

  o Prosecutors included screenshots of messages that FIN7 emailed to victims. One message claimed that a corporate outing to a restaurant ended with the entire group falling ill. The message included a malicious attachment disguised as a lawsuit.

  o For another message, they spoofed an email address from the SEC. The email was sent to the in-house corporate counsel at a publicly traded company who was responsible for the firm's securities filings.

  o As the business model proved successful, the group updated its phishing messages to include Microsoft and Google logos to boost their legitimacy.

Arrests had little effect on operations

In May 2019, cybersecurity company Kaspersky reported that the arrests of the two 'group leaders' had negligible impact on FIN7's operations. Attacks continued without significant drawbacks. Kaspersky observed interconnected groups using similar toolkits and infrastructure to conduct their cyber attacks (Namestnikov and Aime, 2019). The phishing campaigns followed a similar pattern of social engineering. In some cases, the operators exchanged messages with their victims for several weeks before sending malicious documents. These were designed to take advantage of a wide range of emotions (fear, stress, anger and so on) to elicit a specific response from their victims. As with the previous fake company, Combi Security, the group created new personas for use in either targeting victims or recruiting hackers under a new brand, IPC.

In October 2021, security researchers from Recorded Future's Gemini Advisory unit identified that FIN7 had set up another fake security company called Bastion Secure and was hiring security professionals under the guise of needing penetration testing services. The job offers ranged between $800 and $1,200 a month, which is a viable starting salary for post-Soviet countries (Seals, 2021). Gemini theorized that paying people legitimate salaries for their expertise was cheaper than hiring people on the dark web. In addition, it would enable FIN7 to keep a larger share of the profits.

FIN7 had gone to great lengths to create a fake company with a striking resemblance to the legitimate company Bastion Security, even going as far as lifting the names of real, albeit closed, offices for Bastion, and putting these on their website. In effect, FIN7 adopted disinformation tactics so that if a potential hire or interested party did a cursory internet search, it would reveal true information for at least one company with a similar name.

FIN7 reinventing itself

In December 2022, security research firm Prodaft performed a deep dive exposé into the group. Having analysed thousands of inside conversations between members, it showed FIN7 to be a ruthless criminal gang with links to global ransomware cartels such as LockBit, Darkside, REvil and MAZE, even motivating its members with death threats.

Prodaft researchers told Cybernews (Petkauskas, 2022): 'We think FIN7 consist of real-life gangs, not only cybercriminals. They operate safe houses, conduct money laundering activities, use guns, or make kidnapping attempts, so their activities span beyond the cybersphere.'

Group chats revealed that FIN7 decided to pivot into ransomware to maximize profit. According to the research, the group's boss lives in Russia, while most of the developers and affiliates are in Ukraine. Prodaft describes the leader as a mastermind of infiltration and ransomware, who plays a key role in the planning and execution of these operations. Another member of management is known for his expertise in tailored initial-access operations, responsible for assigning tasks to the group's members and overseeing their execution.

Prodaft highlights how FIN7 pivoted from spear-phishing campaigns to using social engineering and exploit skills, then into developing ransomware, using a range of attack vectors, modules and payloads. Actors even scrutinized the validity of stolen credentials to select the organizations with the highest revenue in order to maximize their profits, and would sell access on to other attackers by keeping open back doors to their victims.

The sinister side of the chat logs reveal that group leaders kept members in check by giving them ultimatums and threatening their families, especially those living in Russian-occupied regions of Ukraine. One FIN7 administrator wrote: 'If you suddenly do not work or disappear, then we can go to extreme measures, at first we will kill one of the closest relatives (parents), and we will put you in the basement and [you] will slave for free. This is not a problem. We have all the information about you from our databases.' The escalation of threats appears to coincide with Russia's war on Ukraine, although the leaders refer to the invasion indirectly as a 'serious situation' or 'bad environment'.

In May 2023, Microsoft Threat Intelligence revealed that FIN7 had resurfaced again, deploying ransomware for the first time since 2021. In the ransom notes, FIN7 claimed they had exfiltrated data from the compromised systems, and included extensive details about the stolen data, with a custom set of threats for each victim. This could be indicative of how the group continues to reinvent itself with new campaigns and malware to continue the cybercrime spree.

Analysing FIN7

Both Ukrainian nationals accused of being directors of the fake Combi Security company were in their thirties at the time of arrest, suggesting that they had risen through the ranks and had been entrusted to the recruitment of other 'hackers' into the company, under the guise of professional and legitimate jobs. This indicates how some people can be drawn into this activity for extended periods. While the recruitment of unwitting individuals as puppets has been a common component of some criminal schemes, FIN7's attempt to masquerade full-scale fraud as legitimate security penetration testing engagements is particularly notable. So too is the ability to pay people a 'wage' rather than a cut of the profits, revealing how those at the top of the pyramid have refined their approach so that most of the money is funnelled in the right way – into the hands of those that are masterminding operations from afar.

Such activity helps to explain why some people are not aware that the 'enterprise' that they work for is a front for organized crime. Similarly, it can explain how criminal gangs are able to get access to people who are highly skilled in cybersecurity. This shows that not only do attackers socially engineer, and manipulate their victims, but they use similar techniques to entice people to work for them, some unwittingly.

Subsequent research would show once more how disconnected some individuals are from understanding the remit of the group, even that the true ringleaders were in Russia. It also highlights how group leaders control their members to keep them involved in illicit activity, either by threatening violence or through other levels of coercion.

Despite the success of not one but three fake security companies (that we are aware of), and the vast sums being made through those, it did not stop the attackers wanting even more, presumably because of the success of ransomware operators. From the 'seven sins of attackers' in Chapter 2, the attackers have moved from 'greed' to a level of 'gluttony', driven by relatively easy success and a constant desire for more, seemingly with little regard for how they obtain it.

Conclusion

As well as evolving business models and tactics, we have seen that, far from individual or small-group cyber attackers and organized crime working as rival gangs, they work in conjunction with each other by sharing exploits and selling access.

As discussed in Chapter 5, naming a threat actor after the ransomware or malware family they have utilized can be dangerous as it makes tracking of specific groups and their tactics difficult for law enforcement, and can also imply that the attacker is bigger than they are. FIN7 is also known as, or linked, to various groups and malware such as the 'Carbanak Group' named after the malware. This simplification can lead to security researchers, as well as law enforcement, working at cross purposes to identify the perpetrators behind the attacks. The next chapter looks at some of the additional headaches for law enforcement in bringing such groups to justice.

References

Carr, N, Goody, K, Miller, S and Vengerik, B (2018) 'On the hunt for FIN7: pursuing and enigmatic and evasive global criminal operation', Mandiant, 1 August, mandiant.com/resources/blog/fin7-pursuing-an-enigmatic-and-evasive-global-criminal-operation (archived at https://perma.cc/F3QX-7THM)

Department of Justice (2018a) 'How FIN7 attacked and stole data', press release, 1 August, justice.gov/d9/press-releases/attachments/2018/08/01/fact_sheet_how_fin7_attached_and_stole_data_0.pdf (archived at https://perma.cc/78QD-UVPY)

Department of Justice (2018b) 'Three members of notorious international cybercrime group "FIN7", in custody for role attacking over 100 companies', press release, 1 August, justice.gov/opa/pr/three-members-notorious-international-cybercrime-group-fin7-custody-role-attacking-over-100 (archived at https://perma.cc/YC73-XM26)

Department of Justice (2018c) United States v Kolpakov, indictment, 27 July, justice.gov/opa/press-release/file/1084316/download (archived at https://perma.cc/WXA3-D3BT)

Department of Justice (2021) 'High-level member of hacking group sentenced to prison for scheme that compromised tens of millions of debit and credit cards', press release, 24 June, justice.gov/opa/pr/high-level-member-hacking-group-sentenced-prison-scheme-compromised-tens-millions-debit-and (archived at https://perma.cc/DJ47-QBC8)

FBI (2018) 'How cyber crime group FIN7 attacked and stole data from hundreds of U.S. companies', News, 1 August, fbi.gov/contact-us/field-offices/seattle/news/stories/how-cyber-crime-group-fin7-attacked-and-stole-data-from-hundreds-of-us-companies (archived at https://perma.cc/AH38-Q6H4)

Microsoft Threat Intelligence (2023) Twitter post, 19 May, twitter.com/MsftSecIntel/status/1659347799442432002 (archived at https://perma.cc/CHA9-U2FP)

Namestnikov, Y and Aime, F (2019) 'FIN7: the infamous cybercrime rig "FIN7" continues its activities', Securelist by Kaspersky, 8 May, securelist.com/fin7-5-the-infamous-cybercrime-rig-fin7-continues-its-activities/90703 (archived at https://perma.cc/65EY-UDNK)

Petkauskas, V (2022) 'Inside FIN7 gang: death threats and Colonial Pipeline links', Cybernews, 22 December, cybernews.com/news/fin7-death-threats-colonial-pipeline (archived at https://perma.cc/U5WQ-4Y3V)

Prodaft (2022) 'Fin7 unveiled: a deep dive into notorious cybercrime gang', 22 December, prodaft.com/resource/detail/fin7-unveiled-deep-dive-notorious-cybercrime-gang (archived at https://perma.cc/3BA6-NKDM)

Seals, T (2021) 'FIN7 lures unwitting security pros to carry out ransomware attacks', ThreatPost, 22 October, threatpost.com/fin7-security-pros-ransomware-attacks/175681 (archived at https://perma.cc/333Q-PLHW)

Stone, J (2020) 'FIN7 recruiter Andrii Kolpakov pleads guilty to role in global hacking scheme', Cyberscoop, 17 November, cyberscoop.com/fin7-recruiter-andrii-kolpakov-pleads-guilty-role-global-hacking-scheme (archived at https://perma.cc/3WCB-4GZD)

09

Brokers – law enforcement headaches in tracking cybercrime and money laundering

CHAPTER OBJECTIVES

We have seen how attackers are motivated by different things, whether it's financial gain, kudos or something else. At some point, the attacker needs to raise their head above the parapet if they are to successfully achieve their objectives. Whether it is to buy or sell credentials and exploits, or to flaunt the proceeds of crime, each time they raise their head, they run the risk of being identified and caught by law enforcement.

This chapter explores how law enforcement is working across jurisdictions to follow and dismantle criminal networks, and the burden of proof when it comes to successfully attributing and prosecuting criminals.

We have examined how multiple groups have become prolific at providing different models, exploits and kits. Some actors have turned this into a fully fledged empire operating across multiple countries, while others are just trying to make a quick buck, or a name for themselves. For those that are financially motivated, what do they do with the proceeds of crime, and how do they spend the money without it flagging up to banks and law enforcement agencies?

Money laundering as a service

The United Nations Office on Drugs and Crime (UNODC, 2023) highlights that organized crime groups do not only *provide* illicit goods and services;

they use intimidation, violence, corruption and duress to *create a demand* for their services. Let us have a deeper look at money laundering as a service – whereby criminals can have their money 'washed, laundered and returned' for a fee.

Understanding the money-laundering cycle

The cycle is performed in three distinct stages:

1 **Placement** – moving the funds from being directly associated with the crime. This serves two objectives: it relieves the criminal of holding substantial amounts of illegally obtained cash, and it inserts the money into the legitimate financial system. Money launderers are most vulnerable to being caught at this stage.

2 **Layering** – disguising the trail to hinder pursuit. This is the most complex stage and often entails moving illicit funds internationally. The primary purpose is to separate the illicit money from its source. This is achieved by layering financial transactions to conceal the audit trail and break the link with the original criminal activity.

3 **Integration** – making the money available to the criminal. Money is returned to the perpetrators from a legitimate source. The criminal proceeds, which were initially placed as cash and layered through financial transactions, are now fully integrated into the financial system and can be used for any legitimate purpose.

Some of this may be achieved by making use of 'money mules' – individuals who deliberately or innocently help a crime syndicate launder money by transferring funds secretly from one nation or bank account to another – and 'cash couriers' – individuals who deliberately carry money in suitcases across borders.

To avoid detection, this money-shuffling is sometimes conducted through cryptocurrency exchanges or anonymous wire transfer services. Funds are frequently divided into smaller batches and moved through multiple channels. More sophisticated launderers may use automation so they are less reliant on chains of people and can keep a greater share of the profit.

Anti-money-laundering laws

Laws against money laundering require the recipients of funds to exercise reasonable care in monitoring financial transactions. Given the threats of transnational crime, corruption and terrorism, many countries have expanded their money-laundering controls beyond banks to include other businesses that move large amounts of cash (for example, cheque-cashing companies, jewellers, pawnbrokers, casinos, credit card providers).

United Nations members are required to adopt in their domestic laws principles and legislation that criminalize money laundering and profiteering from the proceeds of crime and aiding in the concealment of such crimes. The requirements and disclosures for anti-money-laundering can often be quite complex and vary by country.

The threat from money laundering

According to the UK National Crime Agency (NCA, 2023a), money laundering underpins and enables most forms of organized crime, allowing groups to further their operations and conceal assets. The impact runs into the hundreds of billions of pounds, undermining the integrity of the entire financial system.

All high-end money laundering schemes abuse legitimate processes and services. Accounting, legal professionals and estate agents are often criminally exploited, whether this is complicit, negligent or entirely unwitting. These can function as intermediaries, using their skills and knowledge to draft documentation and disseminate funds, and can be used to store substantial amounts of criminal money and conceal ownership.

The aim of the NCA is to provide a hostile environment for money laundering by:

- targeting individuals engaged in money laundering by prosecution and conviction and disrupting their techniques
- recovering and confiscating assets
- training financial investigators from law enforcement
- making it harder to abuse the financial system.

The identification of money launderers disrupts criminal activity, while recovering and confiscating assets cuts criminal networks off from their money laundering routes.

One way in which law enforcement agencies can work in unison is by disrupting the criminal networks and infrastructure that disrupts the initiation of the cybercrime. One such method is to dismantle the criminal marketplaces used on the dark web to buy and sell illicit services such as stolen credentials and exploit kits. Let's look at some examples of law enforcement and intelligence agencies working together, before considering some of the additional challenges they are facing.

Disrupting criminal dark-web marketplaces

Takedown of Genesis Market

On 4 April 2023, an international operation involving 17 countries led to the takedown of the Genesis Market, which hosted approximately 80 million credentials and digital fingerprints stolen from over 2 million people. The investigation was led by the FBI and the Dutch police.

Launched in 2018, Genesis Market was one of the top-10 dark-web marketplaces. It specialized in the sale of login credentials, cookies, device fingerprints/trackers, website vulnerabilities and other sensitive data (Webz.io, 2022).

Genesis Market sold 'bots' that stored stolen credentials, which gave buyers access to other people's accounts. There were over 400,000 bots for sale, with prices ranging from 70 cents up to hundreds of dollars, depending on the nature of the stolen data. The bots gave criminals access to all the data pertaining to an individual identity, such as cookies, saved logins and autofill form details. They collected information in real time and notified buyers of any change of passwords.

Genesis Market was unique in that it provided users with a custom browser that would mimic that of their victim. This allowed the criminals to masquerade as the victim, making it appear that they were accessing their account from the usual location, thus not triggering security measures. Criminals could also use information about a victim – obtained from various accounts, such as interests, names of friends and family and personal circumstances – to socially engineer them for further offences.

As part of the joint investigation, the NCA identified hundreds of UK-based users of the platform, resulting in 31 warrants and coordinated raids. The NCA Director General commented (2023b):

> Behind every cybercriminal or fraudster is the technical infrastructure that provides them with the tools to execute their attacks and the means to benefit financially from their offending. Genesis Market was a prime example of such a service and was one of the most significant platforms on the criminal market. Its removal will be a huge blow to criminals across the globe.

The removal of Genesis Market follows a previous large-scale takedown.

Takedown of DarkMarket

In January 2021, Europol announced that DarkMarket, the world's largest illegal marketplace, had been taken down as part of an international operation involving Germany, Australia, Denmark, Moldova, Ukraine, the UK and the US. Since May 2019, when DarkMarket was created, it had amassed:

- 500,000 users
- over 2,400 sellers
- over 320,000 transactions
- more than 4,650 bitcoin and 12,800 Monero transferred. This corresponds to more than €140 million.

The sellers on the marketplace traded in drugs and sold counterfeit money, stolen or counterfeit credit cards, anonymous SIM cards and malware. DarkMarket prohibited the sale of weapons, fentanyl and images of child abuse (Caesar, 2021). DarkMarket also advertised itself as being the only site administered exclusively by women, to gain users' trust – but it was untrue. The founder was an Australian man, who was later arrested by German authorities.

The investigation and takedown allowed officers to locate and close the marketplace, switch off more than 20 servers in Moldova and Ukraine and seize the criminal infrastructure. The stored data gave new leads to investigate moderators, sellers and buyers. Prosecutors understand, however, that every time they take down a criminal marketplace, others spring up in its place. If people continue to have illicit desires, the internet will find a way to satisfy them, and so it often feels like a game of whack-a-mole.

This position was echoed by Peter Anaman, Microsoft Digital Crimes Unit Lead Investigator, when he described some of the novel ways in which Microsoft and law enforcement agencies have worked together to identify and dismantle criminal infrastructure in such a way that hinders the attackers' operations. In one such example, Anaman describes how, in 2010, he was given the challenge of taking down an organized crime group in Russia, which was illegally selling counterfeit Windows licences. It had over 2,000 websites and was making over £3 million a month. Some websites were hidden, so, as one was taken down, another could spring up in its place. Another approach was required.

While studying law in the UK, Anaman came across the Proceeds of Crime Act (POCA), which makes it illegal for anyone to profit from a crime, whether directly or indirectly. It dawned on Anaman that, each time someone paid for an illegal download or CD, the credit card merchants were probably getting commission, which may put them in violation of the POCA. Anaman reported the case to the FBI and the Metropolitan Police, who were investigating the network, and they contacted Mastercard in New York to explain the situation. Mastercard was happy to help, and by collecting the merchant numbers, which in essence is what allows the money to move from credit cards to banks, Mastercard was able to shut down 15 accounts across the Seychelles, Spain and other countries. A joint operation with Interpol helped to shut down the next wave of infrastructure and accounts in the UK, Ireland and France, which caused severe disruption to the attackers' business model and ability to access funds, thus shutting down their illegal piracy business. The ROI just didn't stack up for them any more.

This highlights two positives for defenders: first what can be achieved when law enforcement, financial institutions and tech companies work in collaboration, and second, that it is possible to outsmart criminal gangs. It requires the ability to think 'outside the box', which may be a cliché, but it really does work.

Nigeria's celebrity scammers

Imagine a country where scammers are so prolific they have earned a certain celebrity status – well, that country is Nigeria (BBC News, 2019a). On 23 August 2019, the BBC reported that US authorities had charged 80 people, most of whom were Nigerian, with participating in a conspiracy to steal millions of dollars. They were accused of using business email compromise and romance frauds to con victims. Prosecutors said it was one of the 'largest cases of its kind in US history' (BBC News, 2019b).

When these Nigerians first attained notoriety for defrauding Westerners of millions of dollars, the frauds were known as '419' after the Nigerian law that tackles such crimes. The frauds were mostly online, via email and messaging apps, and are now referred to as 'Yahoo-Yahoo', or 'Yahoo Boys'.

The first wave of Nigerian 419 scammers were mostly uneducated criminals. The second wave comprised young, educated men who were frustrated by the lack of formal jobs in an economy ruined by a series of military dictatorships and years of mismanagement. They noticed that uneducated fraudsters were accumulating wealth and esteem and decided to join them. The third wave seemed simply to admire the scammers. They observed that these people were able to establish legitimate businesses from fraudulent funds and become respected philanthropists or politicians in senior leadership positions. Far from turning people away from crime, 419 provided inspiration for many up-and-coming fraudsters.

The FBI's intermittent interventions led to national shock and embarrassment, and a period of collective soul-searching, before the cycle continued as there was simply too much at stake for some people to stop. This further demonstrates the benefits for many attackers to work across multiple jurisdictions, to enable them to work in more innovative ways.

Among these were a new wave of organized crime and violent gangs that included groups known as Black Axe, Eiye and Vikings. The Black Axe gang has been operating for decades in Nigeria and is among the country's most-feared organized crime syndicates. It is known for its street crime and brutality and alleged links to politics and business. Many of these suggested links are murky and unsubstantiated, but include allegations of fraudulent internet scams, bribery and assassination attempts (BBC Africa Eye, 2021).

The case of Obinwanne Okeke

Most shocking for Nigerians was the arrest of their internationally celebrated business tycoon, 'Obinwanne Okeke', the head of Nigeria's Invictus Group and named by *Forbes* magazine as one of its '30 under 30 top African entrepreneurs'.

Okeke was arrested by the FBI in Virginia, in August 2019, just before he could board a flight back to Nigeria. On 16 February 2021, he was given a 10-year jail sentence by a US federal court for masterminding an $11 million fraud on a British company.

Okeke and other conspirators had engaged in a BEC scheme targeting Unatrac Holding, the export sales office for Caterpillar heavy industrial and farm equipment. In April 2018, a Unatrac executive fell prey to a phishing email that allowed conspirators to capture login credentials. The conspirators sent fraudulent wire transfer requests and attached fake invoices. Additionally, Okeke had engaged in other forms of cyber fraud, including sending phishing emails, creating fraudulent web pages and causing losses to numerous victims.

The FBI stated: 'This sentencing demonstrates the FBI's commitment to working with our partners at the Department of Justice and our foreign counterparts to locate cybercriminals across the globe and bring them to the US to be held accountable' (Department of Justice, 2021).

The case of Ray Hushpuppi

Another high-profile Nigerian arrest was Ramon Abbas, popularly known as Ray Hushpuppi, who flaunted a lavish lifestyle of private jets, designer clothes and luxury cars worth millions of dollars. Abbas found fame as an Instagram influencer, and had amassed 2.5 million followers (Karimi, 2020). He told fans that he was a real estate developer, but the truth is that he stole millions of dollars from major companies in the United States and Europe. He is also alleged to have laundered money for North Korea (Dawkins, 2021).

In June 2020, investigators from the United Arab Emirates swooped into Abbas' Dubai apartment, arrested him, and handed him over to FBI agents, who flew him to the United States. Investigators seized 41 million dollars, 13 luxury cars worth $6.8 million, and the email addresses of 2 million victims on confiscated phones, computers and hard drives. 'This case targets a key player in a large, transnational conspiracy who was living an opulent lifestyle in another country while allegedly providing safe havens for stolen money around the world,' the US Attorney said in a statement (Department of Justice, 2020).

In February 2021, the US Justice Department alleged that Abbas had also taken part in a cyber-enabled heist of $14.7 million from the Maltese Bank of Valletta in February 2019. Abbas' name emerged among details of a larger international criminal conspiracy involving Lazarus, the North Korean military hackers involved in 'a series of destructive cyberattacks, to steal and extort more than $1.3 billion of money and cryptocurrency from financial institutions and companies' (Dawkins, 2021). (We shall discuss Lazarus in more detail in the next chapter.)

In April 2021, Abbas pleaded guilty to one count of conspiracy to engage in money laundering. Court documents revealed the crimes cost victims $24 million. The FBI claimed that Abbas was one of the 'most high-profile money launderers in the world', and his guilty plea was 'a crucial blow to this international network' (BBC News, 2021a).

In September 2021, the BBC discovered more about the man behind the heists, from his humble beginnings as a Yahoo Boy in Nigeria to the self-proclaimed 'Billionaire Gucci Master' living a life of luxury in Dubai. Following the Bank of Valletta heist in February 2019, Abbas set up a bank account in Mexico in May, to receive £100 million from a Premier League Football Club and £200 million from a UK firm. The frauds were to be conducted via BEC. But the exploit fell apart when UK banks refused to pay into the Mexican account (BBC News, 2021b).

Abbas' final big fraud came just before his arrest in June 2020. He assumed the identity of a New York banker to entrap his victim, a Qatari businessperson seeking a $15 million loan to build a new school in the Gulf state. Abbas and a gang of middlemen in Kenya, Nigeria and the United States groomed and conned the victim out of more than $1 million. Unearthing the level of abuse and corruption that Abbas had built up, one member of the gang threatened to blow the scam wide open as he was unhappy about the money he was getting. Abbas sent a text to his contact in the Nigerian police saying: 'I want him to go through serious beating of his life. I want to spend money to send this boy to jail, let him go for a very long time.' It is alleged that the police officer did then falsely arrest and jail the intermediary for a month in squalid conditions (BBC News, 2021b).

In November 2022, Abbas was sentenced to 11 years in a US prison. The FBI commented (Department of Justice, 2022):

> Abbas leveraged his social media platforms – where he amassed a considerable following – to gain notoriety and to brag about the immense wealth he acquired by conducting BEC scams, online bank heists and other cyber-enabled fraud that financially ruined scores of victims and aided the North Korean regime. This significant sentence is the result of years' worth of collaboration among law enforcement in multiple countries and should send a clear warning to international fraudsters that the FBI will seek justice for victims, regardless of whether criminals operate within or outside US borders.

Ahead of sentencing, letters were lodged by Abbas' wife and two imams pleading for leniency, citing that Abbas was a frequent donator to local mosques and made other philanthropic gestures. This indicates how some people could see Abbas as a role model, rather than the ruthless criminal he was (Adesomoju, 2022).

Tackling Nigeria's cybercrime

With more than 120 million internet users in Nigeria, the country's anti-corruption agency, the Economic and Financial Crimes Commission (EFCC), is faced with an uphill struggle to contain an epidemic of cybercrime.

Peter Anaman has worked with the EFCC to provide officers with training on cybercrime and how the fraudsters make and receive money. He notes that, although there is a desire by the EFCC to clean up Nigeria's image, it sits against a backdrop of deeply embedded corruption, where criminals can pay their way out of harm, which makes EFCC's job increasingly difficult. It is a challenge that persists despite the organization's partnership with the FBI, Microsoft and Africa's main telecoms company, MTN.

A lawyer in the city of Lagos said that the proliferation of internet-related frauds has seriously hurt the country's image and requires concerted efforts by all stakeholders to stem the trend: 'The level at which cybercrimes are being perpetrated among young Nigerians shows that the society has degenerated into a comatose state. Concerted efforts are needed in combating these crimes; the EFCC alone cannot achieve this. It requires the efforts of every citizen and relevant agencies.' The EFCC's chair noted: 'From January 2021 to July 2021, they [officers] had arrested more than 400 Nigerians suspected of involvement in cybercrime or advanced fee fraud-related offences and that is to tell you how huge the problem is' (Iwenwanne, 2021).

The burden of proof

Law enforcement is often tasked with dealing with the aftermath of cybercrime – fraud and issues associated with drugs, weapons and human trafficking, and the violence that emanates from them. While there is, at the very least, embarrassment for victims, organizations need to be aware of what else happens next, and how cybercrime is often used to fund other crimes.

It becomes more complicated when relying on international law and cooperation. While there are legal instruments that allow for extradition, it takes time and effort and not all countries share agreements. As we shall discuss in the next chapter, even when arrest warrants are made, there is often no chance of bringing some perpetrators to justice if countries refuse to cooperate or are implicit in the cyber attacks being performed.

The biggest challenge comes down to the burden of evidence and attribution. Even if there is evidence at the scene of the crime, there is still a requirement to link that to a specific person by following traditional lines of enquiry. There is a higher success rate when there is physical evidence, such as DNA, fingerprints, fibres from clothing and vehicle tread patterns, that is easier to link. It is much more difficult when dealing with a network intrusion and following a digital footprint, as opposed to a physical footprint, and it is an area where law enforcement is not as well equipped.

The same issue applies in terms of collecting evidence – the burden of proof to track the attack becomes challenging. Even if it is possible to follow the path that an intruder took to get access into the organization, or to steal data, how can that be linked back to a specific person or group?

Proof beyond reasonable doubt

While researching this book, I had the opportunity to speak to Milan Patel, a former cybercrime special agent with the FBI, and co-founder of the managed security provider Bluevoyant. Patel described how difficult it can be for law enforcement to gather information on cybercrime and then to prove beyond reasonable doubt that it was a specific perpetrator, so that they could be charged and prosecuted with a crime.

Patel highlighted how investigators may collate a huge amount of information about IP addresses and computers, and the physical location of a person; they may even know the times they were online and can prove that someone was physically at home during those hours; they may be able to link a social media handle or other account to a physical person; but the onus is still on the investigators to prove that it was that person behind the keyboard at the time of the attack.

In the early days, investigators could perhaps knock on a door, and arrest someone, but proof in cybercrime is a whole other matter. It is a different type of evidence collection and requires a deep level of technical skill and digital forensics, and that all had to be learnt. This includes obtaining physical access to machines and understanding and defeating encryption.

Fingerprints can be gathered from a keyboard, but, in a shared house or workspace and without a photograph or video of that person using the computer at the time of the offence, there is enough reasonable doubt for a judge or jury to acquit.

Where it started

As we have identified, cyber-enabled fraud is often just a mechanism to make and move money. It starts with something separate from the cybercrime, such as setting up shell companies and bank accounts, to prepare to receive the proceeds of crime and laundered money.

Milan Patel explains that the scale of credit card fraud committed against eBay and PayPal was what started many of the large-scale investigations on payment fraud. As these companies investigated reams of fraudulent transactions, they identified that many were from the same computers and IP addresses. They contacted the FBI for help, and the subpoena was written in such a way as to be able to 'collate any and all accounts linked to an IP address'. The FBI ended up with a flow chart of around 50 IP addresses that were accessing another 200 accounts. Many of them started with small-scale fraud on eBay, and then used PayPal to wire payments internationally to move and launder the money quickly.

Ultimately, humans must touch those transactions at various points and that is what law enforcement is looking for. Who are they, how are they linked, and is it part of a larger group?

Dismantling LulzSec

To bring to life some of the challenges of identifying individuals and bringing them to justice, Milan Patel discussed the work the FBI undertook in identifying and turning a member of LulzSec in order that they could learn about and control aspects of the group's operations.

WHO WERE LULZSEC?

LulzSec, short for Lulz Security, was a group of hacktivists that gained notoriety in 2011 for conducting a series of high-profile cyber attacks against government and corporate targets. The group was a spinoff from Anonymous.

LulzSec was known for its brash, irreverent style and its use of humour to mock its targets. The group claimed to be motivated by a desire to expose security flaws in the systems of large organizations and to draw attention to the vulnerability of online security, by literally laughing at their victims, hence the name.

Patel explained that LulzSec was on the FBI's radar as they had attacked one too many US companies. In March 2012, the group's leader, Hector Xavier Monsegur (also known as Sabu), was revealed to have been working as an informant for the FBI, which led to the arrest of several prominent members of the group, leading to their disbandment. The FBI had been monitoring online chats between the group, and it was evident that Sabu was one of the key influencers that they needed to identify and turn.

As former Anonymous hacktivist Lauri Love described in Chapter 6, there is always a fear among attackers that someone will try to dox you to reveal your identity, and that was often used to keep people in line and persuade them to perform specific tasks. It therefore came as a shock to learn that it was one of LulzSec's leaders who had been working with the FBI. It was seen as the ultimate betrayal by some members.

Mirroring what has been identified in previous chapters about how attackers appear to know a lot about the locations and cultures of the organizations they are targeting, investigators were convinced that Sabu was British, by the language he used, his mannerisms, slang and how he spoke with the rest of the group (most of whom were British). It therefore came as a surprise when they discovered that he lived in New York.

What they found was a young man who had to look after his two younger cousins and made ends meet with petty credit card fraud. Despite having the skills to perform deeper and more profitable levels of cybercrime, he was not motivated by financial gain, but by political activism, and would often direct the operations of LulzSec – who it would target and why.

Once the FBI had arrested Monsegur, the intent was to leave him in play so that they could identify other members of the group and provide a redirection on some targets. This was done subtly to avoid suspicion. Monsegur was encouraged to have video calls with other members, but they were reluctant to reveal themselves, so they had to resort to idle chat and other means to identify the members.

Despite trying to keep a level of anonymity, attackers often can't help but reveal elements of their real lives, perhaps what the weather is like, what food they have eaten, and even comments on news stories. In identifying one such individual, the FBI printed over 3,000 pages of chat messages between members, marking in pen every time they revealed something personal or made a connection to the real world, no matter how small. Investigators correlated this across other data sources, until they could narrow down a suspect. That involved liaison with law enforcement in the UK, to share data and intelligence, to enable arrests.

In evaluating the offences that Monsegur had committed, or been involved with, he was initially looking at a 20-year prison sentence. However, in thanks for his cooperation in thwarting hundreds of cyber attacks, and highlighting vulnerabilities in target networks, he only served seven months in prison. Some of his co-conspirators, however, served lengthy jail terms (Neumeister, 2014).

Obtaining a conviction

As Patel highlights from other complex cases, when working across jurisdictions it can be disheartening to know for certain who the attacker is, and what they are up to, but without a chance of conviction because of where they are located and the inability to arrest them or have them extradited.

Sometimes, it just has to be a case of letting them know that law enforcement knows who they are. It may stop some of what they are doing, or they may find a workaround, or tip their accomplices off to cover their tracks.

Patel explains that society is not yet ready to invest the time and resources to tackle the issues of cybercrime. Even if the FBI could commit another 10,000 agents, it would only scratch the service. Cybercrime is happening at a pace that no law enforcement agency can realistically keep up with. There are simply not enough resources, technical talent and political motivation to drive the level of support needed.

The challenges described by Patel, is echoed by Detective Chief Superintendent Andrew Gould, of the City of London Police, which is the national lead police force in the UK for fraud and leads on cybercrime for UK policing. Gould highlighted that as of March 2023, half of all crime reported in the UK is cybercrime and fraud related, yet less than 1% of police forces are assigned to deal with it, as outlined by the UK public accounts committee. Gould explained that, with such a wide range of criminal and terrorist threats to deal with, high volumes of crime, and responsibilities to maintain public order and provide support with the consequences of wider social challenges such as mental health, policing is simply stretched too thinly to adequately resource this area of crime. Assessments of the impact of harm done by different types of criminality mean that cybercrime is, understandably, deemed less of a priority than sexual and violent offences, for example. Prioritization of cyber-enabled and cyber-dependent crime is therefore levied at those committing the highest levels of threat and harm to individuals or organizations (House of Commons Committee of Public Accounts, 2023).

A new wave of cyber sanctions

Where traditional law enforcement and extradition is not an option, a new wave of sanctions have been proposed by the UK and US governments. In February 2023, seven Russian nationals had assets frozen and travel bans imposed. These individuals have been associated with the development and deployment of ransomware targeting UK and US entities. The sanctions follow a complex, large-scale and ongoing investigation led by the NCA. In addition, the sanctions prohibit funds being made available to the individuals such as paying ransoms, including in cryptocurrency (UK Government, 2023).

The individuals identified had links with ransomware groups known as Conti, Wizard Spider, UNC1878, Gold Blackburn, Trickman and Trickbot, and have been responsible for the development and deployment of Trickbot, Anchor, BazarLoader, BazarBackdoor, Conti, Diavol and Ryuk ransomware strains. The group behind Conti extorted $180 million in ransomware in 2021 alone and was one of the first cybercrime groups to back Russia's war in Ukraine, voicing its support for the Kremlin within 24 hours of the invasion.

Conclusion

In this chapter, we have identified that for law enforcement and intelligence agencies to have any success in tracking and prosecuting cybercriminals, they must work in unison.

To support this, law enforcement and intelligence agencies are investing in specialist cybercrime and fraud units, with the aim of dismantling criminal networks and infrastructure, to make it increasingly difficult for attackers to achieve their objectives. This can often be accelerated by the seizure of large sums of money and assets to further disrupt the criminals.

For law enforcement to have any chance of making a serious dent, they would need to increase the number of skilled officers substantially. They are just not there yet, partly due to public perception of the crimes and lack of awareness of the scale of the problem. This means that attackers will continue to fall under the radar and go unchecked. The more time goes by, the more temptations go their way and, like those that preceded them, they will go bigger, and harder, and so the cycle continues when there are limited deterrents to stop them.

This is further compounded by a reliance on target organizations to keep logs and evidence, and knowing what may be useful and why. We shall explore more on this in Part Three, when we consider the strategies that organizations can deploy, not just to help themselves, but to assist in subsequent investigations. This requires organizations to take accountability for self-governance and policing their own environments, and to maintain accurate logs for forensic investigation if there is to be any success in beating cybercrime.

It also relies on organizations being proactive in using specialist agencies and security researchers to assess what information and exploits may be bought and sold on dark-web marketplaces so that they may be better prepared for what may be on the horizon. This may not be possible for some smaller enterprises, so it pays to be well versed in the current threat landscape and what is being reported by the media, law enforcement and technology companies. Having knowledge of the types of cyber attack and the tactics used can provide significant benefits when assessing the effectiveness of the current or required strategies, as we shall discuss in Part Three.

References

Adesomoju, A (2022) 'Hushpuppi's wife, imams write judge a US court sentences fraudster today', *Premium Times*, 7 November, premiumtimesng.com/news/headlines/564013-hushpuppis-wife-imams-write-judge-as-us-court-sentences-fraudster-today.html?tztc=1 (archived at https://perma.cc/VD7C-ERZV)

BBC Africa Eye (2021) 'Black Axe: Leaked documents shine spotlight on secretive Nigerian gang', BBC News, 13 December, bbc.co.uk/news/world-africa-59630424 (archived at https://perma.cc/SSM4-X34P)

BBC News (2019a) 'Letter from Africa: why Nigeria's internet scammers are "role models", 23 September, bbc.co.uk/news/world-africa-49759392 (archived at https://perma.cc/9TCL-A6MN)

BBC News (2019b) 'US names Nigerians in massive fraud investigation', 23 August, bbc.co.uk/news/world-africa-49446845 (archived at https://perma.cc/9WXW-H54W)

BBC News (2021a) 'Hushpuppu: Nigerian influencer pleads guilty to money laundering', 29 July, bbc.co.uk/news/world-africa-58002932 (archived at https://perma.cc/8JXZ-APB8)

BBC News (2021b) 'Hushpuppi – the Instagram influencer and international fraudster', 14 September, bbc.co.uk/news/world-africa-58553109 (archived at https://perma.cc/7Y26-264B)

Caesar, E (2021) 'The takedown of a dark web market', The New Yorker, 23 January, newyorker.com/news/news-desk/the-takedown-of-a-dark-web-marketplace (archived at https://perma.cc/6FLE-3NWP)

Dawkins, D (2021) 'Nigerian influencer Ramon "Hushpuppi" Abbas laundered funds for North Korea hackers, says US Dept of Justice', *Forbes*, 19 February, forbes.com/sites/daviddawkins/2021/02/19/nigerian-influencer-ramon-hushpuppi-abbas-laundered-funds-for-north-korean-hackers-says-us-department-of-justice/?sh=7c92ec141dd5 (archived at https://perma.cc/5NVX-2BFV)

Department of Justice (2020) 'Nigerian national brought to U.S. to face charges of conspiring to launder hundreds of millions of dollars from cybercrime schemes', press release, 3 July, justice.gov/usao-cdca/pr/nigerian-national-brought-us-face-charges-conspiring-launder-hundreds-millions-dollars (archived at https://perma.cc/3MEG-2RCV)

Department of Justice (2021) 'Nigerian national sentenced to prison for $11m global fraud scheme', 16 February, justice.gov/usao-edva/pr/nigerian-national-sentenced-prison-11-million-global-fraud-scheme (archived at https://perma.cc/2WEB-V2PT)

Department of Justice (2022) 'Nigerian man sentenced to over 11 years in federal prison for conspiring to launder tens of millions of dollars from online scams', 7 November, justice.gov/usao-cdca/pr/nigerian-man-sentenced-over-11-years-federal-prison-conspiring-launder-tens-millions (archived at https://perma.cc/G86N-KMH6)

Europol (2021) 'DarkMarket: world's largest illegal dark web marketplace taken down', News, 12 January, europol.europa.eu/media-press/newsroom/news/darkmarket-worlds-largest-illegal-dark-web-marketplace-taken-down (archived at https://perma.cc/Y33A-MUSL)

House of Commons Committee of Public Accounts (2023) *Progress Combatting Fraud*, committees.parliament.uk/publications/34609/documents/190751/default (archived at https://perma.cc/2QJH-444T)

Iwenwanne, V (2021) 'More than email scams: the evolution of Nigeria's cyber-crime threat', The National, 22 July, thenationalnews.com/world/africa/2021/07/22/more-than-email-scams-the-evolution-of-nigerias-cyber-crime-threat (archived at https://perma.cc/RRD4-M7L2)

Karimi, F (2020) 'He flaunted private jets and luxury cars on Instagram. Feds used his posts to link him to alleged cyber crimes', CNN Edition, 12 July, edition.cnn.com/2020/07/12/us/ray-hushpuppi-alleged-money-laundering-trnd/index.html (archived at https://perma.cc/HLY7-9WS9)

NCA (2023a) 'Money laundering and illicit finance: the threat from money laundering', nationalcrimeagency.gov.uk/what-we-do/crime-threats/money-laundering-and-illicit-finance (archived at https://perma.cc/42NP-WJFQ)

NCA (2023b) 'Notorious criminal marketplace selling victim identities taken down in international operation', 5 April, nationalcrimeagency.gov.uk/news/notorious-criminal-marketplace-selling-victim-identities-taken-down-in-international-operation (archived at https://perma.cc/GA89-UZQM)

Neumeister, L (2014) 'Hacker who helped feds gets no more time in prison', Associated Press on Yahoo News, 27 May, news.yahoo.com/hacker-helped-feds-gets-no-163849655.html (archived at https://perma.cc/VPK2-8GHB)

UK Government (2023) 'UK cracks down on ransomware actors', press release, 9 February, gov.uk/government/news/uk-cracks-down-on-ransomware-actors (archived at https://perma.cc/DTD7-9M8C)

UNODC (2023) 'Infiltration of organized crime in business and government', Organized Crime, university module, unodc.org/e4j/en/organized-crime/module-4/introduction-learning-outcomes.html (archived at https://perma.cc/U56T-R2U6)

Webz.io (2022) 'The top 10 dark web marketplaces in 2022', 30 August, webz.io/dwp/the-top-10-dark-web-marketplaces-in-2022 (archived at https://perma.cc/QQX8-26JT)

10

Influencers – how nation-sponsored actors change social dynamics

CHAPTER OBJECTIVES

We have explored many types of, and motivations behind, cybercriminals, and how law enforcement and intelligence agencies need to work together to identify the perpetrators and bring them to justice. But what if there is no justice? What if the very groups identified are controlled and managed by the state? And what if that state has no intention of cooperating with international law; in fact their objective may just be to cripple it?

This chapter explores the issues associated with nation-sponsored actors that have high intent and the resources to commit cyber attacks, and what is driving these attacks against other nations and their citizens.

Understanding strategic cultures

During research for this book, I had the opportunity to speak to Wing Commander Paul Norry from the UK Ministry of Defence (MoD), Development, Concepts and Doctrine Centre (DCDC), where he is leading the Global Strategic Trends (GST) programme. Since its inception in 2001, the GST has undertaken continuous research to identify the key drivers of change that will reshape our world.

This analysis helps the MoD, and cross-government partners, to identify potential future developments, spot likely disruptions and detect weak signals that need to be evaluated. These include what cyberspace may plausibly look like in 2050 to 2055 and how it might affect society, the economy and the environment.

The struggle for power and influence

Part of DCDC's research is to consider different scenarios and the balance between competition and power that exists between nations and which may drive conflict or unity. Two almost opposing worlds are:

- **Multipolarity** – major powers are the main international actors that form blocs with other geographically close or like-minded states. While states within a bloc cooperate under the leadership of the major power, the blocs compete for power and influence.

- **Multilateralism** – states are the most influential actors in the global order. Almost all states use multilateralism to address global challenges, define legal frameworks and settle disputes. Good global governance is a characteristic of this world.

When we consider the world in 2023, we are arguably somewhere between the two. The shifting of powers and alliances means this will be more fragmented before it gets better. With a rising global population and shortage of natural resources, such relationships will determine how well a nation is able to trade and sustain its population.

When a nation feels threatened, it is more likely to take countermeasures, which include forming alliances with other nations or acting aggressively to those they feel aggrieved by. Like-mindedness may be construed as having a similar culture, laws and belief systems. Examples are the UK, United States, Canada, Australia and New Zealand, which formed a 'Five Eyes' intelligence alliance. These are Western democratic societies, influenced by British and European cultures, values and rules.

Paul Norry explained that it is useful to consider research into strategic cultures, and how they can influence how a nation may act or behave in given scenarios. This can largely be shaped through its history and how the state perceives itself.

WHAT IS STRATEGIC CULTURE?

The concept of strategic culture is widely used in the field of international relations to explain the distinctive strategic behaviours of states, by reference to the unique properties that exist across populations. This can help to shape a collective and unique identity and idealism (Lock, 2017).

This is why understanding culture, whether it is at the national or organizational level, is so important to informing strategy, as we shall discuss further in Part Three.

Dominant cyber superpowers

In September 2022, the Belfer Center for Science and International Affairs launched its cyber power index (Voo et al 2022). It argues that governments should be concerned about other states' efforts at surveillance, information control, technology competition, financial motivations and shaping what is acceptable through norms and standards. This means considering cyber holistically. The report notes eight key objectives when considering the intent of each nation:

1 **Surveillance and monitoring domestic groups** – the capability to monitor, detect and gather intelligence within its own borders.

2 **Strengthening and enhancing national cyber defence** – prioritized defence of government and national assets, and systems for cyber hygiene and resilience.

3 **Controlling and manipulating the information environment** – the ability to control and change the narrative of information at home and abroad.

4 **Foreign intelligence collection for national security** – the ability to extract national secrets from a foreign adversary to inform diplomatic activities and military planning and improve situational awareness.

5 **Growing national cyber and commercial technology competence** – the ability to grow the domestic technology industry through legal (investment in cybersecurity research) or illegal (industrial espionage) means.

6 **Destroying or disabling an adversary's infrastructure and capabilities** – utilization of destructive cyber techniques to deter, erode or degrade the

ability to fight in cyber or conventional domains. This includes critical infrastructure and government communication networks.

7 **Defining international cyber norms and technical standards** – active participation in international legal policy and technical debates on cyber norms, including treaties, parties and alliances to combat cybercrime.

8 **Amassing wealth and extracting cryptocurrency** – conducting cyber operations to amass wealth through theft, extortion, data obtained through data breaches, and attacks on digital infrastructure and financial institutions.

When considered overall, the 10 most comprehensive cyber powers with the highest levels of intent and capability are:

1 USA

2 China

3 Russia

4 UK

5 Australia

6 Netherlands

7 Democratic People's Republic of Korea

8 Vietnam

9 France

10 Iran.

Of those, we shall consider the culture and intent of Russia and Democratic People's Republic of Korea (North Korea) further in this chapter. Before then, let's consider the role of offensive and destructive cyber attacks between nations and how that differs from individual or group cybercrime.

The role of offensive and defensive cyber

The Belfer Center notes that the UK has the most 'offensive capability' and intent. While discussing this with Paul Norry, he explained that the role of offensive cyber in a military context differs somewhat from what may be considered an from an organizational and cybercrime perspective. The MoD's 2022 *Cyber Primer* helps put this into perspective, and provides some useful perspectives for comparison.

WHAT ARE OFFENSIVE CYBER OPERATIONS?

According to the *Cyber Primer*, these are:

Activities that project power to achieve military objectives in or through cyberspace [enabled through] cyber and electromagnetic capabilities to shape (defeat, deceive, degrade and deny) adversaries' capabilities... to mould behaviour and the course of events...

They may transcend the virtual dimension (for example, websites and social media feeds) into effects in the physical dimension (for example, causing computer hardware destruction) and... directly influence the cognitive dimension of thoughts, beliefs, interests and perceptions of individuals and groups.

Offensive cyber activity can be used to inflict permanent or temporary effects, thus reducing an adversary's confidence in their networks, information or other capabilities for a specific period.

WHAT ARE DEFENSIVE CYBER OPERATIONS?

These are:

Active and passive measures taken to prevent, nullify or reduce the effectiveness of adversary actions to preserve our freedom of action in or through cyberspace. They may be discrete, episodic or enduring but are... designed to secure our access to, and freedom of action in, cyberspace. They may be undertaken against a specific threat or bounded in scope, for example when in support of a named military operation.

At the strategic level, defensive cyber operations assure freedom of action by protecting digital infrastructure and strategic capabilities from adversarial offensive cyber activity. At the operational and tactical levels, they protect critical computer and communication networks and systems that reside in the sea, land, air and space environments... The need to conduct defensive cyber operations is enduring and non-discretionary.

Note that every cyber superpower has both offensive and defensive capabilities at its disposal, which can be used as a deterrent or incentive, depending on the perspective and point of view.

As Paul Norry highlights, cyberspace can never be considered 'won and held' like vital ground on the battlefield, but it can certainly be lost. There is pressure on governments to ensure that they don't underinvest in their capability, as they risk falling too far behind their adversaries and competitors. In a similar way, organizations must also continuously evaluate and iterate against the latest threats.

Let's now consider the motivation, intent and capabilities of two nations, and how they differ.

Russian Federation (Russia)

The Belfer Center cite Russia as the number two cyber power when it comes to 'destructive capability' and 'information control' (the United States is number one in both these areas).

Russian culture

Russia is the largest country in the world by area, more than double the size of next-largest Canada. It has an abundance of natural resources including vast reserves of oil, gas and precious metals. That richness means there is a stark difference between the wealthy and powerful and the poor and powerless (Britannica, 2022).

The collapse of the Soviet Union in 1991 brought profound political and economic changes to Russia, including the formation of a large middle class. The Russian government implemented radical reforms designed to transform the economy from one that was centrally controlled to one based on capitalist principles, during its shake off of the post-communist era. Meanwhile, its concern with US hegemony in the world system became a constant theme in Russian foreign policy.

Declining US and Russia relations

In July 1998, Vladimir Putin became director of the Federal Security Service (FSB), one of the successors of the KGB. In August 1999, Putin was plucked from relative political obscurity for the post of prime minister. Since then, he has continuously been either prime minister or president.

As Norry (2023) explains, Putin's 1999 manifesto pledged that 'Russia is and will remain a great power' – a position that he has been steadfast to, and one that has arguably influenced many of his subsequent decisions.

There is potentially a fear, paranoia and distrust from Russia's elite that views Western activity with suspicion of undermining the Russian state.

Although Putin hoped to maintain a strategic partnership with the United States, he focused on strengthening Russia's relations with Europe, particularly Germany, France and the UK. Nevertheless, after the 9/11 terrorist attacks on the United States, Putin was the first foreign leader to telephone President Bush to offer sympathy and support in combating terrorism.

Putin has been consistently wary of US unilateralism and has worked to strengthen ties with China, India and Iran. In 2002 and 2003, he opposed military intervention against Iraq by the United States and UK, favouring more stringent inspections of Iraq's suspected weapons of mass destruction, rather than military force.

Despite President Obama wanting to reset relations with Moscow in 2009, tension between Russia and the West remained. This escalated in December 2012 with the US Magnitsky Act, a law that denied visas and froze the assets of Russian officials suspected of human rights abuses. Putin responded by banning the adoption of Russian children by US citizens.

Ties between the United States and Russia were further strained in June 2013, when former NSA (National Security Agency) contractor Edward Snowden fled to Moscow after revealing secret NSA intelligence-gathering programmes. Despite repeated requests, Putin refused to extradite Snowden, who had been charged with espionage by US prosecutors.

Russia cyber operations

Russian culture places a strong emphasis on power, prestige and the pursuit of national interests. These values can be seen in the country's history, which includes a long tradition of authoritarian rule, territorial expansion and strategic thinking.

These values are reflected in Russia's cyber operations. Russian military and intelligence agencies are known for sophisticated techniques such as advanced persistent threats (APTs) – prolonged attacks to compromise network systems – as well as social engineering to gain access to targets. They have been engaged in a variety of attacks, including stealing intellectual property, espionage and interfering in foreign elections and votes, including the 2016 US presidential election, as discussed in Chapter 1. The Russian government has been accused of using cyber attacks to protect its power and influence and advance its strategic interests.

Russia's invasion of Ukraine

In consideration of the 2022 Russian invasion of Ukraine, it is useful to understand the events that led up to the invasion, with the 2014 annexation of Crimea, and how Russia built its offensive cyber capability by effectively using Ukraine as its training ground.

The timeline in Table 10.1 gives a good indication of the attackers' mindset and the intent behind such aggression, which started as a power and land grab, before escalating to a full invasion.

TABLE 10.1 Timeline of cyber events building up to Russia's war against Ukraine

Date	Events
2014	
28 February	Armed men, whose uniforms lacked visible insignia, take control of key sites in Crimea.
3 March	A pro-Russian prime minister is installed as the head of the regional parliament, enabling Russia to achieve de facto military control of Crimea.
16 March	A referendum held in Crimea claims 97% of voters prefer to leave Ukraine and join Russia. It is alleged that voters were coerced, as Russian troops were stationed at polling stations. The referendum result is not recognized by most countries.
May–June	Ukrainian army begin reclaiming rebel-held territory as separatist groups use increasingly sophisticated heavy weapons, including tanks and air-defence systems.
28 August	Ukrainian President Poroshenko states that Russian forces have entered Ukraine. NATO estimates that at least 1,000 Russian troops are actively engaged in operations inside Ukraine.
5 September	Putin and Poroshenko meet in Belarus and agree to a ceasefire to de-escalate fighting and limit the use of heavy weapons in civilian areas. The agreement was soon violated by both sides.
2015	
December	• Russia's rapidly developing cyberwarfare capacity is demonstrated in Ukraine when a cyber attack is attributed to Russian security services using BlackEnergy malware. The incident was attributed to the Russian military group Sandworm (also known as Unit 74455, Telebots, Voodoo Bear, Iron Viking, Iridium/Seashell Blizzard). • The incident marked the first time that a power grid had been taken offline by a cyber attack, and indicated that Russia was using Ukraine as a training ground for more cyber attacks, since much of Ukraine's critical infrastructure stems from the Soviet era, which Russia is familiar with.

(continued)

TABLE 10.1 (Continued)

Date	Events
2016	
December	• A severe power cut at a power station outside Kyiv was blamed on a cyber attack. It bared similar hallmarks to the one in 2015, but was better planned and more organized (BBC News, 2017). • The cyber attack utilized Industroyer malware. • President Poroshenko claimed Russian security services had targeted state institutions 6,500 times in the last two months of 2016, and that Russia was waging a cyber war against his country.
2017	
27 June	• A series of cyber attacks hit Ukraine, swamping multiple websites including banks, ministries, newspapers and electricity firms with the Petya ransomware strain, which had been revamped to spread quickly. • The attack was timed to hit the day before Constitution Day – a national holiday marking Ukraine's break from the Soviet Union (Perlroth et al, 2017). • The cyber attack used a variant of the same NSA hacking tool, Eternal Blue, used by North Korea in the WannaCry attacks that had started the month before. Combining Petya and Eternal Blue created a new malware strain that would be dubbed NotPetya by experts. • Unlike Petya, which relied on social engineering techniques to trick users into downloading malware through email attachments, NotPetya had been modified to exploit back doors and remote access vulnerabilities and to propagate quickly. • Due to the type of propagation used, NotPetya spread from Ukraine, causing collateral damage around the world. Similar infections were reported in France, Germany, Italy, Poland, Russia, UK, USA and Australia as large enterprises reported that they were experiencing multiple cyber attacks. • Security experts believe that NotPetya was designed to act as a cyber weapon, where the malware was used to destruct files and encrypt networks, but without any subsequent extortion demand or decryption key. • As a result, NotPetya would be dubbed one of the most destructive cyber attacks in history, causing billions of dollars of damage, and would again be attributed to Sandworm (NCSC, 2018).

(continued)

TABLE 10.1 (Continued)

Date	Events
2020	
15 October	• A federal grand jury indicted six officers in the Russian Main Intelligence Directorate (GRU) on seven charges: conspiracy to conduct computer fraud and abuse, conspiracy to commit wire fraud, wire fraud, damaging protected computers and aggravated identity theft (Department of Justice, 2020). As well as the attacks on Ukraine, it highlighted Sandworm's involvement in other high-profile cases: ◦ French elections, April to May 2017 – spear-phishing targeting politicians, and local government prior to the French elections. ◦ PyeongChang Winter Olympics, December 2017 to February 2018 – spear-phishing and malicious mobile apps targeting South Korean citizens and officials, Olympic athletes, partners and visitors, and IOC officials. This culminated in a destructive malware attack at the opening ceremony. ◦ UK Novichok poisoning, April 2018 – spear-phishing targeting agencies investigating the nerve-agent poisoning of Sergei Skripal, his daughter and UK citizens. ◦ Georgia companies and government, 2018 – spear-phishing campaign targeting a major media company, and 2019 – efforts to compromise the network of parliament, and a wide-ranging website defacement campaign. • The Assistant Attorney General stated (Department of Justice, 2020): 'No country has weaponized its cyber capabilities as maliciously or irresponsibly as Russia, wantonly causing unprecedented damage to pursue small tactical advantages and to satisfy fits of spite. Today the department has charged these Russian officers with conducting the most disruptive and destructive series of computer attacks ever attributed to a single group, including by unleashing the NotPetya malware. No nation will recapture greatness while behaving in this way.'

Over the next two years, the COVID-19 pandemic would dominate global headlines while Putin took the opportunity to stir up propaganda and disinformation against those nations that had applied sanctions.

2022 began with the prospect of a major war in Europe as Putin ordered a massive build-up of Russian forces along the Ukrainian border. Putin claimed that the deployment of troops was merely an exercise, but, by February 2022, there were 190,000 Russian troops along the border. On 21 February, Putin ordered Russian 'peacekeepers' into Donetsk and Luhansk. While Russia had been supporting separatist movements there since 2014, this marked a dramatic escalation. As a result, Western leaders announced a new wave of sanctions, and the German chancellor suspended certification of Russia's Nord Stream 2 gas pipeline. On the morning of 24 February, Putin delivered a televised address announcing the beginning of a 'special military operation,' and, within minutes, Russian air strikes were carried out against cities across Ukraine. Putin's unprovoked attack was condemned by leaders around the world, and many vowed that even harsher sanctions would follow.

As Paul Norry highlights, from Russia's perspective, subversion, disinformation and sabotage have become almost prerequisite for an attack. The use of non-military tactics in achieving political goals and objectives has been significantly more effective than kinetic attacks. Describing the invasion as a 'special military operation' reinforces Russia's claim that it is increasing stability and restoring the natural order of things by asserting itself as the dominant power among former Soviet countries.

In his speech, Putin stated that modern Ukraine was 'entirely created by communist Russia' and had since fallen into the hands of nationalists and corrupt 'puppets' controlled by the West. He claimed that Ukraine was not 'just a neighbouring country' but an 'an integral part of our own history, culture and spiritual space'. Importantly, Russia's political elite conform to this rhetoric (Talmazan, 2022).

This is a position echoed by James Sullivan, Director of Cyber at the Royal United Services Institute (RUSI), the world's oldest and the UK's leading defence and security think tank. Sullivan argues that Russia was never going to install a new government using cyber warfare. The brutality of modern-day weapons means that devastation can be caused easily by missiles if your objective is to destroy infrastructure or kill people. Cyber operations can provide a non-lethal option for de-escalation. It can almost act as a pressure release system if used effectively. In conversation with me, Sullivan explained that there are typically three elements of cyber operations and campaigns:

1   **Intelligence gathering** – 'traditional' spying and espionage.

2   **Cyber operations** – to destruct and deceive the other state's military.

3   **Psychological warfare** – to undermine trust. This is known as 'compellence', where you take an action that encourages the adversary to take a subsequent action that was not planned, which can lead to changes in patterns of behaviour and changes in policy.

Sullivan argues that psychological warfare can often be the most damaging and likened it to 'death by a thousand cuts', whereby you systematically chip away, to bring the state down by playing the long game. Continual disinformation and dissent among populations can cause citizens to lose trust in their government and force a change in power. This could be the long-term objective of the adversary, to install a government that can be easily manipulated or influenced to change policies or allegiances.

From Russia's perspective, there is no difference on whether to utilize destructive cyber attacks or cyber-influence operations to fulfil its objectives, it is all part of its cyber capability and strategy. In essence, it appears that Russia will utilize any and all tactics to achieve its mission. In addition, Russia seems to view almost everything and everyone as a legitimate target. This is not simply limited to military and defence; and an intelligent adversary like Russia will be more likely to attack the weakest point in the ecosystem, rather than the strongest. This is why it is important to have a strong security culture mindset – to reduce risk and increase resilience to an array of attacks.

To put this into perspective, in March 2023, Microsoft issued a report that examined a year of Russian hybrid warfare, delivered in three key phases (Table 10.2; Microsoft Threat Intelligence, 2023a).

TABLE 10.2 Examples of Russian hybrid warfare tactics against Ukraine, 2022–2023

Russian activity		
Phase 1:	Destructive operations	Influence operations
January – March 2022, Russia's initial invasion of Ukraine	• Hundreds of systems across the Ukrainian government, critical infrastructure, media and commercial sectors are affected by large-scale deployment of destructive wiper malware that permanently delete files and/or renders machines inoperable. • Active incident response and information sharing between Ukrainian and allied defenders thwarts much of the destructive efforts, leading Russia to develop and deploy new and diverse malware.	• Social media flooded with disinformation ahead of invasion. Attempts to dehumanize Ukrainians by calling for the 'denazification' of the country. • Russia shifts blame to the United States, alleging it is creating bioweapons in Ukraine. • This triggers many social media companies to block Kremlin-affiliated accounts.

(continued)

TABLE 10.2 (Continued)

Russian activity		
Phase 2: March – September 2022, focus turns to Kyiv's foreign and domestic logistics	• Russian threat actors direct destructive cyber attacks towards logistics and transportation sector in Ukraine, to disrupt weapons and humanitarian flow to frontlines. • Microsoft observed Sandworm launching destructive wiper attacks and intelligence collection intrusions against Ukraine's transport sector in spring. At the same time, Russia launched missile strikes against transportation infrastructure, to disrupt the flow of goods and people. • Since at least May, phishing campaign compromises organizations that produce or transport weapons, drones, protective equipment and other supplies for US and European military customers.	• Moscow remobilizes propaganda efforts with fearmongering about nuclear attacks. • Aims to garner coverage from international press by sponsoring a PR tour of Donbas in the spring, with press from France, Germany, India and Turkey, among others.
Phase 3: Sept 2022 – March 2023, kinetic operations paired with doubled-down cyber and influence operations	• Following Ukraine's successful counteroffensive, Russia deepens its claims to Ukraine's territory and intensifies military operations designed to break Ukrainian will. • Almost claiming sovereignty over eastern Ukraine, Russia launches missile strikes on critical energy infrastructure across major cities, cutting heat and power to civilians as winter set in. • Outside Ukraine, Sandworm escalated operations to disrupt supply chains to Ukraine while other GRU-linked groups targeted Western defence organizations for intelligence collection.	• Russian agents of influence promote newly launched propaganda to launder Kremlin-aligned narratives in occupied and annexed territory, key to maintaining Russia's PR efforts. • An example is Readovka Helps, an organization led by Alexander Ionov, indicted by the United States for working with FSB. Purporting to maintain a humanitarian mission, Readovka helps to crowdfund supplies for Russian soldiers.

Far from lying in wait, Ukraine has continually built up and adapted its cyber defence capacity since the annexation of Crimea. As a result, the country was able to significantly deter, defend and mitigate many of the cyber attacks unleashed by Russia. Notably, a range of international actors have helped to cultivate and bolster Ukraine's cyber resilience through technical, financial, diplomatic and other legal avenues. International governments, along with organizations and media outlets, have partnered to prevent and blunt the effects of cyber attacks (FP Analytics, 2023). As of October 2023, Russia continues to adapt its cyber operations in relation to Ukraine and its supporters.

A crackdown on dissent

For years, the citizens of Russia and Ukraine enjoyed cordial relationships, having family and friends on both sides of the border. As the invasion of Ukraine intensified, however, and the Russian people had some exposure to the atrocities being inflicted on their own as well as other citizens, many started to protest over Putin's government. The more people hear about civilian massacres and soldiers killed on both sides, the harder it is for Russians to accept that they are not the saviours as they were led to believe, but are the aggressors.

Protests have been met with a heavy-handed response from police, with mass arrests, fines and imprisonment. This has only served to stoke the fires further. The Dance of the Cygnets from *Swan Lake* has become a symbol of deviance for many Russians. A picture of four ballerinas may seem an unlikely choice, but it has a powerful historical reference for Russians. In the Soviet era, the ballet was symbolic of the deaths of Soviet leaders, and it has become a sign today that people are waiting for Putin to die (Aronson et al, 2022).

In July 2023, the *New York Times* revealed how the Russian government was cracking down on those citizens opposed to the war by amassing an arsenal of digital surveillance capabilities (Krolik et al, 2023). The technologies enable police and security services to track encrypted apps like WhatsApp and Signal, monitor the locations of phones, identify anonymous social media users and break into people's accounts. Rather than many Russian people having a paranoia against Western states, the paranoia is now levied at the home state, as internet traffic and calls are heavily monitored.

Much like the 'cyber mercenaries' discussed in Chapter 5, surveillance technology is built by Russian-backed private-sector actors who are developing advanced tools for intelligence and security services. Of concern is that this is being levied at their own people, and, no doubt, that same technology will be utilized to provide advanced surveillance on Russia's adversaries. Could this lead to a new wave of attacks aimed at citizens? Only time will tell.

Let's consider the culture and intent of another nation.

Democratic People's Republic of Korea (North Korea)

North Korea's culture

The nation's economic goals are linked to the general government policy of *self-reliance* (Britannica, 2023). The country has shunned most foreign investment, although it has accepted considerable economic aid from Russia and China, its two most significant allies. Despite its stated policy of self-reliance, North Korea has routinely found it necessary to import fuels, machinery and grain. This ideology of self-reliance means that North Korea is one of the most isolated and inaccessible countries in the world, with severe restrictions on travel in or out, and a totally controlled press.

The country strongly emphasizes military preparedness, and economic plans have been tailored to support military objectives, often prioritizing it above other concerns. All men, and a limited number of women, are subject to conscription for a minimum period of three or four years. The country's internal security system is extensive. People's movements and social activities are monitored and controlled even down to the household level.

The country places a strong emphasis on loyalty to the ruling regime, self-sufficiency and secrecy. These values can be seen in the country's political system, which is based around the ruling Kim family, and in its closed-off economy. There is often propaganda and disinformation surrounding the country's leaders, which makes it difficult to determine just how much of the culture has been informed by its history and how much has been created to serve a specific purpose.

North Korea's class system

Songbun, which loosely translates as 'background' was first developed by North Korea's founder Kim Il-sung, in the late 1950s, and is a socio-political classification system that groups people based on perceived loyalty and whether they can be trusted by the state.

Under Japanese rule – from 1910 to 1945 – landowners, businessmen and intellectuals occupied the top tiers of the social hierarchy, whereas farmers, factory workers and labourers made up the lower classes. *Songbun* effectively reversed that:

- **Core** – the people closest to the Kim family, their relatives, and anti-Japanese resistance fighters, became North Korea's core or ruling class.

- **Wavering** – peasants, labourers and workers were lifted from the bottom of the social order.

- **Hostile** – those who opposed Kim's ascent to power or collaborated with South Korea or Japan could face discrimination. This also included North Koreans who were of high status under Japanese rule and so might be considered 'subversive'.

Over several decades, Kim Il-sung's government classified approximately 3.2 million people as 'hostile', relocating them to impoverished and isolated areas.

When the Soviet Union collapsed in 1991, North Korea lost one of its major benefactors. Coupled with a series of droughts and floods in the mid 1990s, the country was flung into crisis as millions of tonnes of grain were destroyed. Lacking the money to import enough food, Kim Jong-il's government directed scarce rations to those with the highest *songbun*. Many students abandoned their studies to help their families find food, and many North Koreans employed by the state had to start making money on the side to support themselves.

As ordinary people gradually began to earn more money, many realized that by paying bribes to the right officials, they could access privileges that had been reserved for those with high *songbun*. As a culture of corruption took hold, people began to buy things that were unavailable before the famine. This complicated the *songbun* system by allowing lower classes to use private wealth and personal connections to improve social status or avoid punishments.

Controlling citizens

Self-reliance and isolation have meant that successive Kim governments have tried hard to stop citizens seeing what is going on outside the country, while also pursuing a propaganda of benevolence within. This is achieved by exerting rigid control and power over people by restricting access to the internet and media and denying freedom of expression, public assembly and religion.

Dissent is silenced through fear, torture, starvation and forced labour. It is illegal to travel abroad without permission: it is stated as treachery, punishable by death (Human Rights Watch, 2022). Accessing phones, computers, televisions, radios or media content that is not sanctioned by the government is illegal and considered 'anti-socialist' and to be severely punished. The level of punishment for crimes seems to be arbitrary, and depends on a person's record of loyalty, personal connections and capacity to pay bribes.

Building North Korea's cyber operations

Cyber operations are seen as a cost-effective way for North Korea to gather intelligence on its primary targets – South Korea, the US and Japan. In 2013, Kim Jong-un declared that cyber warfare, as well as nuclear weapons and missiles, were an 'all-purpose sword' that guaranteed strike capability. The military and weapons are therefore prioritized over everything else.

The Belfer Center notes that North Korea is the most financially motivated cyber power, and fifth in the world when it comes to advancing commerce. Perhaps not surprising – without the vast natural resources of Russia and no trade access to many of the largest economies, how might a state get funding? One short answer is to steal it, which is why North Korea is so focused on obtaining cash and bringing that into the county.

In addition to military intelligence and cyber operations, Bureau 39 of the Korean Worker's Party engages in illicit economic activities with the aim of raising funds for senior leadership and the elite. Examples include narcotics trafficking and other smuggling. The government engages in deceptive practices to disguise the nature of transactions, using front companies to engage in weapons and missile proliferation and related activities to evade detection by global financial institutions.

These approaches are also reflected in North Korea's cyber operations. The country's military and intelligence agencies have been accused of engaging in a variety of attacks, including stealing money, in the form of cash and cryptocurrency. These attacks support the need for self-sufficiency and to avoid the need for foreign aid or economic assistance.

Since most people in the country don't have access to the internet, or computers, it can be assumed that most cyber operations are state-sponsored or that the state is complicit in any illegal or unethical practices.

As the regime is generally not fearful of sanctions, it is often more reckless than other nation-sponsored actors, and unlikely to succumb to political pressure. The senior leadership go to great lengths to profit from the proceeds of crime, by recruiting people from other countries to perform money laundering, as discussed in the previous chapter.

While researching for this book, I had the opportunity to speak to Geoff White, investigative journalist and author of *The Lazarus Heist* (2022), which provides a detailed exposé of some of North Korea's most prolific cyber attacks, including the Bangladeshi Bank heist, involvement in WannaCry ransomware and a hack on Sony Pictures. What particularly struck me about the book was the research on North Korea's underpinning strategic culture, and revelations of how some people may be forced into working for the regime because of the principles of *songbun*.

WHO IS THE LAZARUS GROUP?

Also known as Zinc/Diamond Sleet, Black Artemis, Labyrinth Chollima, Hidden Cobra and Nickel Academy, among others, the group is attributed to state-sponsored activity associated with Bureau 121 of the Reconnaissance General Bureau (RGB), North Korea's elite security intelligence organization. It is responsible for collecting strategic and tactical information on behalf of the National Defence Commission (Global Security Org, 2023).

Bureau 121 specializes in overseas sabotage and espionage. It includes cyber warfare, physical attacks on key personnel, and extortion of defectors who fled North Korea to the West (Recorded Future, 2023).

Microsoft Threat Intelligence (2023b) has observed the group targeting media, defence and IT industries globally. The focus is on espionage, theft of personal and corporate data, financial gain and corporate network destruction, using a variety of exploits.

Recruiting elite hackers

As White (2022) reports, North Korea has a habit of recruiting gifted individuals in mathematics and computer science from university. As a hierarchal society, the opportunity to work for the military cannot only transform their life, but that of their family too. Simply having access to the internet is a privilege that many don't have.

Military hackers are among the most talented, and rewarded, people in North Korea, handpicked and trained from a young age, since the education system seems to be geared towards creating an army of 'cyber warriors'. It is a sure way of increasing *songbun* and is often seen as a great honour by those selected (Park and Pearson, 2014).

Much of this talent is sent to China so individuals can learn how computers and the internet are used in the 'free world' before going to work for the regime as a hacker. They are given a minder and instructions on what to do. Since North Korean citizens are banned from working in any country, they often travel on fake Chinese passports (NCC, 2023).

Despite being exposed to a different world and way of life, these are only temporary privileges since the recruits are part of the nation's army and treated as such. They are in essence 'state-backed slaves', who must earn at least $10,000 per year for the regime. They perhaps get a salary of $300 a month in return. Even for those that have the benefit of working in foreign countries, the regime ensures they don't have ideas about escaping – by effectively holding their families hostage in North Korea. Any escape would certainly mean severe punishment for those left behind, and stripping of all privileges and *songbun*. To those that loyally return to the fold, there is the chance of promotion, better rations and housing, and so, for the most part, they are compliant.

Analysing nation-sponsored actors

Once the purveyor of stealth and espionage, nation-sponsored actors have evolved their capabilities to deliver an array of offensive cyber and influence operations aimed to drive fear into their enemies. Many actors have shown a willingness and desire to move from 'disruption' to 'destruction', with the aim of causing as much unrest and upheaval as possible. Although not as visible and physically damaging as kinetic attacks, the level of impact can be just as far-reaching. As demonstrated by the two countries examined in this chapter, there is often a rich history and sequence of events that provide a level of justification to what they are doing and how they are doing it.

Widespread disinformation and propaganda campaigns make it hard for people to know what to believe, and they can be misled into turning against their own governments and leaders in times of crisis. Arguably, this level of psychological warfare is the hardest to detect and mitigate against, since it can often be years in the making. Education on historical events, culture and how to provide media literacy are therefore important and should be encouraged so that people have the sources available to them to help them think and act objectively. As we have discussed, the measure of what is right and wrong is often blurred and depends on your perspective.

Organizations therefore need to consider their strategies from two perspectives; first a *microscope* to delve deeper into the here and now and the changing tactics that are being waged on the organization, sector or countries within which they operate, and second a *telescope* to consider what may be on the horizon, as power struggles, conflicts and allegiances continue to unravel and evolve, and what bearing this may have on the overall cyber-threat landscape.

Conclusion

The role of nation-sponsored actors in the cybercrime ecosystem is complex. The people enacting the crimes are instructed by the state and often do not have a choice. Unlike many other nations, where people can choose to leave an establishment if they don't like the work they are undertaking, for many people working in the military or intelligence services in certain countries, this is not an option.

When reflecting on the motivation and intent of nation-sponsored actors, who their targets are, and the lengths they will go to for their objectives, it is necessary to understand the culture. The history of the nation and its changes in alliances can have a huge bearing on what happens and why. When considered against the 'seven sins of attackers' in Chapter 2, there is an inherent and deep-seated level of wrath and even envy from such nations that have been years in the making. While some actions may seem irrational, when viewed through their lens, they feel justified and believe that it is protecting their interests.

Russia and North Korea both have authoritarian and strong-willed leaders. Putin has been in power in Russia since 1999, and the Kim dynasty have been in power in North Korea since 1948. Many citizens of these countries don't know any different, so the stories, propaganda and controlled media keep people in check, and discourage them from questioning authority. Those that do question the nations' leadership often don't fare well.

Although Russia's citizens enjoy many more freedoms than those in North Korea, many are starting to question the rules and policies of the state. Their livelihoods have been severely disrupted, and the level of dissent is rising within the population, but so is the heavy hand that rules them.

Citizens of North Korea are potentially so isolated from the outside world that they are ignorant to what is happening, other than what is fed to them, and hence there may be little opportunity or desire to dissent.

When met with such authoritarian leaders, who have the means and motivation to unleash an arsenal of conventional and cyber weapons, alliances and strong international cooperation are vital for defence and protection. We shall explore more on this in Part Three as we consider different strategies for organizations.

References

Aronson, V, Mielke, B and Deliso, M (2022) 'How "Swan Lake" became a symbol of protest in Russia', ABC News, 29 April, abcnews.go.com/International/swan-lake-symbol-protest-russia/story?id=84401801 (archived at https://perma.cc/MG48-NMUS)

BBC News (2017) 'Ukraine power cut was "cyber-attack"', 11 January, bbc.co.uk/news/technology-38573074 (archived at https://perma.cc/Z5C7-ZZR9)

Britannica (2022) 'Russia', Geography and Travel, britannica.com/place/Russia (archived at https://perma.cc/286Y-YLBA)

Britannica (2023) 'North Korea', Geography and Travel, britannica.com/place/North-Korea (archived at https://perma.cc/J82D-FRA4)

Department of Justice (2020) 'Six Russian GRU officers charged in connection with worldwide deployment of destructive malware', Office of Public Affairs press release, 19 October, justice.gov/opa/pr/six-russian-gru-officers-charged-connection-worldwide-deployment-destructive-malware-and (archived at https://perma.cc/J85Z-U98M)

FP Analytics (2023) 'Cross-cutting responses to strengthen Ukraine's digital resilience', Digital Front Lines, digitalfrontlines.io/2023/06/28/cross-cutting-responses-to-strengthen-ukraines-digital-resilience (archived at https://perma.cc/P63B-SSDZ)

Global Security Org (2023) 'North Korean Intelligence Agencies', globalsecurity.org/intell/world/dprk (archived at https://perma.cc/BL76-TF2H)

Human Rights Watch (2022) 'North Korea', hrw.org/world-report/2022/country-chapters/north-korea (archived at https://perma.cc/9QHR-6KNG)

Krolik, A, Mozur, P and Satariano, A (2023) 'Crackling down on dissent, Russia seeds a surveillance supply chain', New York Times, 3 July, nytimes.com/2023/07/03/technology/russia-ukraine-surveillance-tech.html (archived at https://perma.cc/D3PT-ACK8)

Lock, E (2017) 'Strategic culture theory: what, why and how', *Oxford Research Encyclopedias*, Politics, 26 September, doi.org/10.1093/acrefore/9780190228637.013.320 (archived at https://perma.cc/SNR9-7PP2)

Microsoft Threat Intelligence (2023a) 'A Year of Russian Hybrid Warfare in Ukraine', report, 15 March, https://query.prod.cms.rt.microsoft.com/cms/api/am/binary/RW10mGC (archived at https://perma.cc/C64N-9QSB)

Microsoft Threat Intelligence (2023b) Diamond Sleet internal intelligence profile

MoD (2022) *Cyber Primer, Third Edition*, October 2022, assets.publishing.service.gov.uk/government/uploads/system/uploads/attachment_data/file/1115061/Cyber_Primer_Edition_3.pdf (archived at https://perma.cc/V2DB-LYWC)

NCC (2023) 'The Lazarus group: North Korea scourge for +10 years', nccgroup.com/uk/the-lazarus-group-north-korean-scourge-for-plus10-years (archived at https://perma.cc/Q82Y-FX5T)

NCSC (2018) 'Russian military "almost certainly" responsible for destructive 2017 cyberattack', News, 14 February, ncsc.gov.uk/news/russian-military-almost-certainly-responsible-destructive-2017-cyber-attack (archived at https://perma.cc/3FL8-6Q9D)

Norry, P (2023) 'How far can strategic culture enhance our understanding of states' security strategies?', defence research paper, 18 February

Park, J and Pearson, J (2014) 'In North Korea, hackers are handpicked, pampered elite', Reuters, 5 December, reuters.com/article/us-sony-cybersecurity-northkorea-idUSKCN0JJ08B20141205 (archived at https://perma.cc/P4WN-9V8G)

Perloth, N, Scott, M and Frenkel, S (2017) 'Cyberattack hits Ukraine then spreads internationally', New York Times, 27 June, nytimes.com/2017/06/27/technology/ransomware-hackers.html (archived at https://perma.cc/C42M-E8CT)

Recorded Future (2023) *North Korea Cyber Activity*, go.recordedfuture.com/hubfs/reports/north-korea-activity.pdf (archived at https://perma.cc/595T-V9PJ)

Talmazan, Y (2022) 'From buildup to battle: why Putin stoked a Ukraine crisis – then launched an invasion', NBC News, 25 February, nbcnews.com/news/world/why-putin-invaded-ukraine-russia-war-explained-rcna16028 (archived at https://perma.cc/2G72-YCU7)

Voo, J, Hemani, I and Cassidy, D (2022) *National Cyber Power Index 2022*, Belfer Center for Science and International Affairs, Harvard Kennedy School, belfercenter.org/sites/default/files/files/publication/CyberProject_National%20Cyber%20Power%20Index%202022_v3_220922.pdf (archived at https://perma.cc/MY3H-2H5X)

White, G (2022) *The Lazarus Heist – From Hollywood to high finances: Inside North Korea's global cyber war*, Penguin Business, London

11

Insiders – how attackers take advantage of internal loopholes

---

CHAPTER OBJECTIVES

Much of this book has focused on the role of external attackers – those that have no direct affiliation to the organization, but who wish to gain unauthorized access to systems and data to fulfil their objectives.

But what if the attacker already has access to systems and data from within the organization? What if they are trusted employees that you have brought into your business, and they are the ones that are leaking sensitive data or sabotaging systems? In this chapter, we explore the rise of the insider threat, and question what happens when we give someone too much trust.

What is an insider threat?

Terms that are often used interchangeably are *insider risk* and *insider threat,* and it is worth taking a moment to consider the differences. You may decide to use a different definition for your own organization.

WHAT IS AN INSIDER RISK?

This is the overarching risk that anyone inside the organization (employee, contractor or partner) can pose and that leads to the unauthorized disclosure of sensitive information or other unintended consequences.

This can often be attributed to poor policy and controls, a lack of education and awareness, or someone making a mistake that leads to the resulting damage and harm. Generally, the risk does *not* assume malicious intent by the individual.

WHAT IS AN INSIDER THREAT?

This is the risk that specific individuals (employee, contractor or partner) can pose and that leads to the unauthorized disclosure of sensitive information, or other unintended consequences that may be considered unethical, harmful or illegal.

This can often be attributed to a deliberate action to circumvent poor policies and controls. Generally, the threat assumes there is *deliberate intent* by the individual.

Irrespective of whether the action was intentional or not, the impact can often be the same if there has been a compromise to the organization's networks and systems or a data breach. The ability to perform such nefarious actions generally points to flaws in policies and processes, and the ability to take advantage of such flaws.

Even when considering the will and motivation of an individual to deliberately circumvent a policy, it might not be for malicious purposes. For example, a common issue is when an employee leaves the organization and may take some information with them, such as reports or presentation slides they created, or particularly like, and want to reuse. It may not contain sensitive data, but, technically, this is still the intellectual property of their employer, and could be considered theft, depending on the policies of the organization.

It gets a little more deceptive when people take lists of customers and their contact details with them, especially when going to a competitor organization. It gets even murkier if the employee argues that these were their customers to begin with, as they were encouraged to bring contacts from their previous employment – so who is in the wrong here?

Of course, if an employee exfiltrates sensitive information, such as business plans, pricing lists or sensitive research to share or sell to other third parties, this can be considered a deliberate intent to remove information, especially if they are going out of their way to hide their actions, such as renaming or applying passwords to documents.

So, an organization not only needs to consider the intent and motivation of the person that may have access to sensitive information and systems, but whether they have defined the thresholds and consequences when policies or employment contracts may have been violated, as well as any obligations for internal and external reporting to law enforcement or regulators.

There is a layer in between that we also need to consider in relation to the context of this book, which is the coerced and manipulated insider, and whether there is a deliberate intent to perform a specific action. Examples of a manipulated insider with *no* malicious intent are those people who have been the target and victim of a phishing email or business email compromise where they have been duped into performing actions. An example of a manipulated insider *with* malicious intent maybe someone who has been paid to perform a specific action. There can often be a level of apathy towards the organization, where the employee does not care whether trust has been breached or may not even consider that the resulting action has a high impact on the organization.

The culture of the organization, how they treat people and how they monitor for cases of delinquent or changing behaviour are important factors in how they perceive and manage insider risks and threats. We shall circle back to this in Chapter 14.

WHAT IS THE COST OF INSIDER THREATS?

The Ponemon Institute (2022) notes that insider threats have increased in both frequency and cost since 2020, with the average cost to resolve sitting at $15.4 million, compared with $11.45 million in 2020. The research highlights several interesting statistics:

- Malicious insiders accounted for 26 per cent of incidents.

- Organizations are most concerned about credential theft, which has more than doubled since 2020.

- The most sensitive data resides in employees' email, which is where they store their organization's most sensitive data, such as personally identifiable information, intellectual property and other critical business information. As a result, 74 per cent of survey respondents say malicious insiders emailed sensitive data to outside parties.

- Disruption, downtime and investment in technologies represent the most significant costs when dealing with insider threats.

- Companies spend the most on containment of the insider security incident. The least amount is for escalation, monitoring and surveillance.

Rise of the super malicious insider

DTEX (2022) highlighted how the effects of COVID-19 had left many people stressed and despondent because of dealing with the myriad of issues resulting from the global pandemic. This included the forced requirements to adjust to changes in the workplace, as well as how people interacted and went about their daily lives. DTEX identified that 75 per cent of insider-threat investigations originated from within the individual's home.

The DTEX report, based on real investigations, identified a significant increase in industrial espionage incidents and the rise of the 'super malicious insider', which is a malicious insider threat with superior technical skills and in-depth knowledge of common insider threat detection techniques. Typically, this person has a deep understanding of the technical environment, level of monitoring performed and how to circumvent and bypass system controls. This enables the individual to perform higher levels of espionage, fraud, sabotage and other workplace violations in a more efficient manner. The research identified a noticeable increase in the use of OSINT practices to conceal their identity and actions. DTEX identified that:

- The 'super malicious insider' accounted for 32 per cent of all malicious incidents.
- 42 per cent of actionable incidents were related to IP and data theft, including industrial espionage related to the theft of trade secrets, source code and active collusion with a foreign nexus.
- Most of the super malicious insiders worked in financial services and critical infrastructure industries.

Privilege misuse

The concept of the super malicious user and the abuse of privileged access and controls was also identified by Verizon (2023), in which it reported that 78 per cent of all privilege-misuse cases are financially motivated.

Privilege abuse (80 per cent of cases) is fraudulent or malicious activity enabled because of privileged access rights that enable individuals with higher levels of privilege to steal data. *Data mishandling* (20 per cent) involves insiders handling sensitive data carelessly. Unlike privilege abuse, data mishandling incidents don't usually indicate malicious intent.

Verizon identified instances where organized crime gangs had set the objective of being hired by organizations solely for the purpose of facilitating large-scale frauds. These people can be difficult to spot – they may present and interview convincingly. One of the difficulties in responding to an incident is that no organization's onboarding process is perfect, and most involve adding the new hire to various groups and systems that are not always directly controlled by IT.

Similarly, some nation-sponsored actors may be willing to play the long game by having people planted as international students at prestigious universities so that they are more likely to be employed in high-tech and scientific industries, as discussed in the previous chapter.

How much trust is too much trust?

A case that has brought much condemnation and embarrassment to the US government is that of disgraced 21-year-old national guardsman Jack Teixeira, who was found to have been leaking highly sensitive and top-secret military information, because of abusing the privileges entrusted to him.

Reporting of initial leak

On 6 April 2023, the *New York Times* (Cooper and Schmitt) reported that classified documents detailing secret US and NATO plans to build up the Ukrainian military ahead of a planned offensive against Russian troops were posted on Twitter and Telegram. Military analysts stated that some documents appeared to have been modified, but disclosures of original documents, including photographs of charts of anticipated weapons deliveries, troop and battalion strengths and other plans, represented a significant breach of US intelligence. It was unclear at that stage how the documents had been leaked, but pro-Russian channels had been sharing some of the leaked documents.

The following day, the *New York Times* published another article (Cooper et al, 2023) highlighting that a new batch of classified documents had surfaced. The documents were found on Twitter and other sites and included those labelled 'Secret/NoForn,' meaning they were not meant to be shared with foreign nationals. Even as officials at the Pentagon and national security agencies were investigating the source of documents on Twitter and Telegram, another surfaced on 4chan. US security analysts stated that the leaked information went beyond just the war in Ukraine and included sensitive data on China, the Indo-Pacific 'theatre', the Middle East and terrorism.

By 9 April, Bellingcat, the investigative OSINT group, had revealed that many of the leaked documents were dated from early March 2023, around the time they were first posted on Discord (Toler, 2023). Bellingcat had spoken to three members of the Discord community, where the images had been posted, who claimed that many more documents had been shared across other Discord servers. Bellingcat was able to trace the spread of the documents over a variety of internet forums, including a server called Thug Shaker Central. While the server name kept changing, Bellingcat identified that the administrators and users were a tight-knit community that included 20 to 30 young men and teenagers who frequently posted about guns, games and racist memes. It would be through this group and server that Teixeira would be identified.

A declaration of facts filed by the FBI on 13 April 2023 showed parallel inquiries led to Teixeira's arrest at the home he shared with his mother and stepfather. Teixeira was subsequently charged with 'unauthorized removal and retention of classified documents and materials' under the US Espionage Act.

What ensued was a media frenzy about 'one of the biggest intelligence leaks in US history'. Who was Teixeira? How did he have access to such sensitive information? Why did he leak it? And what was his intent? (BBC News, 2023)

Court documents submitted on 26 April 2023 for pre-trial detention (US District Court) highlight some key aspects on the will, motivation and mindset of the accused before entering the military and while serving. Not only were these felony charges, but court documents reveal a genuine concern that Teixeira would be considered an asset in enemy hands that could offer him safe harbour and attempt to facilitate his escape from the United States. As the court documents show, not only does Teixeira stand charged with betraying his oath and his country, but he had taken numerous steps to thwart the investigation, including smashing up a tablet, laptop and Xbox that were found at his home at the time of arrest.

Teixeira's movements that led to the disclosure

Court documents and media stories would reveal a troubling history of events that led up to Teixeira's arrest. A report from CNN on 28 April 2023 (Bertrand et al) called into question how someone with Teixeira's background was not only recruited into the military but was given the highest levels of security clearance as well as unfettered access to print records, and was able to take them home without anyone noticing.

On 19 May 2023, CNN (Britzky et al) showed newly released memos revealing that Air Force leadership repeatedly warned Teixeira about inappropriately accessing classified intelligence, as documented in the timeline in Table 11.1. Questions have been raised as to how Teixeira continued to hold top secret clearance despite multiple warnings.

TABLE 11.1 Timeline leading to Jack Teixeira's arrest and charges

Date	Event
2018	
March	• Teixeira suspended from high school when a classmate overheard remarks about weapons, including Molotov cocktails, guns at the school, and racial threats.
	• Teixeira applied for a firearms identification card (FID). Application denied due to concerns by local police over high school comments.
2019	
September	• Graduates high school.
	• Applies again for an FID and is denied by local police.
	• Enlists in Air National Guard.
2020	
November	• Reapplies for FID and includes a letter citing his position of trust in protecting classified information in the US government as a reason he could be trusted to possess a firearm (Teixeira, 2020). Application is approved.
2021	
October	• Achieves rank of Airman First Class and is decorated with an Air Force achievement medal. Enters active duty.
	• Provided with TS/SCI clearance (Top Secret/Sensitive Compartmented Information), one of the highest US military and intelligence security clearances available.
2022	
February	• Begins accessing hundreds of classified documents containing national defence information that had no bearing on his role as an 'IT support specialist'.
	• Conducted hundreds more keyword searches to find classified information and even solicited requests from online friends for specific information.

(continued)

TABLE 11.1 (Continued)

Date	Event
September	• In a leaked memo, Teixeira was 'observed taking notes on classified intelligence information' in the unit's sensitive compartmented information facility, or SCIF, and putting 'the note into his pocket'. • He was instructed 'to no longer take notes in any form on classified intelligence information'.
October	• His supervisors believed he was 'potentially ignoring' a cease-and-desist order to stop deep diving into intelligence. • Supervisors were made aware of the second infraction when Teixeira started asking 'very specific questions' after a weekly intelligence briefing and was asked if he had been accessing JWICS (Joint Warfare Intelligence Communications System), a government network for top secret information, to look up classified intelligence.
December	• Posts sensitive government information to social media platforms. Records associated with Teixeira's username show that records, including photographs, were posted much earlier. • Admits in a chat forum that he 'omits a decent amount' of information because he was 'not gonna type out 35 pages of information it's just not happening'. • He went on to state, 'I tailor it and take important parts and include as many details as possible'.
2023 January	• Another leaked memo shows that a senior non-commissioned officer (NCO) spotted Teixeira 'on a JWICS machine... viewing content that was not related to his primary duty and was related to the intelligence field'. • The memo said only that the NCO notified their leader of her observation. There was no mention of additional discussions with Teixeira.
April	• Reports appear in the *New York Times* highlighting multiple leaks (perpetrator not yet known). • Teixeira adopts new username, tells another user 'if anyone comes looking, don't tell them [expletive]'. Encourages that user to 'delete all messages' and tell others to do the same. • The server (where the leaked government information was uploaded) no longer exists, suggesting that Teixeira had deleted the server in its entirety. • FBI arrest Teixeira at his home. • FBI identified that Teixeira kept a gun locker approximately two feet from his bed, which included handguns, bolt-action rifles, shotguns, an AK-style high-capacity weapon and a gas mask. Ammunition and what appeared to be a silencer found in his desk drawer.

(continued)

TABLE 11.1 (Continued)

Date	Event
May	• Courts agree to remand Teixeira into FBI custody until his trial.
June	• Teixeira is indicted on six counts of wilful retention and transmission of national defence information (revised from the previous two he had originally been charged with in April 2023) (Department of Justice, 2023).
	• The charges of unauthorized retention and transmission of national defence information each carry a sentence of up to 10 years in prison, up to three years of supervised release and a fine of up to $250,000.
	• The Attorney General accuses Teixeira of violating his oath to safeguard national security and says the leaks were likely to have caused 'exceptionally grave damage to national security'.
	• The judge rules that Teixeira remain detained while awaiting trial, citing a 'lack of integrity' and stressing that he put countless people in the United States and abroad 'at risk' by allegedly leaking the documents.

Court documents highlight that Teixeira was deceptive and coercive, exposing others to peril in pursuit of his own freedom. He had received training in the fundamentals of information technology, computer system familiarisation, network fundamentals and cybersecurity. Not only did he have the means but the motive and the skills to circumvent any potential restrictions of online activity that the court may impose. As of December 2023, Teixeira is awaiting trial. It is expected that much more will be revealed with regards to his motivations, intent and overall objectives as evidence is collated and shared by the FBI and other parties.

As we discussed in Chapter 2, and the 'seven sins of attackers', it could be construed that Teixeira exhibits a level of wrath with his racist and harmful content and perhaps a profound fascination with reading and copying military intelligence reports. The case certainly suggests that Teixeira may have been capable of much more than has been released so far.

Issues with military vetting processes

As further reported by CNN (Bertrand et al, 2023), the US Senate Intelligence Committee requested an examination of the Pentagon's vetting process and whether any procedures were violated or ignored. After former NSA contractor Edward Snowden had exposed the scope of the NSA's intelligence gathering apparatus in 2013, the Pentagon had rolled out new measures to catch insider threats by detecting when an employee gains unauthorized access to a classified system.

The main government programme for catching someone like Teixeira is a multi-billion-dollar effort begun in 2018. That programme, largely run by the Defense Counterintelligence and Security Agency (DCSA), aims to continuously vet security clearance holders for warning signs rather than periodically investigate them. Background checks include high-level reviews of social media posts, but more invasive searches are off-limits because of privacy safeguards.

Lawmakers as well as current and former US officials state that there is a need to delve deeper into the backgrounds of people like Teixeira who have access to the nation's secrets. There is currently a focus in background investigations on counterintelligence threats and the likelihood that someone might hold foreign allegiances.

A former member of the NSA General Counsel highlighted: 'We do not focus anywhere as much on overall fitness, character [or] trustworthiness… we don't really get into deep psychological profiling of anybody that might, in this particular case, have picked out [Teixeira]' (Bertrand et al, 2023).

Pentagon officials stated that the incident underscores the importance of the Department of Defense's insider-threat efforts, which principally rely on an individual's colleagues and superiors to report any suspicious behaviour. 'This is negligence on the part of the chain of command,' cited a former member of US Cyber Command. 'They had a clear pattern of behaviour,' adding that Teixeira 'should have been cut off at the second incident' (Bertrand et al, 2023). What did or did not happen following Teixeira's actions and the concerns from his supervisors was be part of the Air Force's own investigation.

In December 2023, the Air Force disciplined 15 members of the 102nd Intelligence Surveillance and Reconnaissance Group after a watchdog concluded that they had failed to properly supervise Teixeria's access to classified information, including the ex-commander of the unit, who was relieved of his position (Massie, 2023).

The probe also concluded that several members of the group had failed to report the incidents, in case officials might 'overreact', highlighting that 'had any of these members come forward, security officials would likely have restricted systems / facility access and alerted the appropriate authorities, reducing the length and depth of the disclosures by several months'.

Challenges with monitoring for insider threats

The case of Jack Teixeira highlights many issues that the military, as well as organizations, have with preliminary vetting, as well as ongoing monitoring of personnel when they are actively employed. There is often an assumption, rightly or wrongly, that, once they have joined, someone can be entrusted with access to highly sensitive information right from the outset, even though such trust has not been verified. It also brings into question whether some individuals have deliberately applied to such positions for the sole purpose of getting access to the sensitive information and other resources.

There is often a challenge to balance monitoring behaviour in a work environment with monitoring behaviour across all aspects of someone's life. It brings in issues of privacy and potentially violating someone's human rights. The irony is that even attackers have exercised their rights to privacy when asked by law enforcement to hand over passwords and encryption keys. It therefore requires knowledge on local laws and regulations to determine what may or may not be allowed and under what circumstances.

As we have seen, people reveal different aspects of themselves to different social groups. What we freely discuss with work colleagues will be quite different from that discussed with friends and family at home, and different from what may be discussed in closed forums. Some people may choose to reveal a darker side of themselves to like-minded people that may seem at odds with normal societal values and behaviours.

Not only do people create groups and subgroups on social media sites and forums, but they may look to the dark web to discuss some of their deepest desires, rages and criminal behaviour. Organizations need to be cognisant that what we say and what we do can often be at odds with each other and should not be taken for granted.

Conclusion

In this chapter, we have explored the overall issue of insider risk and how this leads to insider threats. The level of motivation and intent is largely driven by the objective of the individual, and whether they are being manipulated, coerced or acting on their own fruition.

We have seen the case for the super malicious user, and the dangers when people not only have malicious intent but have the levels of technical skill and knowledge that enables them to circumvent and bypass security policies and controls.

There is a compounded issue of the effectiveness of initial vetting, and then ongoing monitoring, as an employee enters the workplace, and for the duration of their employment. This can be intensified by the misguided notion that, if someone wears a uniform, they automatically carry a level of additional trust, which can be very dangerous. It also brings further into debate issues with culture when it comes to understanding the gravity of the threat and the impact that a malicious insider may cause, and whether those that identify wrong-doing feel empowered to speak up.

As we move into Part Three, we shall start to consider the strategies required for dealing with external and internal threats, and how we can help to reduce the vulnerabilities surrounding people.

References

BBC News (2023) 'The biggest intelligence leaks in US history', 15 April, bbc.co. uk/news/world-us-canada-65281470 (archived at https://perma.cc/8LTE-N7XJ)

Bertrand, N, Lyngaas, S, Cohen, Z and Britzky, H (2023) 'Accused Pentagon leaker's violent rhetoric raises fresh questions about top secret vetting process', CNN, 28 April, edition.cnn.com/2023/04/28/politics/pentagon-leaker-red-flags-fresh-questions-top-secret-vetting/index.html (archived at https://perma.cc/ H5M3-8GNB)

Britzky, H, Lyngaas, S, Cohen, Z and Bertrand, N (2023) 'Defense personnel alarmed after memos reveal Air Force leadership warned about accused Pentagon leaker but let him continue working', CNN, 19 May, edition.cnn.com/ 2023/05/19/politics/jack-teixeira-leak-intelligence-unit-warnings/index.html (archived at https://perma.cc/C2DP-EW77)

Cooper, H and Schmitt, E (2023) 'Ukraine war plans leak prompts Pentagon investigation', New York Times, 6 April, nytimes.com/2023/04/06/us/politics/ ukraine-war-plan-russia.html (archived at https://perma.cc/RBM3-EELA)

Cooper, H, Barnes, J, Schmitt, E and Gibbons-Neff, T (2023) 'New batch of classified documents appear on social media sites', New York Times, 7 April 2023, nytimes.com/2023/04/07/us/politics/classified-documents-leak.html (archived at https://perma.cc/88DQ-AF5Y)

Department of Justice (2023) 'Air National Guardsman indicted for unlawful disclosure of classified national defense information', US Attorney's Office press release, 15 June, justice.gov/usao-ma/pr/air-national-guardsman-indicted-unlawful-disclosure-classified-national-defense (archived at https://perma.cc/ SLH6-FCT6)

DTEX (2022) '2022 Insider Risk Report', www2.dtexsystems.com/2022-insider-risk-report (archived at https://perma.cc/L3Q8-YU26)

FBI (2023) Affidavit in support of application for a criminal complaint and arrest warrant, case: 1:23-mj-04293-DHH, storage.courtlistener.com/recap/gov.uscourts.mad.255930/gov.uscourts.mad.255930.3.1.pdf (archived at https://perma.cc/H66G-WEZF)

Massie, G (2023), The Independent, 12 December 2023.'https://www.independent.co.uk/news/world/americas/crime/teixeira-pentagon-classified-information-leak-report-b2462259.html', (archived at https://perma.cc/JLX6-M9P6) accessed 17 December 2023

Ponemon Institute (2022) '2022 Cost of Insider Threats Global Report', static.poder360.com.br/2022/01/pfpt-us-tr-the-cost-of-insider-threats-ponemon-report.pdf (archived at https://perma.cc/S5H2-EG9U)

Teixeira, J (2020) Letter to police accompanying fire arms license request, 15 November, media.wbur.org/wp/2023/04/Teixeira-letter-seeking-gun-permit.pdf (archived at https://perma.cc/K28F-XMPJ)

Toler, A (2023) 'From Discord to 4chan: the improbable journey of a US intelligence leak', Bellingcat, 9 April, bellingcat.com/news/2023/04/09/from-discord-to-4chan-the-improbable-journey-of-a-us-defence-leak (archived at https://perma.cc/CNF9-XPS5)

US District Court, District of Massachusetts (2023) *USA v Jack Teixeira*, motion in support of pretrial detention, 26 April, storage.courtlistener.com/recap/gov.uscourts.mad.255930/gov.uscourts.mad.255930.19.0_3.pdf (archived at https://perma.cc/R8QJ-ZJTK)

Verizon (2023) '2023 Data Breach Investigations Report', verizon.com/business/resources/reports/dbir (archived at https://perma.cc/R5TX-TSFH)

PART THREE

Strategies to counteract the criminal mindset and build resilience

12

Why your security awareness training sucks, and education is the differentiator

CHAPTER OBJECTIVES

I'm sure Part Two gave you plenty to think about when it comes to the different threat actors, their motivations, and their tactics. As we head into Part Three, we discuss the strategies to counteract the human adversary and prepare your organization for such attacks.

In this chapter, we address traditional cybersecurity awareness training and why it, quite frankly, sucks! I'm being deliberately provocative here to address some of the fundamental issues that organizations face and what they can to do improve awareness.

We also explore why education is different from training, and why it might just be the differentiator we are looking for when it comes to changing perspectives and the future of cybersecurity.

Playing with emotions

If we assume that key benefits of performing security awareness training include promoting a good security culture and empowering people to have the confidence to detect and respond to an array of attacks, why do some organizations try to catch people out?

Don't get me wrong – we want people to understand the form of social engineering and manipulation that attackers use to lure them into acting, but when we deliberately use these tactics to play on people's emotions, and then ridicule them for being caught out, we just build distrust. Rather than increasing awareness, and motivating people to learn more, it only serves to isolate them further, and they are more likely to consider security in a negative light. Let's look at an example of how the promise of a bonus during the COVID-19 pandemic backfired.

In May 2021, the TSSA rail union hit out at the 'cynical and shocking stunt' after West Midlands Trains sent an email to staff, purportedly from the managing director, thanking them for their hard work in keeping the rail networks operational during the pandemic, and promising everyone a one-off bonus. People were invited to click on the link to read more details, but, instead of bearing good news, those that clicked were instead told that they had failed a 'phishing simulation test' and there was no bonus (Topham, 2021).

The union highlighted that it was 'totally crass and reprehensible', given that one worker had died during the pandemic and many more were taken ill yet staff continued to operate critical services.

In Chapter 4, we saw how attackers used COVID-19 as a phishing lure to entice people into taking specific action by playing on people's emotions and fears. A company spokesperson for the train company used this to explain why they had performed the phishing simulation. So, let me explain why this approach doesn't work:

- First, it leaves people despondent because, if a company can use a traumatic event to prove how its staff can be manipulated, then staff members will believe that the company does not care about their feelings.

- Second, what did it change? Do we think that people were more engaged and motivated? Do we think that they now see security in a positive light, and do we believe that they feel more empowered to report a phishing attempt? Or did it have the opposite effect?

Why security awareness fails

Beyond the emotional manipulation and stress that people find themselves under when confronted with phishing and awareness training that catches them out, let's look at other factors that may get in the way of a successful training strategy.

Too simplistic

While wanting security awareness to be accessible and understandable, there is often a tendency to oversimplify the types of cyber attack and what to look for, for example that phishing messages contain poor grammar, spelling mistakes and poorly designed logos. However, with the advent of phishing-as-a-service, many emails are purposely created and engineered to look like an exact replica of the organization's standard emails or text messages. Some even go so far as to redirect people to the correct website, after they inadvertently enter their credentials into the fake website. As training evolves, so does the attackers' ability to counteract it. Therefore, relying on people to spot a fake message is getting much harder.

One size fits all

Many organizations deploy the same level of training to every employee, irrespective of role or relevance. Therefore, people are not engaged in the training and don't understand or care about the outcomes expected of them. What may be applicable to someone in accounting would differ from someone in human resources. There will undoubtedly be common *foundational* levels of training that may be required for all employees, but the security awareness programme needs to operate beyond that, to cater for different requirements.

Counter-intuitive advice

Many programmes remind people not to click links or respond to unsolicited emails, which, in a digital environment, is both counter-intuitive and unhelpful. Many people will feel confused about what to click and when and so are more likely to rely on instinct, or be too busy and stressed to care. Remember what we covered in Chapter 3 about the language that attackers use, and sending messages at times of the day when people may be off guard. Unless the individual is the specific target of the message, attackers tend to cast the net far and wide to see who bites.

Tick-box for compliance

Many security awareness programmes are driven by a need to demonstrate compliance to a specific framework and policy. Metrics are driven by how many people successfully completed the training within a specific time frame. Success may be determined by a *simple* multiple-choice quiz, as opposed to practical application. If the training is too simplistic, some people are likely to go directly to the quiz or backtrack to get the correct answers. So, think about the measures you may be utilizing and what purpose they serve. A more effective measure might be to identify whether there was a marked increase in people that reported phishing messages, whether real or part of a simulation. Should the person do so, it is also a good idea to follow up with them, to assess what made them believe it was phishing, and to thank them for being security aware.

Awareness delivered only once a year

Many programmes are delivered on an annual recurring basis, rather than in relation to the changing and dynamic risk as it happens. As we have discussed, attackers vary their techniques and exploits to follow the news of the day and what is most likely going to get a reaction. Often organizations will deliver a campaign to coincide with 'cyber awareness month' and then forget about it for the rest of the year. As well as varying the frequency, and topics for awareness, analyse changes in language or lures from real phishing attempts to determine what factors changed and whether these were successful or not.

Delivery mechanism

Many programmes are delivered in the same way, for example e-learning, and so people know what the format will consist of. These are often dull and repetitive and don't grab the attention of the person, and they can often feel disengaged as a result. As we have identified, some neurodiverse people may not respond in the same way to the emotional cues that attackers may utilize to manipulate people, so, as well as a range of delivery mechanisms, we need to ensure that training is inclusive and caters for different accessibility needs. For people that find it hard to engage in group exercises or concentrate for long periods, it may be helpful to offer bite-sized learning that can be taken at different times. By varying the type and style of training, it will lead to more active participation.

Focusing on the negative

All too often, cybersecurity awareness focuses on the pessimistic, where only bad things happen and where there are negative consequences when things go wrong or when people fail to follow policy. The threat of disciplinary action only serves to turn people off the subject, hence why they are less likely to engage. By concentrating on the positive influence that security has on the individual, they feel more engaged.

But what if your role does require more in-depth training, and what if security, resilience and privacy is fundamental to your role? What is going to be required to meet the needs of those people, and how will that evolve over time, to cater for the types of threat and attack that we are being exposed to?

The power of education

Think back to what ex-fraudster Tony Sales said in Chapter 2, where he mentioned that 'education educates out crime'. This was made in reference to the circumstances that many people find themselves in when they feel that they have limited social standing and opportunities, and hence are forced into making difficult choices.

Education is about *obtaining broad knowledge and theory*, while training is about *applying practical skill*. Both are important, but, arguably, many cybersecurity awareness programmes do not go far enough to educate on the theory and knowledge required to understand *what and why* before people can apply those skills in the workplace. As we shall discuss in Chapter 13, it is not enough to just touch on the practicalities of cybersecurity, it is necessary to also consider the real-world human impact and the complexities of the human attackers and their motivations.

In addition, we have identified that there are many young people with high intellect and inquisitive minds for learning. Yet frustration, and boredom, means that technical skills are being misdirected and misused (as well as abused by peers). In Chapter 6, we saw how some teenagers have already learnt how to be prolific attackers, so a question to ask ourselves is whether education on cybersecurity is being taught at the right level and at the right time? Arguably, if we wait until people join organizations before they receive appropriate education on the issues identified, it is already too late.

Quite often, seeing is believing, and by visualizing the art of the possible and how they might use those skills in different ways, people may choose a different path. We therefore need to consider how we influence the next generation to move away from a career in cybercrime to one in cybersecurity.

Of course, you are not going to be able to influence the entire education system, but you may have the opportunity to enable people in your organization to attend career fairs, speak at events and mentor young people. The same goes for older people who have already embarked on a different path, or lost their direction, who are yearning to put their skills to use or gain new ones.

Changing mindsets

One fantastic way to bring this to life is through the story of Sarah Morris, Professor of Digital Forensics and Director of Enterprise for the School of Electronics and Computer Science at the University of Southampton. I have known Professor Morris for several years, having taken an avid interest in the 'weird and wonderful' world of digital forensics that she helped foster and build.

In a surprising twist of fate, this is also a tale of two halves, since Professor Morris and Lauri Love, the former Anonymous hacktivist we met in Chapter 6, studied at college together. It is testament to how two gifted people, with similar skills and an aptitude for maths and computers, can go on to lead parallel lives, as each decision took them on a separate journey. Let's explore that journey further.

Navigating childhood and college

From a young age, Professor Morris became hooked on coding and what computers could do. She took any opportunity to finish her lessons early and go to the computer room to learn more. At the age of 16, she enrolled in sixth form, but she struggled on which subjects to choose. She was adamant that she wanted to take maths and law, but was struggling for the third subject, and was over the moon to find that she could study computer science. Studying computer science and maths was how she met Lauri Love.

Studying with Lauri Love

Professor Morris describes how she and Lauri Love often felt like outcasts and developed a kinship.

Affectionately, she recalls how Love appeared to be in a world of his own, finishing assignments quickly, but looking bored, as if it was all too easy for him and he was not challenged by the activities. In retrospect, and reflecting on what Love said in Chapter 6, he acknowledged his struggle to balance 'extreme arrogance and humility' and had a level of untapped skill beyond what he learnt in the classroom. It is perhaps no wonder that he found solace online with like-minded peers and found new ways to utilize his skills.

From college to university

When determining what degree to take, Morris landed on computer science, specializing in AI.

She didn't know it at the time, but AI was about to take off in a big way. Her undergraduate project was to design a poker player using a Darwinian type of AI – utilizing the principle of adaptation and 'survival of the fittest' to determine how to outwit the opponent.

Professor Morris recalls that some friends were building their own casino games, but they ended up putting their own money into it and betting on their own algorithms. As she explains, you can see how people with such skills could be swayed into serious gambling, fraud or addiction. You know how to build, and break, the system – it's what makes it fun and scary at the same time. You are taught to explore and to take it to the next level, but you don't really understand the consequences of your actions yet, or how others might take advantage of you.

This bears a striking resemblance to that of Navinder Sarao, who we also met in Chapter 6, where learning how to beat and spoof financial trades was just a game to him, yet fraudulent investors were able to take advantage of his skill. It is a reminder of how vulnerable many young people can be and how others might wish to exploit their newly found skills if they are not being adequately supported.

The transition to digital forensics

Professor Morris turned down the opportunity to study for a PhD in AI, because her heart was not in it, so she decided to work as a teacher in the interim.

When she was ready to think about a PhD again, she applied for lots of different placements until she had an interview at Cranfield University's Shrivenham campus, based at the Defence Academy of the UK. Little did she know that the panel she interviewed with had several PhDs available. While she had applied for electronics and networking, it was halfway through the interview when the professor of cybersecurity and digital forensics stated that he had a PhD available in forensic computing, and which would she prefer? She didn't even know what forensic computing was, and, after what felt like a long pause, the professor looked at her A-levels – maths, computing and law – and said that was exactly forensic computing!

Professor Morris studied for her PhD in forensic computing at Cranfield University, and spent 14 years there, working on police cases. The setting being a military academy meant that the police could be assured over the strict levels of physical and logical security required to deal with complex and difficult cases, which includes child abuse and murder.

Try as they might, some criminals are not good at covering their tracks, or they have a level of arrogance that assumes they won't get caught. We will dive into this aspect further in Chapter 15, where we discuss some of Professor Morris' notable cases, and lessons learnt on the importance of collating evidence and forensics.

But first, I want to discuss her late diagnosis with autism. Not just how this was a revelation for her, but how, ultimately, it enabled her to thrive in the field of forensics.

An autism diagnosis and the stigma of neurodiversity

Just like Lauri Love, Professor Morris was not diagnosed with autism until later in life. After being on anxiety medication for three years because of the pressures that came with some of the police cases, a doctor stated they were treating the symptom and not the cause and suggested an autism test. Professor Morris had identified coping 'systems' that would manifest to help her deal with anxious situations, even to the point of analysing the sensory feel that she associated with clothes and how certain garments would either calm her or lead to stress.

She explains that there is a whole generation of people who have yet to be diagnosed, and who don't yet understand why and how they feel or act differently from those around them. They often know that they feel different, but they don't know what to do about it, and there is generally a stigma surrounding people who identify as neurodiverse.

Dealing with traumatic cases

After finally being diagnosed with autism in 2019, things started to make sense for Professor Morris. For example, her desire and gift for working on complex cases came with an innate ability to disassociate herself from the harmful and graphic content that she was exposed to during investigations. She identified that people who are openly neurodiverse often find digital forensics easier than their neurotypical colleagues because they can switch off, up to a point, and they don't experience the same emotional connection to some cases.

When Professor Morris took over the Digital Investigation Unit at Cranfield, it mostly examined criminal cases. Being acutely aware of the graphic content of the case work and wanting to ensure that people were not overly exposed to such images, a decision was made to perform more civil case work, such as forensics work for organizations, museums and newspapers. They ended up doing all the 'weird and wonderful' cases, which Morris openly asked for.

Becoming a professor

After a long tenure at Cranfield, it was time for Professor Morris to try something new.

The University of Southampton was looking for seven new professors across different fields. Morris identified that they didn't teach digital forensics, and so she pitched it to them. When she was offered a professorship, she was over the moon. Not only has it become her dream role, but the university is building an array of specialist labs for case work and research and a crime-scene room where students can reverse engineer and reassemble devices and machines to see how they work and how they might be tampered with.

Professor Morris is also creating a range of short courses to encourage more people to learn about different aspects of forensics. When you learn about how such technology works, however, you are also learning how to bypass system controls, and so students are strictly vetted before joining. Morris is aware of some people who have unfortunately used such skills for nefarious purposes.

Through her years of teaching, Morris identified that there is a high proportion of people who are neurodiverse who are drawn into electronics and computer science. She says that Southampton University has adapted to people's different needs without making a big deal of it. It is welcoming and inclusive without people feeling like they are being singled out. It really brings to bear what Tony Sales said about education 'educating out' crime if people know what opportunities are available and how they might be supported.

There are a few important aspects we can draw from this, not just in terms of the power of education, but how people with the same skill and aptitude can make different life choices. Without strong guidance, it is easy to see why some people can be persuaded to use their talents for nefarious purposes. We therefore need to consider how we identify the potential in individuals, by articulating how their skills and interests can lead to fulfilling careers in technology and cybersecurity. For Professor Morris, it took over eight years of study before someone helped to fully connect the dots.

Sharing such stories can help people overcome their doubts that they can switch subjects, or careers, to one that fits their aspirations. What started as a teenage obsession for Sarah Morris has turned into a career with passion. How many others might resonate with that?

Making security relevant and engaging

We have discussed why your security awareness training might not be working and how education has the power to waken the senses when provided as early as possible, so let's consider how to make security relevant and engaging for all, no matter the background.

Everything starts with why

Think back to how West Midlands Trains used an email purporting to be from the managing director promising a bonus as part of a phishing simulation. What could have been done differently?

One key technique in cyber defence is to explain the *why* right up front, by analysing attackers' motivations. Why might attackers use a Covid phishing lure? Why would they use the promise of a bonus to entice people to click on a link, or open an attachment? And why might this be dangerous for the company if they unwittingly enter their credentials? Let's consider this further.

Think about your current corporate policies, whether that is security or other policies. It will no doubt be filled with a list of dos and don'ts, reminding people that they might be disciplined if they don't follow policy. But do you explain why? What is the rationale and reason behind the policy, and what problem are you trying to solve? Why are you asking people to perform a specific action? How does the policy or required action help to improve the overall security posture?

Remember what we discussed in Chapter 2 about social sciences and how humans have an innate need to create social bonds with like-minded peers. That applies equally well in a security setting because we want people to have a sense of purpose, to understand where they fit in and how they contribute – not just in terms of their specific role but in their overall contribution to the success of the organization and how that helps to inspire trust with consumers and the brand.

Sir Richard Branson, founder of the Virgin empire, once famously said: 'By taking care of employees, everything else will take care of itself' (Krapivin, 2018). As we will explore in Chapter 15, how we think the business works and how it actually works are two different things. In addition, leadership and culture can either make or break the company. As we identified in the previous chapter, when an employee, or group of employees, shows apathy, it increases the insider threat. Not only because people are being less diligent and are likely to make mistakes, but, if they become despondent and pessimistic, it can lead to malicious behaviour. We will discuss more on strategies for enabling effective leadership in Chapter16.

Bear in mind that, despite training and education, there will still be people who fail to follow, or care about the policies, and will continue to do what they want and in their own way. This is where technology plays its part, acting as the safety net and guardrail, by embedding policies into system controls and default settings. We will discuss more on defending through the layers in Chapter 15.

Establishing relevance

So, how can we make security more relevant to those in the organization? In essence, what does it mean to me personally and professionally, and why should I care?

In the digital era, it is getting much harder to separate work life from personal life. There is a high likelihood that people will engage across a multitude of social groups and forums. Security has a role to play across all those areas.

Being relevant means removing the oversimplicity associated with training and awareness exercises, enabling people to understand the realities and complexities of security, and how they are not just part of the problem but a critical aspect to enabling the solution.

Learning from actual events and near misses

Often, there is a tendency to want to come up with elaborate stories and scenarios that often do seem exaggerated or contrived. There is no better way of increasing awareness than to learn from real incidents and events that have happened within the organization or to others. You can even use the case studies and anecdotes in this book to understand the will and motivation of attackers, some of the methods utilized, why they work and how to overcome them. It is also important to note the positives, like the story of Professor Morris.

While there is often a stigma with being a victim of cybercrime or fraud (as we discuss in the next chapter), stepping through the aspects of each attack, and being objective on what happened and why, can help to put things into perspective. There are two things to consider here:

- How actual events played out within the organization that was attacked.
- How such an event could play out in your organization, accepting that you have different technologies and controls, but envisioning each of the steps required to thwart the attack.

This level of sharing and collaboration works both ways, and, for you to learn from others, you need to be willing to let others learn from you. For example, following a severe attack in May 2021 by the Conti ransomware group, which impacted the systems of multiple hospital trusts during the height of the Covid pandemic, the Ireland Health Services Executive made the decision to publish the entire 150-page post incident review performed by PWC (2021), without redactions. This included the sequence of events and decisions that led up to and happened during the ransomware attack, as well as the impact to hospital trusts and patients that were dealing with the pandemic. This level of transparency helps to reinforce the scale of such cyber attacks and helps to identify and heed the warning signs.

The interesting thing about near misses is that you rarely hear about them unless they have made front-page news, and they can quickly be forgotten about, but they are an incredible source of information and education.

Near misses should be treated like the real thing; they must be logged and analysed and actions recorded. A slight change in parameters could have led to a different outcome, so take the time to explore the possibilities. When considering the context of the near miss, and what could have happened if the incident were not resolved or contained, it is necessary to look forward and consider the consequences and impact if those actions did not take place (Armstrong-Smith, 2022). This is why learning from actual incidents and near misses can be a valuable tool in support of security awareness and education at all levels.

It is worth bearing in mind, however, that when evaluating lessons learnt from actual events or near misses from within your own organization, some people can be stuck in hindsight. Once they know more about the details of an event, they may look back with emotions of guilt or shame, which is normal. In the next chapter, we shall discuss how to avoid victim blaming and scapegoating through the power of introspection. This emotional disassociation helps people to focus on the lessons learnt and overcome the shame, regret, or guilt – so they can move forward and learn from the experience.

Conclusion

In this chapter, we have performed a critical analysis of why many security awareness programmes fail to yield the required results, and why playing with emotions can often backfire. It can create division between the very people that we need to protect and secure, and it can cause untold reputation damage if such stories were to reach the media.

We have explored how education differs from awareness, and, if we can identify and nurture those that exhibit exceptional skills much earlier, we have an opportunity to change their mindset. This relies on not just educating people in the workplace, but considering how we can broaden this much wider, to have more relevance across all aspects of people's lives, including how people might influence and help their own children to be more digitally literate and cyber aware. Envisioning the type of careers that people can have can also help those with exceptional skills.

Being openly transparent about real-life events and near misses, and having a willingness and desire to learn from mistakes, requires us to consider how we identify and deal with such mistakes, and how our own culture might be contributing to those failings. It might be hard for us to comprehend, but that is exactly what we will discuss over the next two chapters, to determine what we can do about it.

References

Armstrong-Smith S (2022) *Effective Crisis Management*, BPB Publishing, London

Krapivin, P (2018) 'Sir Richard Branson's five billion reasons to make your employees and candidates happy', *Forbes*, 9 July, forbes.com/sites/pavelkrapivin/2018/07/09/sir-richard-bransons-5-billion-reasons-to-make-your-employees-candidates-happy (archived at https://perma.cc/8MQW-8DWY)

PWC (2021) 'Conti Cyberattack on the HSE: Independent Post Incident Review',
    3 December, hse.ie/eng/services/publications/conti-cyber-attack-on-the-hse-full-
    report.pdf (archived at https://perma.cc/WW38-L3GJ)

Topham, G (2021) 'Train firm's "worker bonus" email is actually a cybersecurity
    test', *The Guardian*, 10 May, theguardian.com/uk-news/2021/may/10/train-
    firms-worker-bonus-email-is-actually-cyber-security-test (archived at https://
    perma.cc/BWK7-V7YD)

13

Are people really the weakest link?

CHAPTER OBJECTIVES

In this chapter, we challenge the adage that people are the weakest link when it comes to cybersecurity. When faced with a major incident, there is often an inherent need to seek justice and to hold someone to account. We are quick to jump to conclusions before investigating the full facts.

We shall explore the issues when it comes to victim shaming and scapegoating and how to overcome these through introspection.

Some security practitioners believe that the human is always the weakest link because they are driven by instinct, and curiosity leads to mistakes. While people will make their own decisions, these are not always rational or bound by logic, as we have discussed. It is easy to apply a label to unilaterally blame people, but situations and solutions are much more complex than that. Let's consider why.

Victim blaming and shaming

Reflecting on what Dr Elisabeth Carter discussed in Chapter 3, generally, less than 5 per cent of fraud is reported to law enforcement because of the shame, embarrassment and stigma that surrounds victims, especially individuals who may have had their identity or money stolen.

Dr Carter believes that, as a society, we have left victims of cybercrime and fraud unprotected, as the onus is on them to report the crime, fight their cause and repair their identity and reputation. Often police may look at them with a degree of scepticism. Meanwhile, some victims of violent crimes are given emotional support and access to specially trained officers who can assist with the negative feelings that may arise.

To bring clarity to this subject, Dr Carter collaborated with the UK National Trading Standards Scams Team to highlight the level of coercion in romance and financial scams, and how ill-equipped the victim is to deal with the situation (Hawkswood et al, 2022). The research has been adopted as an All-Party Parliamentary Group report on consumer protection.

Simply labelling victims as *naïve, stupid* or *greedy* ignores the reality that we are all vulnerable to a persuasive approach, regardless of status or circumstance. We all have the same emotions and stressors that can make us act impulsively or irrationally. Key life events, such as marriage, divorce, redundancy, bereavement, can all increase someone's susceptibility to an attack. Now imagine how these stressors were amplified during the Covid pandemic.

The reason why frauds are so successful is nothing to do with the capabilities of the victim. It is the perpetrators' ability to effectively groom people into thinking they are making good, reasonable choices and empowered decisions, by engineering the situation to their advantage. If victims were able to determine that they were being manipulated or groomed, they would not be in that position in the first place. The fact that they don't see it, or how precarious the situation has become, only adds to the deep feelings of shame that can manifest. This can be particularly prevalent in younger, as well as older, generations. Due to the low levels of reporting, public perception surrounding cybercrime, and the tactics utilized, people may not even realize they are a victim of an attack. There is limited information available in the public domain from which they can learn.

As well as the financial and emotional impact, people often report that an attack impacts their health and well-being. The research highlights that using a trauma-informed approach in how we work with victims helps to avoid re-traumatizing people. Instead of using language that belittles or shames victims, consider how you can reassure, encourage and empower the person. This helps them to learn from their experience and build resilience. It can also help them to become champions for other victims.

WHAT IS A TRAUMA-INFORMED APPROACH?

Trauma-informed approaches have become increasingly cited in policy and adopted in practice as a means for reducing the negative impact of traumatic experiences and supporting mental and physical health. Trauma-informed practice is an approach to health that is grounded in the understanding that trauma exposure can impact an individual's neurological, biological, psychological and social development. The practice acknowledges the need to see beyond an individual's behaviour and ask, 'What does this person need?' rather than 'What is wrong with this person?' (UK Government, 2022)

Strategies for avoiding victim blaming

So, what can be done about this, and how can your strategy help?

- Shift the focus from what the victim did to make them so vulnerable towards how the attackers are so powerfully manipulative. This involves evaluating the technical and non-technical skills utilized by attackers to create and use fake profiles, their trust-building social engineering skills and their use of language. There is often a 'set up and drip feed' of disinformation to distort the victim's reality. The attacker needs the victim to be a willing participant to avoid arousing suspicion. This means that attackers are often willing to put the time into ensuring the victim is primed for, and receptive to, sending money (Carter, 2021). This forms part of the powers of persuasion we discussed in Chapter 3.

- Determine whether there is an inherent blame culture within the organization, and how that has manifested. Are there previous cases from within the organization that can be researched to establish what improvements could be made?

- Take steps to educate people into changing the language and removing the stigma about how we speak to and treat victims. This includes the perception that only naïve or greedy people are victims of scams.

Scapegoating

In a similar way to victim blaming, scapegoating is typically used by an organization to apportion blame to a specific person or group for their mistakes, misgivings and wrongdoings. The principle of scapegoating is often used in response to a large-scale, distressing event. Typically, this is in the public domain, with media attention. There may be cries of outrage as people demand answers and they want them quickly. The use of a scapegoat can often be appealing as a defence mechanism as it deflects the issues onto someone else or another group.

The 'best' scapegoat is one that has limited means and resources with which to defend themselves. It is rare that a scapegoat is a member of the elite or leadership, since they often have the means and resources to retaliate and defend themselves. Individuals or groups who are subservient are more likely to find themselves victims of scapegoating. Those that find themselves labelled in such ways are also the subject of harsher policies as everyone in that group gets labelled in a similar way, for example how people are labelled 'repeat offenders' during phishing exercises or other security-related tests. By labelling them as such, we are criminalizing their behaviour rather than examining why it happens.

Rather than benefitting from investment in the time and resources to tackle the underlying causes and issues, the scapegoat becomes a symbolic reference. It gives the organization a way of directing frustrations away from the actual issues, to refocus attention and stabilize the situation. By focusing on the scapegoat, who may have left the organization or been prosecuted, it creates a sense of closure from the figurative sacrifice that has been made.

What happens when that one person or group that you have tried to scapegoat takes a stand and turns into the whistleblower – the aggrieved insider who has nothing to lose and everything to gain? There is nothing that society loves more than to get behind the plight of the underdog or someone facing an obvious abuse of power and hierarchy. The use of social media can often act as a force multiplier when people decide to get behind and support the scapegoat.

Just like victim blaming, utilizing a scapegoat shifts accountability and actual blame away from the attacker. Not only is the attacker free to continue their path, but nothing has changed – it merely shifts the problem.

How to avoid scapegoating

So, what can be done about this, and how can your strategy help?

- The first thing is to acknowledge whether your organization has a history of scapegoating, and what is driving this. Analysing previous incidents can help to identify common factors.

- Bring the issues and dangers of scapegoating to the forefront, and how such practices rarely lead to a positive outcome.

- Establish the motivation behind the scapegoat, and what it is trying to achieve. How might alternative approaches deliver a better resolution?

- Remove the emotion from the situation by establishing facts and timelines. Remain objective with regards to performing an unbiased investigation with no preconceived ideas on guilt or blame.

- Embrace the fact that people will make mistakes, that there are flaws in processes, and therefore you can identify what steps need to be taken to drive effective change and avoid repeat incidents.

- Even in the case of wilful deception and deceit, there will still have been errors in the process, which enabled events to manifest in the way they did.

Introspection

The practice of overcoming or avoiding victim blaming and scapegoating requires a degree of introspection. Looking inward doesn't come naturally for many people; it is something that you must actively do and participate in. It is often easier to deflect from the situation outwards and become defensive, which is why people look for someone else to blame.

When people fear consequences, such as being ridiculed or disciplined, they are less likely to come forward and are less willing to state what they really think or what the issues are. Without time for introspection, things will bottle up and invariably get worse. We often end up repeating the same cycle and looking for another person or scapegoat to blame.

Keep in mind that we are often our worst critics. We choose to be more critical and harsher on ourselves than others would be. We may be inclined to just blame ourselves, which might not be wholly accurate. Some people may obsess over specific details, playing things over and over, which increases the stressors.

To provide people with assurance about how introspection will be utilized, it is good practice to remain objective. Rather than thinking negatively about what went wrong, consider the opportunities to improve. This encourages people to consider the process positively and assume a level of responsibility. Bringing people together also helps to overcome our natural biases by evaluating different perspectives.

Strategies to enable introspection

The challenge is not to wait until there is a major incident, but to make introspection part of how we do things by having a debrief during or after each major change and project, encouraging people to have a voice and share opinions. The key is the commitment to take affirmative action, otherwise it will have limited value. Focusing attention on safety and security builds resilience by asking: 'What did we miss? What did we take for granted? How can we change?' Note the emphasis is on *we,* not *you* – focusing on the individual can be construed as accusatory. Remember what we have noted about apathy and what happens when people feel threatened, stop caring or no longer take an active interest.

When performed in a calm, controlled manner away from the stressors that gave rise to the incident, introspection can help people to acknowledge and process what they did in a rational way, and explore whether under different circumstances they may have made different decisions.

Some other positive factors include:

- **Combine the *why* with the *what.*** Rather than simply asking, 'Why did this happen?', consider, 'What are the circumstances that enabled this to happen?' The second question is worded in a way that encourages a range of scenarios, rather than being a singular answer.

- **Encourage a natural curiosity.** Get people to reflect on the past, and challenge the status quo, by asking exploratory questions. 'This is the way it's always been' is a defensive answer and doesn't address the why.

- **Take time out.** If the world surrounding you is too busy and stressful, you need to take yourself out of it. This means taking periodic breaks, and agreeing a schedule with peers, so that each person is taking their allotted break. Encourage people to use the time to do something they enjoy, so that it becomes something they look forward to.

The follow-through

Having considered all the above, if you really believe that people are the weakest link, what will you do next?

If we consider that anyone and everyone can be a victim, the objective is to assess the organization's disciplinary procedure and the consequences if people don't follow company policies and protocols. Does this range from performance improvement, warnings and dismissal, and are you prepared to follow through on this?

Is the process applicable to every person without bias, or are you excluding people based on their position and authority?

If you exclude certain people, such as the CEO or the board, it creates a vulnerability that can be exploited as it falls outside the monitoring loop. Remember that people in authority can be impersonated in cases of business email compromise, and super malicious users are fully aware of where the gaps and loopholes are.

Attackers will find any way of getting access to the organization, so how easy or difficult are you going to make it for them?

As we discussed, we don't know how people will react on a given day, what decisions they will make under duress, and how that may affect the organization. What we do know is that we are all human, and no one should be excluded. With an assume-compromise mindset, we consider that any person can be targeted and manipulated and that an attacker has used social engineering to illicit information.

Conclusion

Often, we are so focused on what people did wrong that we forget to consider what the attacker did well. We must not lose sight of who the actual perpetrators are and how they were able to achieve their objectives by analysing what they did, and how, and what we need to do to strengthen our defence capability.

Rather than simply looking to apportion blame, let's consider the mechanisms and processes surrounding the event, and whether these are working as intended, or whether the attacker has identified and exploited the gaps.

As we discuss in the next chapter, it is necessary to consider the culture of the organization and leadership and how that may influence the policy of victim blaming and scapegoating. Consider that whatever the process or culture, victim blaming and scapegoating rarely have a positive outcome for any party.

References

Carter, E (2021) 'Distort, extort, deceive and exploit: exploring the inner workings of a romance fraud', *British Journal of Criminology*, 61 (2): 283–302, doi.org/10.1093/bjc/azaa072 (archived at https://perma.cc/6JVS-YLMG)

Hawkswood, J, Carter, E and Brown, K (2022) *Coercion and Control in Financial Abuse: Learning from domestic abuse*, National Trading Standards Scams Team, October

UK Government (2022) 'Working definition for trauma-informed practice', Office for Health Improvement and Disparities guidance, gov.uk/government/publications/working-definition-of-trauma-informed-practice/working-definition-of-trauma-informed-practice (archived at https://perma.cc/JWJ6-ZYXU)

14

The human factor – mindset, cultural variances and what factors tip people over the edge

---

CHAPTER OBJECTIVES

In this chapter, we discuss how strategic culture and organizational culture play a pivotal role in the success or otherwise of the security strategy and programme.

We explore whether we are effectively tuned into culture, how people react to what is going on around them, and how that may help or hinder their actions on a given day. When people don't feel adequately supported, they stop caring.

We establish the key stressors, triggers and concerning behaviour that turn a risk into a serious threat, and how you might overcome this with empathy.

So, let's start by asking ourselves whether we are tuned into culture, how we deal with conflicting cultures and how well we really know our people.

Are you tuned into culture?

While researching for this book, I spoke with Nadja El Fertasi, former stakeholder engagement executive with NATO Communications and Information Agency, and founder of Thrive with EQ, where she prioritizes building human resilience within the sphere of cybersecurity. As a result, El Fertasi has a unique perspective on culture and leadership.

While working for NATO's cyber executive, El Fertasi was responsible for providing guidance on the digital impact of political and military priorities for the alliance, designing strategic away-days and seminars for senior military and political leadership, with a focus on cybersecurity and disruptive technologies.

The underpinning mission of NATO is to 'guarantee the freedom and security of its members through political and military means', but this comes with challenges as each member has a unique culture and agenda. This is important when considering the role of strategic culture, as discussed in Chapter 10, since a key mandate of the treaty is to consult and take decisions on security at all levels, with a view to obtaining *consensus* and common consent. Any agreement is the 'collective will' of the sovereign states that make up the alliance and has been the sole basis for decision-making since NATO was created in 1949 (NATO, 2023).

I want to reflect on a few aspects of culture and stakeholder engagement that I discussed with El Fertasi. During the last five to six years of her tenure, NATO was focused on adopting cybersecurity as a key operational domain. El Fertasi worked with key decision-makers, such as ambassadors, military committees and private sector entities, to transform and develop the cybersecurity programmes. This meant shifting mindsets to work more securely, which was a complex dynamic since there was a cultural issue about information and intelligence sharing, even across the alliance. Many nations were naturally quite hesitant about intelligence sharing due to national interests and running different classifications of systems and networks.

Dealing with conflicting cultures

Imagine how difficult it can be to reach a consensus inside your own organization. Now imagine how difficult it is to reach a consensus across all member states of NATO.

El Fertasi explains that the delegations within NATO share information and intelligence through a hierarchal and classified system to preserve national interests. Each nation has its own computer systems and networks, each with different security classifications. Sharing intelligence, and in a format that is useable, is incredibly difficult. The other issue is that NATO is often seen as a 'fighting machine', but the main objective is to de-escalate situations using political persuasion.

This requires cooperation and collaboration across multiple stakeholders. Most ambassadors are non-technical, so, rather than telling them how cybersecurity operations work, El Fertasi showed them. It is the same principle with military exercises – it is great having a strategic plan, but the camaraderie only shines through by conducting large-scale immersive exercises.

El Fertasi likens this to the c-suite in most organizations. Unless they are the CISO or CIO, they are likely to find cybersecurity complex. They may not want to deal with it, or don't know how to deal with it, in case it reveals how much they don't understand, and so it is easier for them to delegate. But, as we have identified, cybersecurity is not just a technical issue – it affects the entire business. Therefore, top-down leadership members need to understand it, as, otherwise, how can they make effective decisions about the security and resilience of the organization?

As El Fertasi highlights, if you left geopolitical decisions to military commanders, many of the issues that NATO deal with would have very different outcomes and most likely would include military action without taking into consideration the full political impact. This is why the level of in-depth discussion and debate is required with ambassadors to ensure there is a level of accountability in the actions and outcomes proposed.

The other key aspect is the level of preparedness that comes with the ability to take actions. Let's take Russia and the war in Ukraine as an example. NATO spends a lot of time performing risk assessments and calculating the likelihood and impact of a nuclear bomb versus a missile strike, or a terrorist attack versus an offensive cyber attack. It is important to understand that every action causes a chain reaction, so you don't just have to be prepared and accountable for the decision made but what is likely to come next as a result.

There is much we can learn here regarding organizational leadership, preparedness and accountability, which we shall explore further in Chapter 16. But first, let's discuss issues with public perception and how this has a bearing on effective decision-making.

Dealing with public perception

As you might expect from an alliance such as NATO, there are many secrets and much information that is kept away from the public. As Nadja El Fertasi commented, however, we are moving into an era where people are more socially and geopolitically aware. They want more transparency and to be able to hold nations and elected officials to account. A mindset of 'what you don't know won't harm you' doesn't work any more, particularly when considered next to the level of psychological warfare and cyber influence operations that many adversarial nations are adopting. The ability to control and influence how the public think and act, through social media and carefully crafted news stories, is having a large impact on how people make sense of the world around them. When their own nation keeps them in the dark, it only serves to compound the issue.

El Fertasi believes that we are living in a 'world of influence', where everyone is trying to entice you. In particular, the world of digital influencers, and the sheer volume of social media channels, means we develop a need for instant gratification, when we see likes and followers, and succumb to ways in which such accounts or organizations try to engender brand loyalty. Is it any wonder, therefore, that attackers try to mimic that loyalty and gratification by effectively turning a person's emotion up or down depending on how they perceive the organization or brand?

It makes sense, when we think back to Chapter 2 in terms of why certain attacks are so successful, but also why victim blaming and shaming is not the answer, as discussed in the previous chapter. So, bringing this closer to home with your organizational culture and brand – how well do you really understand your people, how they are feeling and how they operate?

Do you really understand your people?

Before we consider in the next chapter the actual roles that people perform, let's think about the people in your organization and the culture surrounding them. Some questions to consider:

- What is the general mood of the people?
- Do they feel motivated, or are there deep-rooted issues that make people feel on edge?
- How do you even know how people are feeling?
- Do you understand what other factors might be going on in their lives, which might be taking a higher priority right now?
- When it comes to the security and safety culture of the organization, is it a general laissez-faire attitude, where people assume someone somewhere is taking care of things, or are they genuinely engaged?

Having a good awareness and understanding of the existing organizational and security culture can help put things into perspective. It allows you to understand how the current security programme is working (assuming you have one), the current barriers to success and how much work may be required to shift mindsets.

Trying to shift the entire culture of an organization is not an easy task, and is not for you to bear alone, as this requires top-down leadership and proactive action to deliver long-term change, but that doesn't mean that you can't influence it. The key is understanding the current state of play and what you are up against. This serves two purposes – understanding the factors and triggers that may make someone susceptible to an external attack and which factors may also highlight a propensity for an insider threat, irrespective of whether the intent is accidental or malicious.

Remember, there are no superhumans, and how the organization overall is feeling also affects those people working in security and technology too. Just like we discussed in the previous chapter, they too can be stressed, tired, despondent or susceptible to making mistakes.

It could be argued that we have more control and opportunity to enable effective change by examining what is going on within our own organization and taking mitigating action. All too often, the focus of organizations is on the external threat, but by paying more attention to the insider threat, we can also enable people to be better prepared for external threats too. Particularly where they are the target of social engineering and manipulation attempts.

It is often difficult for organizations to want to instigate an insider threat programme, in case it is construed as Big Brother watching their every move and impeding on their privacy. It is important to get the balance right. So, let's consider the power of emotions and the importance of well-being, and how we might change people's perceptions on how we think about and manage the insider risk.

The power of emotions

As we identified in Chapter 3, no matter how much you provide awareness on the type and scale of different cyber attacks, nothing can override the strength of the human emotion in that moment – those that have a direct effect on our body and decisions, whether endorphins, adrenaline or stress.

As much as we think we know about how we might react in each situation, when faced with our strongest emotions, we can't say for sure whether we would react in the same way. Both ex-fraudster Tony Sales and criminologist Dr Elisabeth Carter agree that attackers are tuned in to how to take advantage of this – whether through happiness, love and lust, or anger, fear and anxiety. So, is there a way to help people feel and control those emotions and learn how to deal with them as they arise?

This is one of the reasons why El Fertasi developed Thrive with EQ – to provide a mechanism for people to understand what triggers them, and how emotional resilience and well-being can combine to help people stop and think and rationalize their thoughts even when deep emotions arise that may cloud their judgement.

Reflecting on her time in NATO, El Fertasi recalls that she would often clash with certain personalities and she would be drawn into emotiveness that surrounded her. She leveraged her impulse control to proactively train herself to think and act differently. It is a conscious effort that requires introspection, as we discussed in the previous chapter, where you catch yourself in the moment and recognize the triggers. It is this that provides emotional intelligence so that your nervous system is in a calmer state, rather than in flight-or-fight mode.

It takes time and patience to read the signals and to feel the discomfort of an emotion. For example, some people may try to suppress anxiety or fear, rather than letting it out. As El Fertasi states, people are not trained in how to just let it flow, as it feels uncomfortable, then, ultimately, it builds up.

El Fertasi believes that before you can begin to truly help others, you need to help yourself first. Since manipulation and coercion techniques are based on emotion, and we are not going to eradicate that, it is OK to be kind, but also to be alert. As El Fertasi teaches, there is a difference between being *nice* and being *kind*. If I'm being nice, I'm trying to get you to like me. If I'm being kind, I can still treat you like a human, but I'm going to be more assertive, by asking questions: 'Why are you asking me to take this action, and for what purpose?'

El Fertasi suggests that the best way to get to know someone quickly is to say no to them. When you don't give that person what they want, see how they react. Will they take it gracefully, or will they push harder? Another tactic is to stop responding and reacting to messages or requests as soon as you receive them, to allow yourself time to think. This does two things:

- It removes yourself from the immediate situation.
- It helps to determine if the person is respectful of your time or pushes harder with their request.

Living by your values

Reflecting on the power of emotions, let us think back to the 'seven sins of attackers' in Chapter 2, and how each sin or temptation could lead to another. And how each 'virtue' can act as a counterbalance:

- Pride versus humility.
- Greed versus charity.
- Lust versus chastity.
- Envy versus gratitude.
- Gluttony versus temperance.
- Wrath versus patience.
- Sloth versus diligence.

It stands to reason, therefore, that, when thinking about our deepest emotions and what drives us to act, some of these are positive and some negative and will affect how we see and deal with the world around us. It is important to understand that whether the attacker or the victim, we can all be drawn into these emotional states.

When thinking about the culture of your organization today, and where you want to be, are you acting as a help or hindrance?

- If our culture is one where we win at all costs at the expense of all others, where greed and gluttony is almost encouraged and we will do whatever it takes, is it any wonder that our people are driven by the same wants and desires? That is not to say that a desire to win is bad, but if it becomes the dominant factor above all others, you can see why that could become an issue.
- If our culture is one where we do what is best for our customers and colleagues, have humility when things go wrong, where we think about long-term success rather than short-term goals, then we can see how that same mindset could lead to a more positive culture for our people.
- Now, with a human-centric mindset, if we add patience and diligence behind each of our processes, we are slowing things down to a pace that enables people to stop and think before they act.

Consider what we have discussed about having a counterbalance – the idea is not to have complete opposites and extremes, as this goes too far one way or the other. For example, if you have a culture driven by charity and giving services away, you are probably not going to be very profitable, so, what is the right balance that we want to achieve, which is good for the organization and good for our people? Think of it as a sliding scale and a maturity measure. Where are you today? Where would you like to be? What is preventing those things from happening, and what led to those traits in the first place?

You are unlikely to be able to change the culture of the entire organization overnight, but understanding the barriers and limitations is a good starting point when considering the values and ethos of the organization and whether these virtues are truly being exhibited.

Dealing with the fear factor

So, let's now consider some of the factors that hinder people. A few questions to consider:

- How do you support someone who made a mistake?
- How do you support someone who has a grievance?
- How would you handle a whistleblower?
- How do you enable people to speak their minds while being respectful of others?

The culture of the organization has a large bearing on whether people feel comfortable in raising issues, and how this will be dealt with. If people don't feel supported, they are less likely to report issues. When people feel empowered to come forward, and highlight their mistakes, concerns and grievances without being punished or humiliated, or made to feel like a scapegoat, it can lead to *psychological safety*.

That means that people can take reasonable risks and go outside their comfort zone, but are also accountable for their actions. People need to be able to face their own fears and doubts and be transparent about them.

The fear is often personal to that person. For example, what is the greater fear between a person thinking they will be reprimanded for not meeting an urgent deadline versus the fear of breaking a security policy by taking sensitive documents home in order to fulfil their objective? They probably did their own subconscious risk assessment: what is best for them, rather than what is a risk to the organization.

It is akin to how we defend our actions because the ends justify the means, and therefore it is OK to break a few rules and amend the process if it helps to do our job. But can you see the issue here, because isn't that exactly what attackers do to justify their actions – that it is OK to steal from an organization because the end victim will get their money back, and so they can disassociate themselves from thinking about the consequences? So, you can see how small things become a pattern and how it escalates.

We will discuss how the occurrence of shadow processes in an organization can impact the effectiveness of security in the next chapter. The objective is not to remove the fear factor completely, as that can lead to complacency, but it is important to be able to notice changes in behaviour and understand how these might be triggered.

Spotting changes in behaviour

When determining the changes in behaviour that could increase insider risk, it is necessary to consider several key factors:

- Determine whether there is a **predisposition** for violating security policies, and why. This can start with small violations and escalate. Consider how you are monitoring small infractions and identifying what the cause is. This might be a case of simply not knowing or understanding the policy through to someone who is deliberately evading the policy to circumvent a specific control.

- Establish the type of **stressors** that may increase the risk. Has there been a negative event at work or in the person's private life that is making them more anxious? Examples of stressors in the workplace might include a poor performance review or a disgruntled employee being passed over for promotion. Examples of private-life stressors might be financial or medical concerns or a relationship breakdown. Such stressors may not be known if the person does not openly share information, but you could notice that they are more withdrawn, or perhaps using more profanities and airing their grievances publicly.

- Which of the stressors could become a motivating **trigger**? Think back to the 'seven sins of attackers' and how some people can be motivated by heightened levels of greed, envy, wrath or sloth as examples. Perhaps they are so adamant of what they believe in, pride gets in the way. So, consider what actions can be taken to help people manage a stressor before it leads to a triggering event.

- Have there been instances of **concerning behaviour**? In many cases of insider threat, concerning behaviour had been flagged by a supervisor or colleagues but the organization had failed to follow up or take appropriate action. Think back to Jack Teixeira in Chapter 11, where concerns had been raised three times about the airman inappropriately accessing highly classified information, yet he continued and supervisors took no action to remove his access or discipline his behaviour.

- Consider the level of **planning and preparation** that the person might do to fulfil their objective. Examples might be higher levels of data searches, mass printing and downloads, attempting to access data outside their authority, copying data to other devices or practising obfuscation techniques such as emailing documents or information to personal email boxes, changing file names or adding passwords to documents.

When we consider the planning and preparation phase, these are similar tactics and techniques that an external attacker might also use to hide their tracks.

So, how do we know the difference between a *malicious* user and a *compromised* user? In some cases, they may even be the same thing, as we saw with Lapsus$, where the attacker was willing to pay large sums of money to obtain credentials to target organizations or for the employee to upload software for the attacker to gain back-door access.

It will probably not surprise you that most organizations only become aware of an insider threat when it is too late – once the data has been leaked or destroyed and systems have been sabotaged, or after the employee has left the organization. Some actions may be so subtle that they may never be identified, and some organizations may not be monitoring for internal threats at all.

Your ability to spot those who have a predisposition for policy violations will largely be affected by the success of your security awareness programme, how you monitor policy adherence, and whether you have taken the time to explain *why* such policies are important and *why* they are relevant to them.

When we consider the strategy of how to reduce insider risk, and increase internal security, we need to consider two things:

- building an insider risk programme (which we discuss further in the next chapter)

- employee assistance and well-being programmes – such schemes can provide additional help and support to people who are feeling an array of stressors, but only work if they are readily available and proactively offered. This is a key component of being an empathetic leader, as we shall discuss next.

Establishing empathy

Empathy is so much more than just saying and doing the right thing. It is about having a deeper appreciation and understanding of how each interaction impacts people. Your words and actions have a lasting effect, whether you realize it or not (Armstrong-Smith, 2022).

Having empathy for another person, and their situation, is not just good for the people in your organization but is essential for the business too. Being able to pre-empt and manage the stressors that people may be facing can help to address and alleviate insider risks. This does not mean that an individual's manager needs to be personally accountable for that person's emotional state, but it does mean that the organization needs to have a range of mechanisms in place to identify and reduce stressors and triggers, before they become a threat. Nadja El Fertasi believes that practising empathy is core to emotional resilience, and the more we understand ourselves, the better we can all navigate stressful situations.

Humanizing the attacker

Another key aspect of empathy is to remove the fear factor we associate with cyber attackers. Consider that there is still an actual human behind the attack, and what may be motivating them.

Our perception of a criminal or terrorist is often quite different from reality, and because we have an image in our head of how we expect them to look and act, we often let our guard down and become over-trusting when faced with something different. For example, although most of the attackers discussed in this book have been men, attackers are women too. El Fertasi explains that part of the briefings at NATO was to understand this. Many women were used to influence Russian spies, as they were not expecting their counterparts to be women. In addition, some terrorist organizations would use women as suicide bombers, partly because men were more likely to be stopped and searched on patrols, as women were not associated with being terrorists. It is therefore important to highlight that no one is above suspicion.

We have been conditioned to think in a similar stereotypical way about cyber attackers – that they are faceless young men wearing hoodies, who operate from within enemy states; whereas they can easily be operating within our own nations and organizations and may be people we know. The more we can humanize the attacker, the less power they hold over us, and the more we can make informed and rational decisions.

Conclusion

In this chapter, we have considered the role of culture and how it has a bearing on a security strategy.

By taking a moment to slow down and consider how collaboration and communication helps effective decision-making, we are also empowering people to do the same. When considering the types of stressors that people are under, remember that these can be personal to the individual concerned as well as collective, based on current social, economic and geopolitical tensions that could influence organizational decisions.

When faced with a lack of transparency, people lack control. This can increase the fears and the doubts and even the shame that people may feel when faced with stressful events. Such events can trigger concerning behaviour if not effectively dealt with.

So, before we can consider whether we truly understand our business, let's first ask ourselves whether we truly understand our people and what it's going to take to make them feel safe and secure. Then we can do the same for the organization. When we are more tuned in to culture and how people are operating, we can be more self-aware regarding which strategies are going to be most effective at dealing with the human adversary.

References

Armstrong-Smith, S (2022) *Effective Crisis Management*, BPB Publishing, London

NATO (2023) 'What is NATO?', nato.int/nato-welcome/index.html (archived at https://perma.cc/5F9P-M67H)

15

Strategies for counteracting human adversaries

CHAPTER OBJECTIVES

In this chapter, we ask ourselves whether we really understand our business and how it operates.

When putting ourselves in the shoes of an attacker, we need to think holistically from inside out, and outside in, because, if people in the business can find a loophole without anyone noticing, then so can an attacker.

We explore the core strategies and how you can defend through each of the layers to slow the attacker down and recover quickly.

For any strategy to be successful, it requires people, process and technology, but, for many organizations, the security strategy tends to be heavily focused on technology. This is important, but we shall principally focus on the people element – to be more precise, *human-centric security*, which puts people front and centre of the strategy. It is about optimizing the relationship between humans and technology and the processes that fuse them together.

Since this book is about understanding the cyber attacker mindset, we need to reflect on the human behind the attacks, and their will and motivation. The other element is thinking about the people that touch your organization, such as employees, consumers and partners. We are thinking about who is most affected by any strategic decision because everything we do has an upstream and downstream impact. Whether that is a positive or negative experience depends on what you do next and what you deem as a priority.

Do you know your own business?

There is often a thought process in security that an attacker knows your business better than you. Realistically, how can that even be possible? You have people that have worked in the organization for many years and understand the processes implicitly. Some even designed the processes! So how could someone external to the organization really understand this better?

Well, the short answer is that we see things through a business lens – about how we presume things work, as opposed to how they might work in practice. Also, we are not looking at it from an attacker's perspective and standpoint. Attackers are looking at how they can bend or break a process to their advantage and how they can circumvent and take advantage of weak controls.

Many organizations use commercial IT software and products that attackers are familiar with. If they know the operating system or application, what version it is running and how it is configured, they can probably find an exploit for it. Initial access brokers in particular have a very clear objective on what their business model is and what they are trying to sell.

So, the first thing we want to think about is whether we have an inventory of assets and what is running on those assets; not just in terms of infrastructure and applications but what is hosted on them regarding business data, and the value of that data. That may sound obvious, but you might be surprised at how many organizations don't have an inventory, or at least one that is up to date and regularly maintained. The obvious question, therefore, is, if you don't know what you have, where it resides or how important it is, how can you secure and protect it?

Identifying shadow processes

How people do their role is often different to how you think they do it or what is documented about it. Just like shadow IT – when people download unauthorized applications from the internet – if you don't know about it, it is not a recorded asset or process. Therefore, how are you able to monitor it, know whether it is effective, or if it is being exploited? If people can circumvent technology and processes, and have done so regularly, it is a good indicator that perhaps the process or policy just does not work for them.

This is not about looking for ways to catch people out; it is about understanding the realities of the situation and the issues that may be prevalent. This is a great way of getting the people themselves to think about what they do and how they do it, and how an attacker could use the shadow process to their advantage. Of course, that can also highlight gaping holes in security controls because shadow processes were created with ease and without anyone noticing. So, let's consider their *why* and *intent* – what made them decide they needed to work in a different way?

Ultimately, if a person in your organization can figure out a workaround and find the path of least resistance, then why not an attacker? Most people create shadow processes without malicious intent. Instead, they may have just found a way to make these processes easier or more efficient. However, let's also consider the *super malicious insiders,* those individuals with deep technical knowledge who not only know how to circumvent existing controls but may have created new ones to fulfil a specific objective. So, we need to consider the fact that we have shadow IT and processes and what added functionality it may provide, and how that may change our perception of risk. For example, does it enable someone to make system configuration changes without authorization?

Let's take an example of how an Amazon manager not only identified loopholes to commit a $9 million fraud, but then recruited people from within the business to be party to the theft. Kayricka Wortham worked as an operations manager in an Amazon warehouse, which enabled her to set up and approve new vendors and invoices. Wortham told unknowing subordinates to input false seller information into the Amazon system, which she would then approve. Fake invoices were filed to Amazon, which enabled money to be transferred to bank accounts that she and her co-conspirators controlled. Wortham was assisted in the scheme by an Amazon employee working in loss prevention and one working in human resources. These co-conspirators provided names and social security numbers that were used to create the fake vendor accounts. For her part in the scheme, Wortham was sentenced to 16 years in prison (Jiménez, 2023).

There are several reasons why shadow processes may be formed. They can include:

- poor management practices
- lack of protective security controls

- poor security culture
- poor communication between business areas
- lack of awareness of people-risk at a senior level
- inadequate governance and audit processes.

Strategies for dealing with shadow processes

You may think the best option is to lock down devices and systems to prevent people from creating shadow processes, but this is probably why we got into this position in the first place. Onerous policies that work against how people need to operate are more likely to lead to frustration. Security is seen as a blocker rather than an enabler. There are two issues that we need to address here, both of which require open and transparent discussion:

1 Identifying where shadow processes already exist.

2 How to prevent a recurrence.

Consider how you might simplify the current procedure for addressing and evaluating users' requests for change. This might include common technology challenges and some approved alternatives or workarounds.

When you help people to identify the shadow processes they use and understand why these might be a risk, they assume a level of responsibility and are more likely to feel involved in assessing the mitigation. Remember what we said about how positive reinforcement is a better tactic than jumping to conclusions or looking for a scapegoat.

You may need to acknowledge and accept that there will be shadow processes that you don't know about and things that may never be revealed to you. A super malicious user knows all the loopholes but is not going to reveal them willingly. The fact that they know you are looking and monitoring may be enough for them to stop or rethink their actions. Either way, they are now on the back foot, just like other attackers who may intend to cause harm. Conversely, that one person who was despondent and showing apathy might be the key person that you get on side, as someone is now taking an avid interest in what they do and is listening to them.

It may take some time to understand the extent of shadow IT and processes, so this will need to be acknowledged as a risk. This is why you need to look at things objectively and without preconceived ideas on what is or is not in place.

Think like an attacker

If we accept that, realistically, we really should know our business, then we need to model this from *inside out* and *outside in*. How attractive might we be to an attacker and from what viewpoint? Perhaps something has changed in your business model or chosen markets or in the media that makes you a higher value target, or perhaps the attacker merely purchased access on the dark web.

The first thing to do is model the business from our perspective, so *inside out*. Then we need to pivot this to *outside in*, from an attacker's perspective. If you didn't have the benefit of foresight, to know what you have and where it resides, what steps would you need to join the dots together?

Many organizations start from outside in, by utilizing security penetration testing to reveal all the vulnerabilities. So, let me explain why it is useful to consider this from a different perspective. By starting from *inside out*, we already have a good idea of the path that an attacker would need to take and the potential vulnerabilities, and hence the priorities for closure. This is a more proactive way of looking at things, as we are much more prepared, and can use the security test to validate our understanding.

We know that attackers have different motivations: some may be stimulated by greed or gluttony, while others may be driven by kudos, wrath or envy. The truth of the matter is that you may never know *who* exactly is attacking you, or *why*. Whether you are the intended target or just unlucky, it therefore pays to have an open mind. Consider what the impact would be from an opportunist, activist, organized crime, nation-sponsored actor or insider. If they had unfettered access to a specific system or data, what could they do with it, and why might they be motivated to do so? This 'what if' and 'so what' analysis aims to consider and prioritize a range of plausible scenarios and helps to prioritize remediation. If your organization has a business continuity and risk function, they are likely to have information on business impact analysis that can support this task.

Now that we have a business perspective on priority, we want to see how this aligns to the security view of services. For example, the business continuity programme may have based the criticality and sensitivity of systems and data on *availability* and *urgency*. While the business process may be required quickly, is it also sensitive from a *security* and *privacy* perspective? Does that reinforce or change the risk as a result?

When we have a common understanding of the priority and sensitivities of different processes, systems and data, we can think about the controls in place today and whether they are effective. So, while we may not be able to stop every attack, our objective is to slow them down, since this has a direct impact on the attacker's return on investment.

Now that we are more aware of the existence of shadow IT and processes, how easy might it be for an attacker to also circumvent controls and how might such an action be detected, and prevented? Bear in mind that an attack is not always linear, and the attacker may have a range of exploits and tools at their disposal. This may include a move laterally from person-to-person or system-to-system to achieve the level of access and control they need.

Ultimately, *human defenders* need to be able to counter the *human adversary*. While there are various tools and technologies that can counteract the outcome of an attack, the human defenders need to understand and be cognisant of the evolving tactics to enable investment decisions to be made on what people, process and technology will be most effective. Defending against attacks requires a curious mindset and diversity of thought.

Before we look at the types of technology that will be useful in your security strategy, let us round out the conversation that we started with Professor Sarah Morris, and some of the notable cases that digital forensics helped to unravel.

Notable cases and lessons learnt

As Morris Professor Morris highlights, many criminals and attackers think they are cleverer than they are when it comes to their knowledge of how computers work or how they think they are covering their tracks. Simply deleting a few files or internet history does not override many of the system programs and logs embedded in memory. This in essence is what digital forensics is reliant on. Many opportunists buy exploit kits and may not know how to cover their tracks, while others with deep technical skill may be arrogant about what they can do with that skill.

What brought Professor Morris the most acclaim was the 'washing machine case'. When the suspect was caught, they claimed to be at home doing their washing at the time of the alleged activity. There was nobody else in the house, and there was no other evidence that could link them to the crime scene. Law enforcement wanted to know if they could tell the difference between someone physically pushing a button and someone using their mobile phone to activate it. Professor Morris ended up taking the washing machine apart, re-boarding the data chip, working out the language that it had been programmed with, and reading the logs. From there, she was able to tell that the button had not been pressed. Not only did this prove that a mobile phone was used to remotely turn on the washing machine, but it also evidenced that the phone was located at the crime scene, establishing the suspect's guilt.

As both Sarah Morris and former FBI special agent Milan Patel highlight, getting hands on a physical device is crucial for investigations, but it is also incredibly hard to 'place hands on a keyboard'. Many systems will retain logs and are time-stamped, but confirming the device where the commands originated from are crucial. Even if we can pinpoint the account and the device that the suspect logged in from, it is difficult to state categorically that a specific person is tied to that account. So, a combination of digital and physical evidence is required to be most successful, yet many criminals don't think that law enforcement will ever catch up with them, so don't fully consider endpoint security controls. The attackers may think about end-to-end encryption on the network, but they don't consider security across the layers, and this is what gives us the advantage.

One of Professor Morris' most memorable cases involved a person who had amassed a huge array of indecent images. They were adamant that they didn't know how the images had got there, and that malware had infected their machine. However, when the person had downloaded each image, they added keywords and placed them into separate folders so it was easy for them to search. Malware just isn't that efficient and organized! It was a relatively easy case in retrospect for Professor Morris to prove, as there was no encryption on the files, but she highlights this as a prime example of how some people just don't think they will be caught.

Professor Morris accepts that, when people think of *forensics*, they picture the detectives at crime scenes on TV shows, but that really doesn't show the in-depth work that is actually required to prove a case. She feels there is often a disconnect between security and forensics; not just in terms of knowing how computers work and how to configure them correctly, but by learning from previous cases and how they were unravelled.

She argues that even journalists have learnt to exploit security flaws: if they get hold of devices, they can find all sorts of things. They use forensics to identify what shouldn't be there; they pull data from it and use it for salacious stories because they know what sells newspapers. People are reluctant to get rid of information. So, when Professor Morris' team is investigating cases, they find old and draft versions of documents, which are often enough to reconstruct sensitive data.

Professor Morris explains that, if a device was properly configured and secured, she might not be able to get evidence from it, but that also means that an attacker can't either. It may sound like Professor Morris is talking herself out of a job, but she firmly believes that, by understanding more about *how* things work, security practitioners can be more tuned into *why* certain policies and logs are required, and how to retrieve and analyse them in the event of nefarious activity.

Professor Morris believes that it is this gap in knowledge that gives some attackers the advantage – not necessarily the ones that perform the last stage of the attack, but the skilled specialists who design the exploits, malware and scripting that underpins many of the 'as-a-service' models, because, if they know how to reverse engineer systems, it gives them the ability to design exploits and workarounds that other attackers are willing to pay a lot of money for.

If we want to get better at understanding attackers, it means having a deeper appreciation of the technical skill set required and linking it back to the business in terms of the value of systems and data. Not only do attackers need to know how to exploit a vulnerability, they also need to know how to monetize it.

Defending through the layers

We have discussed why human-centric security means putting people first, and why we need to think like an attacker, so let's now consider the core strategies required to counteract potential breaches.

Core security strategy

Believe it or not, there is no overarching standard when it comes to what good security looks like and what it should be modelled on. Most countries will, however, have their own overarching national strategy when it comes to their policy and stance on defensive and offensive cyber capability. They will also have national cyber committees who have been tasked with supporting organizations across the public and private sector. This may include access to good practice guidelines and resources that organizations can take advantage of. In addition, regulated entities will be governed by legislation in the countries where they operate.

So, the idea is not to replace that, or come up with a new standard or approach, but rather to look at a level of commonality and good principles that exist across all these areas, which would be applicable to any organization, of any size, accepting that each organization differs in terms of its risk appetite and access to resources. In terms of establishing the core strategy and principles, it is quite simple:

Stop the access in and exit out.

Use Figure 15.1 to help you think of all the ways in which an attacker might get access to your organization and what they are after. They need to exfiltrate something of value to achieve their objective, be that information, assets or money. This also includes anyone already operating within your organization. This is why I wanted you to think about your business from *inside out* and *outside in*, so you could begin to map this for the most critical and sensitive services.

FIGURE 15.1 Defending through the layers

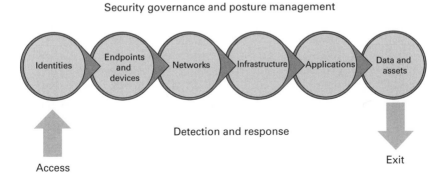

Having a good appreciation for the two outer points and thinking of these as the core areas for your strategy means that you can work backwards from those two areas to close the gaps with regard to the networks, infrastructure and applications that host and support these services. This is not unique to IT infrastructure; it also applies to operational technologies such as industrial control systems, as well as smart technologies such as IoT (Internet of Things) devices – even washing machines. If it has a connection to the outside world and can transmit data, then it has vulnerabilities that can be exploited. It may sound extreme, but there is a precedent there, so it pays to think holistically, because the attackers certainly will.

Think of these as the foundational levels of security, the building blocks if you like, as the stronger the foundations, the stronger everything is on top of them. It stands to reason, therefore, that, when we have weak foundations, cracks can appear, and this is how vulnerabilities set in. Get enough of those, and the cracks can cause fundamental issues in the stability and protection of the business. Some practitioners refer to this as 'basic hygiene' measures, but 'basic' may be misconstrued as 'easy', which is why I prefer to call them foundations.

The most efficient way to deal with cyber attacks is to use *preventative measures* to reduce or slow down the probability of an attack, along with *proactive measures* that enable fast recovery should the attacker prevail. With a mindset of 'assume compromise and failure' we can consider that no person, process or technology is infallible to an attack, especially if there is enough motivation and sufficient resources. Based on what we know, and why many human-operated attacks are so successful, we can build resistance and resilience to such attacks by pre-empting them.

It is important to note that cybersecurity is an ongoing process that requires constant vigilance and regular updates to keep up with the evolving threat landscape. Organizations will need to adopt a comprehensive approach that combines a range of strategies to mitigate the risk from human adversaries.

Before you think about investing in new technologies, it pays to spend time analysing what you have already deployed and how it may be working, especially how people are interacting with the systems as well as each other. It is often the case that organizations are not fully utilizing or optimizing the tools and technology they already have at their disposal. The underlying issues when it comes to effective governance and modelling expected behaviour don't change because of a new tool, but it can help to identify current gaps and *why* you may need to invest in other areas.

SECURITY GOVERNANCE AND POSTURE MANAGEMENT

One of the core principles of any strategy is to consider the governance, risk and compliance structure and how that dovetails with and complements the wide business governance and risk structure. The aim is to set the overall objectives and how these will be measured, taking into consideration how the people and organization works, as well as the overall culture of the organization, and whether this may help or hinder the efforts of the programme.

While we may have a utopian vision of what we would like to be in place, we need to be realistic in terms of the potential challenges and how we might overcome those. This is about establishing the overall context within which the security strategy and programme will operate, including account-abilities, responsibilities and authorities, throughout the organization.

There will inevitably be resource and budget constraints that most organizations must contend with. However, don't think of security as a cost centre but rather an essential service for the entire business that enables trust. A sustainable programme is one that provides longevity in systematically reducing risk while increasing resilience. Consider what will have the biggest impact, in the shortest amount of time, and whether there are quick wins, such as security education, training and awareness, to fill gaps in knowledge and preparedness.

Some of the strategies that can be deployed to manage security governance and compliance are:

- **Human risk programme**. Remember what we said about understanding how the business operates *inside out* and *outside in*. An important element is understanding the insider risk before it becomes a threat. While many organizations want to implicitly trust employees, we also know that everyone can be prone to making mistakes, and everyone can be prone to manipulation. We also know that, given the right stressors and triggers, this could lead to malicious behaviour. A proactive programme not only helps to reduce those stressors but can help to evaluate where the internal vulnerabilities are and how to overcome them (PWC and Microsoft, 2020). Consider this as a proactive and positive action, as opposed to one that feels like Big Brother. Perhaps a more friendly term is to think of this as a 'human risk' programme, as opposed to an 'insider risk' programme, to reflect more accurately what it means to have human-centric security. Much of what we are trying to do here is changing mindsets and thinking about the human elements more holistically, which includes how and why shadow processes occur.

- **Dynamically evaluating risk**. Organizations that rely on static policies and reporting may not be able to react quickly enough to the changing threat profile. Not only is it time-consuming to create manual reports, it is often a point-in-time assessment and may not reflect the current or evolving state. Consider how information is currently collated and where there are opportunities to aggregate this data directly into dashboards. Reflect on the very essence of *why* such policies exist, whether they are still fit for purpose and what positive behaviour we expect to see as a result. Let's also reflect on what Professor Morris said earlier in this chapter with regards to how we log, analyse and collect evidence, and how this can help us measure the effectiveness of policies and security controls through tests and audits. This can also be done in a fun and engaging way to establish the many 'weird and wonderful' ways in which it could be broken.

Potential ways of optimizing your current strategy may include:

- **Realtime posture management.** Telemetry data can be used to dynamically understand the current state and identity gaps in coverage, validate existing controls and correlate data across all layers of the environment. This provides the ability to scan for updates and identify where services are outside policy, either to provide recommendations to improve the posture or to automatically place the service back into policy. A drop in posture could also be indicative of an unauthorized change or one not implemented properly. Many cloud services, for example, provide the ability to scan connected resources to identify vulnerabilities and offer recommendations.

PROTECTING IDENTITIES

Identity is a wide concept, and many people will consider it in the context of someone's physical and personal identity – what makes them unique. Your name and biometric identifiers such as DNA, face, fingerprints or palm prints are all attributes that help to identify you as an individual. But there are additional attributes that can be used as identifiers too, which include login credentials that you use at work or in your personal life to gain access to services.

Many non-human 'things', such as devices, endpoints and servers also have unique identifiers and attributes that enable organizations to identify each of the components. Some of these may include unique names and IP addresses, as well as additional login credentials. These come under the broad banner of 'identity', which gives authority to access services, and it is also through identity protocols that organizations can verify and authenticate whether an identity is a legitimate one.

It stands to reason therefore that the stronger the verification and authentication process, the harder it is for attackers to 'guess' or 'brute-force' their way in. This can happen when people choose weak or common passwords (such as children's or pets' names or 'Password123' or 'admin'). Remember what we said about attackers using social engineering tactics to either learn more about individuals through information posted up on social media sites and other forums, or how they may entice them into unwittingly giving up credentials through phishing and other means.

There are several strategies that can be utilized to protect identities, as well as to slow the attackers down should an identity be compromised, so let's consider some of those:

- **Multi-factor authentication (MFA).** Relying on passwords alone is not an effective way to authenticate access to services. Implementing MFA adds an extra layer of security by requiring additional credentials, such as a fingerprint, facial recognition or a one-time code, in addition to the password. This makes it more difficult for attackers to gain unauthorized access, even if they obtain a valid password through social engineering or other means. Using the concept of 'MFA fatigue', however, attackers may attempt to generate multiple requests for MFA to the victim's device, hoping that the victim will accept the request inadvertently or because of fatigue. This is also known as 'push bombing'. This attack can be prevented by using passwordless authentication, combined with features such as 'number matching', where the person needs to physically interact with the device to match a number shown on their device to that shown on another screen.

- **Role-based access controls.** Limit access to only the applications, services and infrastructure required to perform the specific job function. This means granting access to the right resources at the right time for the right purpose. When someone changes roles, it is important that the level of permissions is evaluated and revoked where necessary. This means that should an attacker be able to obtain access to the credentials, they are limited by what they can do with them.

- **Privileged access strategy.** If the attacker has obtained initial access to the environment, the objective is to prevent them from gaining full control to key resources and assets by limiting their ability to laterally move across the network, exfiltrate data or sabotage systems. Taking away the attacker's ability to utilize privileged accounts lowers the chances that they will be successful in achieving their objective. This extends to business executives, system developers and IT system administrators, as well as OT and IoT operators. This is a multi-part strategy:

  o The account that the person uses to access corporate services such as email and collaboration tools should not be the same account they would use to gain access to, and control, production environments.

This prevents the attacker from being able to pivot between different networks, and forces the attacker to obtain additional layers of access. Tightly protect, closely monitor and rapidly respond to incidents related to these types of privileged roles and accounts.

o   Mitigate lateral movement through segmentation of access, to prevent a single compromised device from being able to control multiple devices in the event of self-propagating malware or other methods that an attacker might utilize to obtain control of the network.

o   Research conducted by Microsoft (2022) identified that 100 per cent of customers who experienced a cyber attack did not have privileged access workstations. Validate the trust of people and devices before allowing access to administrative interfaces by utilizing privileged access workstations that are logically separated from the internet.

Potential ways of optimizing your strategy may include:

- **Passwordless authentication**. By removing the password in favour of biometric authentication, attackers are unable to rely on password-based attacks.

- **Behaviour-based analytics**. By first determining what are normal patterns of behaviour for an identity or entity, it can help to identify anomalous behaviour and increased risk factors.

- **Continuous validation and dynamic enforcement**. When risky behaviour is identified, it may be indicative of a compromised identity. Take evasive action by restricting or quarantining the account or device until the identity has been verified.

PROTECTING ENDPOINTS AND DEVICES

An endpoint can refer to any device that can connect to a network, including desktops and laptops, printers, mobile phones, IoT devices and more. A person may use an endpoint to obtain access to the network, or the endpoint itself may have access to other services hosted on the network, whether on premises or in cloud environments. Any endpoints that are not onboarded or outdated serve as potential entry points and access routes for attackers.

COVID-19 accelerated the use of hybrid working, which has meant that many people now work from a variety of devices and locations. These can be corporate devices or those that belong to the person – typically known as 'bring your own device' (**BYOD**). While this can help improve the user experience and productivity, by effectively allowing them to work from *any* *device at any time from any location*, it can also increase the risk if devices are not strictly managed and controlled. Even if an employee wants to use their personal devices to access corporate resources, the devices should be enrolled and adhere to the same device-health policies that govern corporate-owned devices.

Historically, the process to manage and configure IT devices and endpoints has been more developed than IoT devices. However, it is important to remember that the level of security and controls applied to such devices needs to be to a similar level as IT. From the attacker's perspective, it is just another access point, and they are more likely to favour those devices with weak controls.

Let's consider some of the strategies that could be deployed to manage endpoints.

- **Endpoint management**. Internet-exposed endpoints are a common entry vector for attackers, as they take advantage of vulnerabilities in operating systems. It is therefore important to apply security baselines to harden internet-facing servers, devices and applications, rapidly deploy security updates and systematically remove or isolate unsupported versions of software. Confirming that devices are properly configured and 'healthy' as a condition of access can help to limit unauthorized access and malware.

- **Endpoint protection and anti-malware**. One of the core objectives for attackers is to get malware deployed on an endpoint or device. The malware can be utilized for a variety of purposes, depending on the objectives of the attacker. Some might be used to control the device and open back doors; some may steal or wipe information. It is therefore important to deploy security software that can identify and block known and unknown malware from infecting the device.

- **Endpoint detection and response (EDR)**. An EDR solution is often complementary to endpoint protection as it can help to detect and monitor for any suspicious activity, as well as enable proactive hunting for known indicators of compromise or signs that the endpoint or device has been tampered with. Depending on the chosen solution, this can also provide contextual telemetry and historical data to aide with forensic investigations and recovery. While advanced solutions are key for detecting and remediating attacks, they still rely on basic security configurations to be turned on.

Potential ways to optimize your current strategy may include:

- **Access control gated on the device.** This means removing the requirement for passwords in favour of stronger levels of authentication such as biometrics and facial recognition. Having access controls on the device can reduce the probability that an attacker can utilize a lost or stolen device to gain unauthorized access to services.

- **Automated provisioning, registering, monitoring, isolating and remediating of assets.** This enables endpoints to be built and deployed in an effective manner. Once the device has been enrolled, this can enable automated updates, where necessary. In the event of suspicious behaviour detected on the device, it can also take evasive action to quarantine or even remotely wipe the device if compromised.

- **Continuous asset analysis.** In a similar way to auto-provisioning for corporate devices, continuous asset analysis can be used to detect when new devices are added and connected. This can also detect when an attacker might be trying to add or enrol their own devices should they have obtained privileged access.

PROTECTING NETWORKS

A network refers to any open communications channel – including internal networks, wireless networks, cellular networks and the internet – that can be used to transport messages. Such messages can be *person-to-person* or *machine-to-machine*. All data and services are ultimately accessed over network infrastructure. Networking controls can provide visibility of what is connected to the network and help to prevent attackers from moving laterally.

The proliferation of devices, as well as new applications and services coming online every minute, only increases the attack surface and the opportunities for attackers to exploit vulnerabilities. Since most external attacks originate from the internet, a key requirement for network controls and scanning is to determine what is internet facing and what is vulnerable to attack.

Let's consider some of the strategies that could be deployed to manage endpoints.

- **Network discovery and vulnerability management.** Often, organizations are unaware of the extent of assets they own and what is attached to the internet. Unpatched and unsupported assets can introduce vulnerabilities that can be exploited by attackers. Organizations need to perform regular scans of the network, and raise alerts when assets are added or removed. The key is to understand which assets have the most value or disruptive capability if compromised, and translating this into supporting IT assets (applications, files, servers and so on) and business services.

- **Segmenting access controls.** A key lesson Microsoft has learnt about network access is to use layers of network segmentation. This includes segmenting users and devices across purpose-built networks, migrating employees to use the internet as the default network and automatically routing users and devices to appropriate network segments. This serves two purposes. First, it improves productivity with how users access their services, and, second, network traffic is not being routed via corporate services, creating less of a dependency and a bottleneck.

Potential ways of optimizing your current strategy may include:

- **End-to-end encryption.** As messages are being transported through different networks and devices, attackers may look to intercept messages in transit. They may use this to spy, sabotage or divert the message. This is often referred to as an 'adversary-in-the-middle' attack. Since the attacker is often sitting between networks, this can often be difficult to detect. End-to-end encryption that protects data in transit, at rest and in use can help to reduce interception. This should evolve in line with cryptography practices and encryption key management since advanced attackers look to obtain the keys and certificates that are used to authenticate both parties.

- **Conditional access and validation.** As a result of monitoring changes in behaviour to identities and devices, this information can be relayed to control network access. This is useful when combined with network segmentation, as you may decide to limit access to critical services rather than restrict full access, depending on your policy.

PROTECTING INFRASTRUCTURE

Infrastructure can include on-premises servers and cloud-based virtual machines, as well as operational technology. In many ways, the requirements for infrastructure follow a similar requirement to that for networks, in that you will need to determine which components are internet facing, such as web servers, and which infrastructure needs to be segmented. As well as core production environments, this includes test and development areas. These often have lower levels of security controls attributed to them, but they can hold just as much value to attackers if they can get access to system code or data. Think back to the case study on Lapsus$ and how the attackers were targeting technical companies to obtain source code, as well as proprietary information on upcoming releases. This is why it is important to think holistically.

When scanning for vulnerabilities, attackers may often choose to launch an attack from an on-premises perspective and either stay within the network or use their administrative permissions to move laterally to the cloud or other environments. They may choose to do this because they can stay hidden for longer, as the organization may be responsible for performing its own network and infrastructure monitoring. However, when services are hosted from the cloud, some of those services transfer to the cloud or application service provider, depending on the contracted level of service.

Irrespective of where the infrastructure is hosted, the organization is always responsible for assigning the user accounts and permissions, and what people are doing with those, as well as any data they host in those services. It is a good reminder of why protecting *the access in and the exit out* are fundamental strategies, and why segmentation between networks and infrastructure is also important to reduce the risk.

Let's consider some strategies that could be deployed to manage infrastructure:

- **Security baselines.** With the continuously evolving security threat landscape, there is an increasing need for security controls to be configured by default to manufacturers' recommended settings and baselines to improve cyber resilience. Historically, machines included built-in security features that the IT professional was expected to configure to their own desired level. This approach may no longer be adequate, as attackers are using more advanced tools in automation, cloud infrastructure and remote access technologies to achieve their aims. It has become critical that all layers of security, from the chip to the cloud, are configured by default. Although many organizations adopt an array of regulations and standards, these often do not reflect the current and evolving tactics and techniques utilized by attackers, so it is important to understand that compliance does not necessarily mean secure.

- **Protect and secure backups.** As attackers become more aligned to our defences, they look for workarounds to force the organization into taking an action they would not normally take. A good example is ransomware operators who deliberately try to corrupt or delete backups so that the organization is more likely to pay an extortion demand if they feel that they have no alternative. To safeguard from deliberate erasure or encryption, use offline immutable storage, as well as MFA or a PIN, before permitting any change in backup regime.

- **Continuous monitoring and auditing.** Implementing continuous monitoring can help to detect anomalies or suspicious activity in real time, allowing for prompt response and remediation. This includes monitoring logs, system events and network traffic for signs of unauthorized access or other security breaches.

- **Regular security assessments.** Conducting regular assessments, such as penetration testing or vulnerability scanning, can help to identify potential weaknesses in an organization's systems and processes, which can be addressed before they are exploited by attackers.

Potential ways of optimizing your current strategy may include:

- **Blocking unauthorized deployments.** Attackers may attempt to fraudulently deploy or utilize infrastructure into a customer's environment, such as enabling them to use it for *cryptojacking* – a type of cyber attack that uses cloud computing power to mine cryptocurrency. As well as monitoring for unauthorized changes and deployments of virtual machines, organizations should monitor for early signs of resource abuse (Microsoft Threat Intelligence, 2023).

PROTECTING APPLICATIONS

Applications include computer programs that execute on endpoints and infrastructure and provide the interface by which data is consumed. These may be hosted on premises, in cloud workloads or delivered through modern software-as-a-service (SaaS) applications. It is typically through the applications that the business users can perform their operations.

Let's consider some strategies that could be deployed to manage applications:

- **Monitoring email and collaboration tools.** Attackers frequently enter the environment through phishing campaigns. Since the rapid deployment of hybrid working, many organizations have adopted collaboration and messaging tools, as well as social media and chatbots. Organizations need to consider each method of communication, as well as the messaging platforms, as an attack vector. As well as limiting the type of sensitive information that may be transmitted over such channels, consider the users of such platforms in case they are targets for business email compromise, and whether you have mechanisms to scan inbound and outbound messages for malicious content or programs.

- **Preventing shadow IT.** This can happen because of people downloading applications from the internet without the approval or knowledge and authorization of the IT or security department. Not only are these not monitored, but data could be leaked or stolen through these applications. This requires cloud-based monitoring to check for sanctioned and unsanctioned applications, as well as protocols that prevent data from being uploaded or downloaded into such applications. While there are technical controls that can detect and block such actions, this doesn't negate the need to assess *why* they are being downloaded in the first place.

Potential ways for optimizing your current strategy may include:

- **In-session monitoring.** While many organizations will monitor access to the application, they may not monitor for changes of behaviour while in use. This includes files that someone doesn't normally access or trying to change permissions such as password controls, and whether this could be indicative of a compromised or malicious user. After all, it is easier for an attacker to simply log in than it is to break in.

- **Content-aware protections.** These should be tailored to the application and sensitivity of the action. For example, rather than preventing the ability to copy, paste or print all data, it is only restricted to specific files or data types.

- **Automated processes for software development.** Many organizations are in a dilemma as to whether they build or buy applications. Those that are building their own applications may choose to utilize open-source software or code to speed up the development and deployment of software packages and capability. Attackers can often inject malicious programs or scripts into code to launch nefarious attacks. Perform automated vulnerability scanning and testing across code repositories.

PROTECTING DATA AND ASSETS

This includes structured and unstructured files and information that resides in systems, devices, networks, applications, databases, infrastructure and backups, as well as the associated metadata. This may include data that resides in shadow IT. The value of data will be different depending on the type of attacker and their objective. You should consider what data you hold and the value of it if placed in the wrong hands.

Increasingly, attackers are finding value in email and collaboration tools, as these enable them to intercept and impersonate individuals for business email compromise and other types of attack. They could act as a beacon for those attackers looking to gain access to information that could be used for espionage or extortion.

Let's consider some strategies that could be deployed to manage data:

- **Data classification and labelling.** All data should be classified according to type and sensitivity, for example whether it is personal data, financial data or intellectual property and so on; whether it is generally available to all people, confidential or secret, and to what extent. Relying on people to know what classification to put on a document, and enforcing the policy, is often a challenge for organizations. Consider tools that can automatically detect and classify different data types, based on your policies and controls.

- **Data lifecycle management.** Many organizations have requirements for documents and information to be retained for specific lengths of time for audit and legal purposes. There may also be requirements to prove who accessed a document and at what time, or to prove that it was not altered or tampered with. This requires additional controls to track and monitor the data from the point of creation to the point of destruction. Even when a document has reached the end of its retention period, steps need to be taken to determine whether it needs to be archived or whether *all* copies need to be destroyed. Data that resides in non-production environments also needs to be considered because this is still valuable to attackers, as Professor Morris highlighted. In a similar way to data classification and labelling, consider tools that allow you to track and audit documents as new ones are created.

- **Information protection.** Many people have far more permissions than they need, for example whether someone can simply view a document or whether they have write/delete permissions attributed to documents and file shares. People in positions of authority may also have permissions to authorize or override transactional data, such as authorizing invoices and payments to third parties. Not only is the data high value, but the people with permissions are also high-value targets for manipulation and control.

- **Data loss prevention (DLP).** This is the practice of detecting and preventing data breaches and exfiltration or the unsafe and inappropriate sharing or transfer of sensitive data. This may include mass downloads and printing, uploads to unsanctioned applications or attaching sensitive documents to emails, collaboration tools or external media. Often, this is the final point of exit from the organization and is where many organizations face the most issues because, if they are unable to prevent and block data from leaving the organization, and unauthorized transactions from being made, they are then dealing with the aftermath.

Potential ways for optimizing your current strategy may include:

- **Automated data inventory.** This is an essential part of data lifecycle management, which identifies and records when new documents are created by automatically applying data-classification controls and rules. This includes differentiating between documents in personal drives and those in formal repositories.

- **Dynamic and automated DLP.** An issue with traditional DLP solutions is that the policy can be binary in terms of whether to allow or block a transaction. Dynamic protection means being adaptable to changing behaviour and taking evasive action to protect the data. This may include stopping a transaction that is in progress or triggering a rule to record all activity over a specific period for forensics investigation. Some people will try to obfuscate their actions by adding passwords, or even running a slow exfiltration rather than a mass download, in the hope that they may not be noticed. This means that access is governed by behaviour, not just data-classification types or rules.

DETECTION AND RESPONSE

These require rapid and responsive detection and remediation of common attacks on identities, endpoints, networks, infrastructure, applications and data, to limit the attacker's ability to laterally traverse IT and OT environments in order to achieve their objective. In addition, it requires keeping up to date with the latest threat intelligence, such as evolving tactics, techniques and procedures used by attackers, so that organizations may proactively evaluate their strategy, policies and awareness training. This may include monitoring industry reports and sharing and collaborating with other organizations, as well as leveraging threat feeds and tools.

Many security tools that offer proactive detection and response will have a degree of threat intelligence included. The best results come from analysing alerts and whether there are opportunities to refine policies and processes as a result. Often, this can be indicative that, rather than an increase in nefarious action, policies are set too high or too low.

Let's consider some strategies that could be deployed:

- **Extended detection and response (XDR).** Many organizations will have invested in tools and technology. However, an attack can originate from anywhere, so visibility is required end to end in order to detect and respond to incidents at each stage and provide correlation to incidents, hence the value of an XDR solution. For example, malware may have originated from a phishing email that provided back-door access. Some of these events may happen at different times and may not be obvious. Ideally, we want to centralize the alerts into one platform, where integration allows. If that is not feasible, consider whether this increases the risk in terms of how quickly you can detect and respond, in case this requires increased monitoring or controls. It is also important to ensure that system logs are analysed to detect whether there have been any attempts to amend permissions, disable tools or bypass controls. This can be indicative that an attacker is trying to cover their tracks.

- **Practise responding to attack simulations.** Practising how you would respond to pre-defined attack scenarios enables you to validate the detection and incident response capability, as well as how the security team will also detect and respond. This includes mimicking the *red team* (attacker), *blue team* (defender) and *purple team* (combination) for the best outcome to yield a higher return on investment and success. This needs to be validated from an operational perspective, in conjunction with other IT teams, before validating the wider business response. The idea is to build confidence at each stage and through each layer of defence.

- **Incident response plan.** Having a well-defined incident response strategy and plan helps to ensure that the organization can respond effectively and efficiently to a cyber attack. This requires identifying key personnel and their roles, establishing communication channels and outlining steps to contain, mitigate and recover from the incident. This includes the steps required to evict an attacker. The way in which an organization responds to an attack is often just as important as the attack itself, so preparation and exercise of the incident response plan is paramount, not least because attacks can happen at any time. It is important to note that a cyber incident response does not work without a coordinated business response, as any action that may be taken to contain the incident, such as shutting down parts of the network or quarantining devices, will have a knock-on effect on how the business can perform its task. We shall discuss more on the board-level response in the next chapter.

Potential ways for optimizing your current strategy may include:

- **Security automation and orchestration.** Just like across the other layers, this means being dynamic and taking real-time evasive action as an attack is happening, which does not rely solely on a human to intervene. There will often be complex events and incidents that you will want an analyst to investigate, but, for less complex incidents, or where incidents can quickly escalate, it can often be more efficient to set policies that allow for automated action and remediation to reduce analyst fatigue and the time to detect and respond. This is aided through machine learning and behaviour analytics that help to identify and correlate anomalous activity and recommend mitigating actions. This is most effective for mature organizations that have refined many of their policies and processes.

Conclusion

In this chapter, we have discussed why it is important to truly understand how the business operates, whether shadow IT and processes have developed, and how this could undermine the efficacy of our strategy.

Thinking like an attacker requires us to think inside out and outside in, as well as about the weird and wonderful ways in which an attacker may try to obtain access or socially engineer their way into the organization.

We have explored core strategies and how we should defend through the layers, taking the time to consider the foundational level of security policies and controls required before we can consider how to optimize our investments. We have concluded with building effective detection and response, and seen why it is important to link the overall security strategy and response back to the business.

In the next chapter, we shall establish how we gain and maintain top-level commitment to the security strategy and how these key people will respond in a crisis.

References

Jiménez, J (2023) 'Ex-Amazon manager sentenced to 16 years in prison in $9million theft scheme', *New York Times*, 6 July, nytimes.com/2023/07/06/us/amazon-manager-scheme-sentencing-atlanta.html (archived at https://perma.cc/63GZ-EN26)

Microsoft (2022) 'Microsoft Digital Defense Report 2022', p 90, https://query.prod.cms.rt.microsoft.com/cms/api/am/binary/RE5bUvv?culture=en-us&country=us (archived at https://perma.cc/5V9W-VEQ6)

Microsoft Threat Intelligence (2023) 'Cryptojacking: understanding and defending against cloud compute resource abuse', 25 July, microsoft.com/en-us/security/blog/2023/07/25/cryptojacking-understanding-and-defending-against-cloud-compute-resource-abuse (archived at https://perma.cc/HTY2-LLL2)

PWC and Microsoft (2020) 'Building an effective insider risk management program', pwc.com/us/en/services/alliances/microsoft/cybersecurity/insider-risk-management.html (archived at https://perma.cc/2GD9-YKWZ)

16

The board-level response – how decisions are made in times of crisis

---

CHAPTER OBJECTIVES

To make the security strategy a success, we need buy-in and support from senior leadership, not just in terms of sponsorship for the programme but their reaction in a crisis. The way in which an incident is handled is often more important than the incident itself and is ultimately what your organization will be remembered for.

So, now it is the time to consider the board-level response when going head to head with a human adversary.

Decisions on how best to respond to a large-scale cyber attack should not happen when multiple services are already down and you have myriads of stakeholders vying for an update. Of course, you want to be safe in the knowledge that you have a good cybersecurity strategy and a recovery plan for when things go wrong, but how do you know? Have you taken the time to truly understand the possible extent of such a situation? Have you been asking the right questions to obtain the assurances you need, or do you assume that someone will just take care of it? This is why due diligence is so important, as we will explore.

Due diligence

Performing effective due diligence requires deep introspection. It does not come naturally to most people, and is a proactive and thoughtful process that requires a willingness and desire to dig deep and face up to the reality of a situation.

Often, board-level reporting is 'sugar-coated' to provide more palatable reading for the recipients. After all, nobody wants to hear bad news, and we want to feel assured that our investments and decisions are paying dividends – *pun intended* – because we want stakeholders to remain happy. However, there are a few issues here that we will discuss.

Most members of the board are not technical or cybersecurity experts, so this is often delegated to those people that are – the CIO, CTO and CISO. However, cybersecurity touches every part of the business and therefore ignorance is not bliss, neither is it a defence since executives are entrusted to act in the best interest of the company. There are many statutory obligations when it comes to duties and liabilities of directors, and an organization can risk being found negligent in how they handle a major incident. There is even increasing pressure on CISOs that they will be found personally liable. For example, in 2022, Uber's CISO was found guilty of failing to adequately report a data breach and obstructing the Federal Trade Commission with their investigation. The CISO was given three years' probation, 200 hours of community service and a $50,000 fine. The judge presiding over the case highlighted that company officers should not expect such leniency going forward and should even expect to spend time in custody (Department of Justice, 2022).

This has led some CISOs to seek assurance from organizations that they will be protected from liability following a cyber attack. It also raises questions over the impact that such responsibility can have on the mental health of individuals who are working under increased scrutiny, shrinking budgets and mounting expectations (Proofpoint, 2023). So, how do we get better alignment between the CISO and the board?

While each organization will have its own view on reporting lines and accountabilities, cybersecurity is an issue that affects every person and every process, as well as every technology. Some institutions are beginning to see the value of having a Chief Security and Resilience Officer as a direct report to the CEO or board in acknowledgement of the broader requirements of security and resilience as business-enabling functions that need to be fully aligned. You may not be able to influence the specific reporting lines, but this is an important factor in how risks and issues are being discussed and considered holistically.

To support this, we need to ensure that cybersecurity is not seen as a risk that can be fixed with technology, since many key aspects of the strategy cover people and business processes. This goes far beyond implementing security awareness and education, and is dependent on the overall culture of the organization and how this can help or hinder what we need to achieve. Strategic culture, as discussed in Chapter 10, is founded in the deep roots and history of the organization. Typically, it has formed over time and is what provides a sense of belonging, or otherwise, for people. The following are some questions for us to consider.

What are you reporting to the board and why?

- What is the story we are trying to portray to the board when it comes to articulating the actual risk, the current state and the level of assurance that you have in preventing and recovering from an attack?
- If you are not being factual about the reality of the situation, it is unlikely that you will obtain buy-in or investment for the strategy and recovery plan.
- Is what you are reporting aligned and explained in relation to business risk, and in a common language that is easy to understand?

How can the board contribute to prioritizing risk?

- What is the overall strategy when it comes to enterprise risk and reputation management?
- What do the board members consider the most important assets for protection, and does this align to the business and security view? Consider what may be driving a difference in perspective if these are not aligned.
- What do they consider to be the highest operational, geopolitical, social and economic threats, and how might these impact the prioritization of the security strategy?
- What are the key reporting metrics and information that they are going to require in order to help them understand the current and future state?

Does the security, awareness and education programme extend to the board?

- 'Why should I care, and what's in it for me?' Think about the role and responsibilities of each board member, and what is going to resonate most with them. This may need to be tailored, depending on whether you are focusing on the legal, financial or operational risk, for example.

- Don't assume that people on the board know about cybersecurity threats, why they personally may be high-value targets and how they can protect themselves, as well as the company, from attacks.

- Remember what we said about ensuring that training is not too simplistic or one size fits all.

What experience does the board have in managing major incidents?

- Board members are senior people who are well versed in managing day-to-day operations. Responding to a crisis is different, and some may not have experienced what it is like to be on the front line.

- Most exercises are not immersive and may not consider the nuances between dealing with a human adversary, intent on doing harm, and the response to a natural disaster, for example. Both are stressful, but only one is trying to control and manipulate the situation to their advantage.

- Conversely, there may be people who have experienced this type of event and can share their lessons learnt. Perhaps they can even act as a champion for you and other board members.

Lead by example and from the front

To pick up on the conversation we started with Nadja El Fertasi, former stakeholder and engagement leader at NATO (Chapter 14), I wanted to get her perspective on the issues that confront business leaders when it comes to making strategic decisions.

When you look at the industry, and the leaders at the helm, they may have 'group think', based on where they have come from and what they have seen previously. As El Fertasi has highlighted, if military personnel make political decisions, the outcome is very different from when these are made by ambassadors. It stands to reason, therefore, that, if we are reliant on security decisions being made by technical personnel, we will get a different decision and outcome than one made by the whole board. Of course, the knowledge of such people is invaluable in terms of their recommendations and experience, but decisions can't just be delegated, as it has repercussions for the entire organization.

As El Fertasi explains, and to use NATO as an example, she identified that there were people with a 'cold-war mentality' in terms of who the enemy was, who they were fighting and why. There is often a crossover from the military into those that find themselves working in a security leadership role, and they too may have a view on who the enemy is and what they are fighting. And that's OK to an extent, because they have valuable perspective, but it is perhaps narrow in scope if it does not consider the full range of attackers and motivations that we have been discussing. The 'enemy' could just as easily be your own children who are experimenting with hacking systems online, without you realizing it. When faced with that reality, does your perspective change on how they should be treated and punished? This is why we have also discussed the need to humanize the attackers, so that we might consider things from their perspective.

The emotional challenge is to bridge the fear and uncertainty that comes with unknown territory, and to come to a common understanding and consensus on what it means and how to deal with the situation. There can be an overwhelming fear that the wrong decision will be made in terms of the strategy and direction that the company should take during normal business operations, and those decisions that you need to make when you are staring down the barrel of a gun, figuratively speaking. But the fear can be real and paralysing all the same, if you don't feel in control or someone is quite literally holding you and your organization to ransom.

Managing the response to a crisis

Let's say you have a typical hierarchal structure where the CEO is expected to make the final decision, but under what advisement? There is huge emotional pressure on that individual to make the right decision, especially if the incident is playing out in the public domain.

Let's take an example that many organizations tend to fear the most – where an attacker has seized control of corporate systems and exfiltrated large swathes of data, an extortion demand has been made and the organization is at the mercy of what the attacker does next. There are the obvious debates in terms of 'pay or don't pay' and the repercussions of that – ethically, as well as operationally. What if the attacker is listening in to everything you say and then takes evasive action to delete the backups or publish the data anyway? Such 'what if' questions are great, and they should be explored and mitigations put in place to counteract the attacks, but the first time to be thinking about it is not when you are in the middle of a cyber attack.

When people are under pressure and feeling stressed, they may not make sound and rational decisions. Therefore, looking at the situation from the attacker's perspective, you can see why it is in their best interest to apply as much pressure as possible, to force you into a decision that you might not otherwise make.

Think back to what we said in Chapter 3 about the different types of cyber attack and why they work: the common factors that they deploy to socially engineer the situation, and the people, to their advantage. Perhaps, like Lapsus$ in Chapter 7, they deliberately triggered the crisis response to see how you would react, they listen to see how confident you are, they pre-empt your next move and they have taken safeguards to ensure they can play their next card. Think of it like a game of chess if you will, where you are not just thinking of your next move but the next few ahead.

Remember, it is all part of the attacker's game plan, all part of their strategy, so you need to know this and be prepared for how you will respond as a result. Of course, that does not make it any less demanding when you are in the situation. You will still need to make difficult and tough decisions, so we will discuss two key areas to help with that:

- Dealing with the emotional stress, and being able to stay calm and think rationally.
- Being prepared and armed with the decisions you will need to make.

Dealing with the emotional stress of a crisis

Board members are human, just like the rest of us. They have issues in their work and personal life that may be getting in the way of their decision-making. If you are leading a company, and facing a real cyber attack, you are going to feel the emotional response of it, and that is going to drive your behaviour. If you have people around you that are not accustomed to this level of response, they are going to feel that stress too.

Nadja El Fertasi found herself in this situation when conducting table-top exercises at NATO. When exercising in this way, there is no pressure. You can chat through the practical things, you may even disagree, but there is no consequence to anything. The time may be ticking, but nothing is going to happen. There is nothing to test the emotional response, so, when something does happen for real, it is overwhelming.

When faced with the fear of making a wrong decision, El Fertasi uses a reflection and visualization technique in her role as a professional coach, by looking at the decisions that need to be made. What are the potential consequences of that action? What are the different outcomes and consequences of those decisions? How did the situation make them feel? What did they learn when they visualized each action? El Fertasi then uses the answers to help people think about how to correct course and deal with the emotions as they arise.

If we let the emotional weight of what we carry influence our decisions, we need to correct that. Sometimes, the situation pans out as we expected; sometimes it doesn't; but we need to consider what will enable us to be more effective in the moment. It comes back to the overarching vision that you have for yourself and the company and being true to that. Once you have been able to visualize different outcomes, it is less uncomfortable when faced with those decisions in real life.

Just as you might tell someone who is being pressurized to take time out, take a break, get help, it is important that we practise what we preach. It is also important to empower and trust ourselves and our judgement. When the decision is sound, reasonable and well thought-through, you can stop second guessing. Even the best athletes need coaching and training and need to adjust their technique to that of their opponent or the conditions. It is an ongoing and iterative process, but the more we practise the more effective we will be in the moment.

Consider what decisions you will make by yourself, and what needs to be a collective decision. If you don't have the knowledge or the expertise, who does, and what help or information might you need to increase the confidence in those decisions?

It is easy to be dismissive and state that we have insurance, we have the tech, we'll be ok. But if we focus just on the technical and not the personal aspects, we are not going to get enough people to care. We need to make it real for them, and we are going to have to ask challenging and probing questions, but, once people feel and know the discomfort, it reduces the emotional intensity. It is an important factor of crisis management training because, by its very nature, a crisis delivers a level of intensity where difficult decisions must be made. So, how can we reduce that intensity and be better prepared?

Being armed and prepared in a crisis

Part of being prepared means being honest about the current situation: what we absolutely know to be facts versus what we don't know and need to find out. The objective is to remove assumptions because we need to be clear about what we are basing our decisions on. How can you decide what the best course of action is if you are not presented with the truth? And, being candid, how much are you a party to that? Do you openly welcome issues and grievances, or do you shy away from them? If we are going to encourage people to be upfront and honest, we need to provide the same level of psychological safety that removes the fear, particularly when there has not been a culture of doing so before. Remember what we said in Chapter 13 about no blaming, shaming or scapegoating.

We know there are ranges of options and decision points in a given situation. Some are linear, some are in parallel. With some of the techniques that El Fertasi mentioned, we need first to visualize the worst-case scenario and then go far beyond it to get us outside our comfort zone. Being frank, I have rarely seen an organization go anywhere near their worst-case scenario. Most organizations probably can't tell you what it is. It might, for example, be a series of events and bad decisions that leads to the collapse of the company, or perhaps a single catastrophic event that leads to multiple fatalities. The point is that, unless you can envisage what this might entail, how will you be able to take preventative actions to stop it from happening?

A crisis rarely happens from nowhere, but when it does happen, and inquiries and investigations are concluded, you can bet that the warning signs were there for all to see. Of course, with the benefit of hindsight, we also have a clear understanding of the catalogue of failings that caused the crisis to manifest in the way it did. One of the common denominators highlighted from multiple inquiries is a history of bad culture and poor leadership. It is why I have dedicated entire chapters to it, and why I want you to understand the reality of the situation.

A key aspect to consider is often the trail of missed warning signs from safety, security, resilience test and audit reports and risk registers: those items that we can't pretend we don't know about. But what if vital information was not escalated to the right level? What if those tasked with receiving such reports did not fully understand the context or the consequences of such reports, or what that could lead to?

Remember that most actions lead to a chain reaction, and *no action* and *inaction* are two very different things: one is a conscious decision to do nothing; the latter is simply doing nothing.

Whether you are the practitioner who is reporting such information, or a leader who is receiving the information, it is important to be very clear and concise about the action you expect someone to take, and that the outcome of that action is recorded. All too often, the answer is, 'transfer it to the risk register', but just think about all the other risks that were treated in that way, how many may be related and whether the risks are being actively managed.

Let me share an anecdote from my own background – a situation I found myself in around 2003, when I was working as a disaster recovery manager for a financial services company. Many changes were already afoot because of the 9/11 terrorist attacks in the United States. I decided to proactively group risks with a common theme together to show the accumulative effect of multiple systems that had ineffective recovery solutions, and how a failure in a data centre would lead to a catastrophic event because we could not recover in line with business, contractual and regulatory expectations. When I presented it to the CTO, he coached me on how to present 'the issues and the asks' inside 10 minutes (the time we had been allocated to present to the board). This may sound like a small amount of time, but it is why you need to be clear and succinct on what the decisions and actions are, and the consequences if not performed. Basing the plausibility on an actual event meant that the board could understand the context and the overarching impact if unresolved.

So, did I get the funding and resource that was needed to fix the issues? *Yes.* Did I get the funding in the timeline that I wanted? *No.* The reason comes down to risk appetite and available resources.

As much as organizations would love to have an infinite pot of money and resources to fix a myriad of issues, this is not reality. Security needs to be balanced against other business issues and requirements that also need investment. You may need to adjust your strategy as a result, but it is important to keep highlighting the current state, what is in progress, what is on the road map, and when the benefits will be realized. Items will be reprioritized, and some may even get lowered, but we must be consistent on reporting on the capability at our disposal and adjusting our confidence levels.

There is a military saying, 'train like you fight to fight like you train'. This means being immersed into training and exercising to such a degree that what you do and how you do it becomes second nature. It also avoids the potential that you will just improvise.

We are tuned into thinking that a cyber attack is big, noisy and visible to us. As we have discussed, however, many attackers rely on stealth and hoping they will not be noticed. Some will steal and divert money from right under your nose, especially in the case of business email compromise, which is the most *financially impacting* cybercrime of all, but not necessarily the most *operationally impacting* or the one that will hit the headlines.

The reality is that you can be faced with a myriad of different types of attack, but the principles by which you detect, respond and recover should be the same, because there are several key priorities that will be the same irrespective of the cause. The assessment of the safety and welfare of people, whether directly or indirectly, should be your number-one priority, always.

Make these the subject of exercises, and consider the range of options that you have at your disposal, based on the capability that you have reported. Don't just think about the easy options but the really difficult ones that might need to be chosen. We want those that will be responsible for making decisions to feel equipped, to understand where the gaps are, and, ultimately, for them to identify and agree on what is going to enable them to feel more confident in making those decisions.

WHAT CAN YOU REALISTICALLY DO TODAY, AND WHAT ARE THE ISSUES TO BE RESOLVED?

Not only are we facing a myriad of attackers, but a cyber attack can come at any time and at the least opportune moment (end-of-year results, product launch, merger – the attackers probably know this if they have done their reconnaissance and will try to catch you off guard). When faced with a real upcoming event, use this to your advantage because you are probably more vulnerable and a high(er) value target. Run through what would happen in this scenario and visualize the outcomes you want to have and those that you want to avoid.

Whatever decision you make, record it and be prepared to explain *why*. What was the decision based on? What were your options? Why did you decide on that specific action? In hindsight, with different information, you may have chosen differently, and that is where we come to that deep reflection and learning once more. Share those thoughts, those lessons; be candid, and do it widely so others may learn, just as you learn from them.

Our objective is to get to the point where we understand the difficult decisions that need to be made: we have already discussed it and agreed the thresholds and the triggers, and we readjust based on our changing risk profile and strategy. As El Fertasi highlights, you can really shift perception and build trust when you act as one entity. Building relationships, as well as remaining humble, is important. The personal connections and knowing who you can call and rely upon in times of crisis can significantly change the outcomes.

So, we have started to consider and prepare for a myriad of attacks, but how do we deal with the unpredictability of a human adversary who is intent on controlling the situation, and is driving their own agenda?

Dealing with attacker manipulation

Our objective is to limit the return on investment for the attacker. Using the extortion example, this means preventing them from obtaining a payment. If the organization can restore business operations without paying a ransom, the attacker has effectively failed. Even if the attacker was successful in encrypting networks and services, they may still try to extort the organization further by threatening to disclose data on the dark web or by selling access and compromised credentials to other attackers. It is perhaps an uncomfortable reality to face, but you should consider any data as already exposed or sold on. Organizations should therefore be aware that they are at heightened risk from other attacks and should assume compromise at any time. The following are some strategies that can be deployed:

- **Do not directly negotiate with attackers.** Extortion is a crime and should be treated as such. Given that you don't know who you are dealing with, or what other criminal activity this could be funding, it is highly recommended that you don't participate in negotiations without legal counsel and assistance from law enforcement agencies. Many countries have sanctions with regards to paying terrorist entities and political regimes, so the organization needs to be cognisant of this. Also consider the role that law enforcement has in reducing cybercrime, which relies on the ability to collect evidence and attribute crimes to specific individuals and groups – which provides mutual benefit.

- **Appeal to the human behind the attack.** While attackers may try to disconnect themselves from their victims, seeing the impact on real people may prompt some to withdraw from the attack. There are examples where attackers have either chosen the wrong target or decided that they did not want to continue, particularly in the case of hospitals, where the prospect of someone dying, for example, may be too much for them to be bear. In the case of FIN7, some people may not even be aware that they are part of a criminal organization and may believe they are performing a legitimate role. Don't assume that the person on the other end of the line knows the full extent of the operation or the impact they are causing.

- **Ring-fence communications.** To prevent attackers from getting the upper hand and listening to your crisis response, stand up separate communication channels. Closely monitor and verify invited attendees, both visually and audibly. Avoid having too many people on a single call by operating separate channels for different groups involved in the recovery action. Remember to grant access to the *right resources* at the *right time* for the *right purpose*. Continuing to observe strict security protocols is important through all aspects of the incident.

Recovering from a cyber attack

In the previous chapter, we talked about defending through the layers. When a layer fails, it increases the ability for the attacker to achieve their objective, and the recovery effort is also made greater because of the level of control that the attacker has obtained. Speaking frankly, if you are in the middle of a ransomware attack, where the attacker has locked and encrypted your systems *and* exfiltrated a mass of sensitive data, multiple things have gone wrong to get to this point.

The attack itself is only part of the problem. The first issue is to contain the incident and 'stop the bleeding'. The next is recovery. Depending on the extent of the incident, what damage has been done and whether you need to restore systems and data, you need to get back control of the layers that have been breached and fix whatever enabled the attacker to gain access in the first place.

Your overarching plan needs to include 'recovery from zero'. This means potentially having to rebuild the entire environment from scratch because we no longer have trust in it. The number-one question is 'How long will it take to recover?' The second is 'Has it been tested?' These are the fundamental questions that the board will need to know the answers to. Recovery is *not* an easy task and even the most mature organization will struggle, so don't underestimate the amount of effort that may be involved. You may need to prioritize, based on the critical assets first. So you can see why we need to be clear on what these are, from a business and security perspective, and that the board is aligned on that, and why preventative and proactive measures to limit both the probability and impact of a cyber attack are preferable to a full recovery. If an attack is something we can't avoid and need to prepare for, what is the cost to the business when it happens?

Can you see why I suggested that a good starting position for your security strategy is one that centres on protecting the *access* and *exit*? What are we doing to understand the vulnerabilities and closing the open doors, and what are we doing to stop the attacker achieving their goal, accepting that the path is often not linear, and the perpetrator may already be in the organization?

By segregating the physical and logical access to networks and infrastructure and protecting backups, we not only limit the attacker's ability to obtain control of the entire environment, we also reduce the probability that we will have to recover and rebuild it. We may not be able to stop every attack, but it is within our gift to manage and control the outcome.

Conclusion

In this chapter, we have reflected on the requirement to achieve board-level buy-in and support to the overarching security strategy, and why it is critical that we utilize open and transparent language to describe current threats and the capability to counteract them. Arguably the biggest test of our strategy and plan will come when faced with a large-scale cyber attack that threatens the very integrity and trust of the organization. Difficult decisions will need to be made, and we need to have confidence in doing so.

We explored that to train like we fight means not only being completely immersed in exercises that enable us to feel and deal with the emotional intensity of a cyber attack, but we are prepared to tackle this head on by visualizing the intended outcomes and how we will collectively respond and recover as one.

Let's bring all these elements together for reflection in the final chapter.

References

Department of Justice (2022) 'Former chief security officer of Uber convicted of federal charges for covering up data breach involving millions of Uber user records', US Attorney's Office press release, 5 October, justice.gov/usao-ndca/pr/ former-chief-security-officer-uber-convicted-federal-charges-covering-data-breach (archived at https://perma.cc/T998-QQDU)

Proofpoint (2023) '2023 Voice of the CISO: Global insights into CISO challenges, expectations and priorities', proofpoint.com/sites/default/files/white-papers/ pfpt-us-wp-voice-of-the-CISO-report.pdf (archived at https://perma.cc/3EH9-4DYV)

17

Final thoughts on the direction and evolution of the human adversary

CHAPTER OBJECTIVES

As we round out Part Three, and the book, let's take a moment for reflection and to gather our thoughts and perspectives on where we've come from and what the future direction may hold.

We explore here how our role as defenders will continue to evolve as the human adversary also evolves their tactics and techniques.

Humans are complex beings driven by a strong desire to build social networks. At our very core, we are driven by an innate set of emotions and desires that provide the motivation and drive to succeed. Our social upbringing, the opportunities we are presented with and the decisions we make are what will ultimately determine our outcome, and history. Some choices we have made ourselves, and some will inevitably be made for us; but each path, and each decision, will ultimately shape our future.

We all bear a level of accountability and responsibility for what we do with our lives and the impact that we have on others. We can choose whether each encounter is positive or negative and how we want others to perceive us. The desires and needs that we all have are what will set us on our path. That may lead us to join different social groups, and the leaders of such groups may influence what comes next; whether it is an authoritarian leader or an empathetic one; whether it is one born from strict rule or one driven by collaboration. While the core of what makes us human has not changed, our thoughts, beliefs and values will continue to grow and expand in line with our communities.

It is an important lesson for us to ponder on, and why this book is fundamentally about understanding the adversary, and, while some humans will do bad things, it doesn't fundamentally mean they are bad. There will always be those that are deeply motivated to do harm, and, where there is strong will, they will find a way, but people can change, and when others believe in them and their capabilities, they can make different life choices.

Our need to build security, protection and resilience into all aspects of our lives is not getting easier, and will never end as a principle, but that doesn't mean that we can't anticipate, and build better defences and teach people how they can secure and protect themselves from harm.

Our greatest opportunity is here and now and influencing what lies ahead. As the organization, and those that lead it, start to think about the future, as they consider building new products and services, entering new markets and embracing new innovations, how might we be central to that? How might we influence the need to have security by design and by default?

The ability to successfully influence those around you is driven by the ability to tap into the emotions that drive behaviours and actions. It is this ability that can improve the situation in the short term and lead to transformation. This means acting as the motivating factor that will offer the vision, excitement and encouragement that people need to deliver change. Often, people need to see a role model, something to emulate, so that they can get behind it (Laker and Patel, 2020).

Transformational leadership is rooted in empathy, which removes the hierarchal decision-making in favour of collaboration and consensus. People are more likely to want to change their behaviour when this is being witnessed from the top down. There is no better way to show this than in times of crisis, as we discussed in the previous chapter.

Removing the fear and uncertainty that often surrounds cybersecurity provides the type of emotional connection and psychological safety that will drive real action. This bond engenders trust, and that is one of the core foundations that will provide resilience.

Building a strategy that is centred on human-centric security means focusing on the most critical yet vulnerable elements of the strategy – our people. By reducing the types of attack that exploit human emotions and psychology, we can positively influence people's behaviour and resistance to such attacks. Once we stop looking at the human as the weakest link, and start thinking of people as our strongest advocates, we are already changing mindsets.

Let us recap on the strategies that we have discussed in Part Three as we close out the book and reflect on all that we have covered:

- Make security awareness relevant and engaging through the power of education and storytelling.

- Have a deep understanding and appreciation for how technology and digital forensics work, so that you may baseline the minimum security controls to protect people and assets.

- Remove the stigma associated with victim blaming and scapegoating by enabling a safe environment for introspection and committing to deliver proactive change.

- Understand the role that culture plays in the success of the strategy, and examine whether we truly understand our people.

- Reflect on whether we are living by our vision and values, and whether our culture is helping or hindering what we need to achieve. How might your actions positively impact those around you?

- Take steps to remove the fear factor by identifying the changes in behaviour and stressors that lead to concerning behaviour. Explore why empathy may be your biggest superpower when understanding the cyber attacker mindset.

- Determine whether we really understand our business, the shadow processes that have developed and how we can work with the organization to close the gaps.

- Think like an attacker by modelling the business *inside out* and *outside in* to determine the vulnerabilities and priorities to be addressed.

- Build the core strategy to *stop the access in and exit out* by defending through the layers, by protecting and optimizing identities, endpoints, networks, infrastructure, applications and data.

- Understand the power of due diligence when it comes to obtaining effective senior leadership buy-in and support for the strategy, which is built on trust and honesty.

- Lead by example and from the front, through consensus and commitment.

- Build effective crisis management through reflection and visualization to reduce the emotional intensity and decisions that will be made under pressure.
- *Train like you fight* by simulating real-world events that build confidence in the security capability and achieve resilience.

You will be amazed at the difference that positive and incremental change can make to the overall behaviour and mindset of the organization. Creating an organizational culture that is receptive and adaptive to change, as well as mindful of threats that may be on the horizon, is key.

The very essence of the human adversary may not change, but your strategy certainly will.

Reference

Laker, B and Patel, C. (2020) 'Strengthen your ability to influence people', *Harvard Business Review*, 28 August, hbr.org/2020/08/strengthen-your-ability-to-influence-people (archived at https://perma.cc/JRN6-9GXX)

INDEX

Note: Page numbers in *italics* refer to tables or figures.

Looking for another book?

Explore our award-winning
books from global business
experts in Risk and
Compliance

Scan the code to browse

www.koganpage.com/risk-compliance

More books from Kogan Page

2nd Edition

CYBER RISK MANAGEMENT

Prioritize threats, identify vulnerabilities and apply controls

CHRISTOPHER J HODSON

ISBN: 9781398613492

STRATEGIC RISK AND CRISIS MANAGEMENT

A handbook for modelling and managing complex risks

David Rubens

ISBN: 9781398609754

CYBERSECURITY FOR BUSINESS

ORGANIZATION-WIDE STRATEGIES TO ENSURE CYBER RISK IS NOT JUST AN IT ISSUE

Edited by
LARRY CLINTON, ISA President

Foreword by Peter Gleason, President and CEO of NACD (National Association of Corporate Directors)

INTERNET SECURITY ALLIANCE

ISBN: 9781398606142

7TH EDITION

IT GOVERNANCE

An International Guide to Data Security and ISO27001/ISO27002

ALAN CALDER
STEVE WATKINS

ISBN: 9780749496951

www.koganpage.com